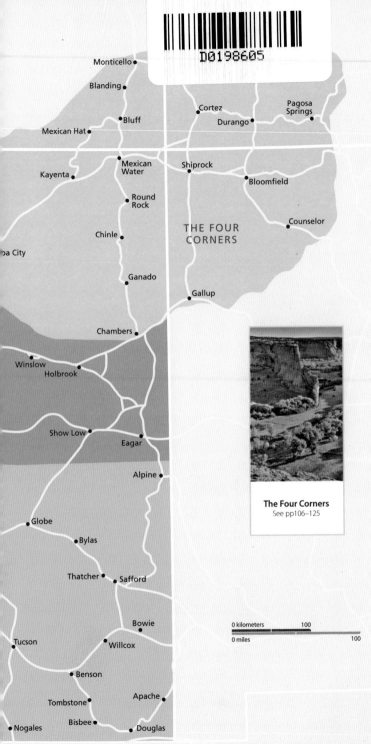

Monticello

Blanding

Cortez

Pagosa
Springs

Bluff

Durango

Mexican Hat

Mexican
Water

Shiprock

Kayenta

Bloomfield

Round
Rock

THE FOUR
CORNERS

Counselor

Chinle

ba City

Ganado

Gallup

Chambers

Winslow

Holbrook

Show Low

Eagar

Alpine

The Four Corners
See pp106–125

Globe

Bylas

Thatcher

Safford

Bowie

0 kilometers	100
0 miles	100

Tucson

Willcox

Benson

Tombstone

Apache

Nogales

Bisbee

Douglas

EYEWITNESS TRAVEL

ARIZONA &
THE GRAND
CANYON

EYEWITNESS TRAVEL

ARIZONA & THE GRAND CANYON

DK

DK | Penguin Random House

Managing Editor Aruna Ghose
Art Editor Benu Joshi
Senior Editor Rimli Borooah
Editor Bhavna Seth Ranjan
Designer Mathew Kurien
Picture Research Taiyaba Khatoon
DTP Coordinator Shailesh Sharma
DTP Designer Vinod Harish

Main Contributor
Paul Franklin

Photographers
Demetrio Carrasco, Alan Keohane, Francesca Yorke

Illustrators
P. Arun, Gary Cross, Eugene Fleurey, Claire Littlejohn,
Chris Orr & Associates, Mel Pickering,
Robbie Polley, John Woodcock

Printed and bound in China.

First American Edition 2005

17 18 19 20 10 9 8 7 6 5 4 3 2 1

Published in the United States by
DK Publishing, 345 Hudson Street,
New York, New York 10014

Reprinted with revisions 2006, 2008, 2010, 2012, 2015, 2017

Copyright © 2005, 2017 Dorling Kindersley Limited, London

A Penguin Random House Company

All rights reserved. Without limiting the rights under copyright reserved above,
no part of this publication may be reproduced, stored in or introduced into a
retrieval system, or transmitted, in any form, or by any means (electronic, mechanical,
photocopying, recording, or otherwise), without the prior written permission
of both the copyright owner and the above publisher of this book.

Published in the UK by Dorling Kindersley Limited.

A catalog record for this book is available from
the Library of Congress.

ISSN 1542-1554

ISBN 978-1-4654-6129-2

Floors are referred to throughout in accordance with
American usage; ie the "first floor" is at ground level.

MIX
Paper from
responsible sources
FSC FSC™ C018179
www.fsc.org

**The information in this
DK Eyewitness Travel Guide is checked regularly.**

Every effort has been made to ensure that this book is as up to date as possible
at the time of going to press. Some details, however, such as telephone numbers,
opening hours, prices, gallery hanging arrangements and travel information are
liable to change. The publishers cannot accept responsibility for any consequences
arising from the use of this book, nor for any material on third-party websites, and
cannot guarantee that any website address in this book will be a suitable source of
travel information. We value the views and suggestions of our readers very highly.
Please write to: Publisher, DK Eyewitness Travel Guides, Dorling Kindersley,
80 Strand, London, WC2R 0RL, UK, or email: travelguides@dk.com.

Front cover main image: Monument Valley Navajo Tribal Park, Arizona

◀ Panoramic vista of Canyon de Chelly National Monument in Navajo Nation, Arizona

Contents

How to Use this Guide **6**

Taking a break in one of the sandstone
chambers of Antelope Canyon

Introducing
Arizona

The 800 ft (245 m) high Spider Rock at
Canyon de Chelly, Arizona

World famous Monument Valley in the Four Corners region

Contemporary glass skyscrapers in downtown Phoenix

Hispanic pottery

Visitors climbing the ladder to Balcony House at Mesa Verde National Park, Colorado

San Xavier del Bac Mission in Tucson, Southern Arizona

HOW TO USE THIS GUIDE

This Dorling Kindersley Travel Guide helps you get the most from your visit to Arizona and the Grand Canyon. It provides both detailed practical information and expert recommendations. *Introducing Arizona* maps the region and sets it in its historical and cultural context and describes events through the entire year. *Arizona & the Four Corners Area by Area* is the main

sightseeing section, which covers all of the important sights with photographs, maps, and illustrations. Tips for hotels, restaurants, shops, entertainment, and sports are found in *Travelers' Needs*. The final section, *Survival Guide*, contains practical advice on everything from personal security and travel information to public transportation and renting vehicles.

Arizona Area by Area

In this guide, Arizona and the Grand Canyon region has been divided into three separate areas, each one identified by its own color code. On the

inside front cover is a general map of the region showing these three areas. All the most interesting places to visit are located on the *Area Map* at

the beginning of each chapter. Finding your way around the chapter is made simple by the numbering system used throughout.

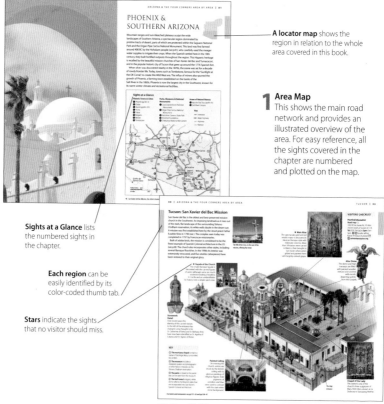

A locator map shows the region in relation to the whole area covered in this book.

1 Area Map
This shows the main road network and provides an illustrated overview of the area. For easy reference, all the sights covered in the chapter are numbered and plotted on the map.

Sights at a Glance lists the numbered sights in the chapter.

Each region can be easily identified by its color-coded thumb tab.

Stars indicate the sights that no visitor should miss.

2 Star Sights
These are given two or more full pages. Historic buildings or those with interesting architecture are dissected to reveal their interiors.

3 Town Maps

Major towns have an individual section where detailed information is provided for museums, important buildings, and other places of interest. The *Town Map* shows the location of the main sights.

The Town Map includes the main roads, along with train and bus stations, parking areas, and tourist information offices.

Practical Information lists all the information you need to visit each sight.

Numbers refer to each sight's position on the *Area Map* and its place in the chapter.

Storyboxes highlight a special feature or interesting story about the town or sight.

The Visitors' Checklist provides the practical information you will need to plan your visit.

4 Detailed information on each sight

All important sights in each area are described in depth in this section. They are listed in order, following the numbering on the *Area Map*. Practical information on opening hours, telephone numbers, websites, admission charges and facilities available is given for each sight. The key to the symbols used can be found on the back flap.

Numbered circles point out features of the sight listed in the key.

5 Arizona's Major Sights

Important sights are given extensive coverage, sometimes two or more full pages. National parks have maps showing facilities and trails; excavated sights are reconstructed; museums and galleries have color-coded floor plans.

INTRODUCING ARIZONA

DISCOVERING ARIZONA & THE GRAND CANYON

One of the best parts of exploring Arizona and the Grand Canyon is simply driving from one place to another through spectacular desert and red-rock canyon landscapes. The following tours have been designed to take in as many of the region's best destinations as possible, while keeping travel distances as short as possible. The itineraries are designed to stand alone, or be combined for a longer trip. The first tour is seven days from Flagstaff to the South and North Rims of the Grand Canyon. There is another seven-day tour through the splendid scenery of the Four Corners region, to the remote Ancestral Puebloan ruins and the hauntingly beautiful Canyon de Chelly. The next two tours explore the modern city of Phoenix and the beautiful deserts of Southern Arizona including the historic Wild West town of Tombstone. The most practical way to travel beyond the cities is by private car, and a high-clearance and/or 4WD vehicle is handy for exploring far-off areas. Some outlying areas are very isolated, so always travel with extra water and keep your gas tank topped up. Pick and follow your favorite tours or dip in and out and be inspired.

Lake Powell
Every year more than a million people visit the lake which was formed by the inundation of the Glen Canyon dam.

Seven Days in Grand Canyon and Northern Arizona

- Hike through beautiful **Oak Creek Canyon** in the Red Rock country near Sedona.

- Tour the Ancestral Puebloan ruins of **Montezuma Castle National Monument**.

- Follow **Hermit Road** along the South Rim of the Grand Canyon to enjoy the views and hiking trails.

- Take a boat trip through the water-filled canyons of **Lake Powell**, to see the graceful **Rainbow Bridge National Monument**.

The Southwest, oil on canvas by Walter Ufe (1876–1936)

Mesa Verde National Park
Once an habitation of the Puebloan people, the well-maintained cliff dwellings are worth a visit.

Seven Days in the Four Corners

- Explore the culture, art, and history of the region at Flagstaff's justifiably acclaimed **Museum of Northern Arizona**.

- Walk among the mysterious ruins of the **Hovenweep National Monument**.

- Tour **Mesa Verde National Park**'s Ancient Puebloan cliff dwellings.

- Visit **Chaco Culture National Historical Park** to learn about the advanced society that lived here a thousand years ago.

COLORADO

Hovenweep National Monument

Mesa Verde National Park

Colorado Plateau

Chapin Mesa Archaeological Museum

Monument Valley

NEW MEXICO

Chinle

Canyon de Chelly National Monument

Chaco Culture National Historical Park

Hubbell Trading Post

Window Rock

RIZONA

Key

═══ Seven Days in Grand Canyon and Northern Arizona

─── Seven Days in the Four Corners

▬▬▬ Seven Days in Phoenix and Southern Arizona

Seven Days in Phoenix and Southern Arizona

- Explore Native American culture at the renowned **Heard Museum**.

- Stroll the centuries-old cobbled alleys of **San Xavier del Bac Mission**.

- Go deep underground at the Copper Queen Mine in historic **Bisbee**.

- Walk the same streets that Wild West legends Wyatt Earp and Doc Holliday strode in **Tombstone**.

Amerind Foundation

chner Caverns e Park

Tombstone

Bisbee

Bisbee
The town of Bisbee witnessed a mining boom in the 1880s and is home to the famous Copper Queen Mine.

Seven Days in Grand Canyon and Northern Arizona

- **Arriving** Most visitors to Flagstaff fly into Phoenix (Sky Harbor International Airport) and rent a car for the 150-mile (241-km) drive to Flagstaff. However, American Eagle flies into Flagstaff Pulliam from Sky Harbor International Airport several times a day.

- **Transport** A rental car is the most practical way for visitors to tour the American Southwest. Rentals are available at most airports and in larger towns. While not required, a high clearance 4WD vehicle can make many remote areas more accessible and easier to navigate. A GPS is a big plus.

Day 1

A self-guided walking trip to historic downtown **Flagstaff** (pp70–71) starts at the train station built in 1926, that now houses the visitors center. Downtown Flagstaff's architecture blends the old west with wonderfully preserved buildings from the Route 66 era of the 1930s to 1950s. In the afternoon, visit the award-winning **Museum of Northern Arizona** (p72) which highlights the art, history, and culture of the Colorado Plateau region.

Day 2

Take a leisurely drive to the beautiful **Oak Creek Canyon** (p75) and hike the West Fork Trail through this lovely western landscape. Continue on to **Sedona** (p74), to spend the afternoon exploring trendy downtown shops, including the galleries of **Tlaquepaque Art Village** (p74).

Day 3

Drive to **Montezuma Castle National Monument** (p77) to explore the ruins of the ancient cliff dwellings. Then head to the historical Fort Verde at

El Tovar Hotel on the South Rim of the Grand Canyon

Camp Verde (p77) to learn how the US Army survived danger and hardship on the western frontier. **Prescott** (p77) is an attractive Victorian town in Arizona's high country where there are three equally interesting museums to choose from: Sharlot Hall Museum (Western history), Smoki Museum (Native art and culture), or Phippen Museum (Western art).

Day 4

Start the day with a scenic drive from Prescott to Grand Canyon South Rim. On arrival, walk the section of the Rim Trail within the Grand Canyon Village and explore the visitors center and nearby historic buildings, including **Kolb Studio** (p56) and **El Tovar Hotel** (p60). In the afternoon, take the shuttle along the impressive **Hermit Road** (p56).

It is possible to get on and off the shuttle at will, and many of the overlooks have trails connecting them.

Day 5

Morning is a great time for a walk along the Rim Trail to watch the morning light fill the canyon. Visitors should note that the total trail is 13 miles (21 km). A more challenging trek is of hiking down a section of the **Bright Angel Trail** (p55) into the canyon. Carry water and remember that going down is easier than up. In the afternoon, take a helicopter tour for an unparalleled view of the canyon. End the day at **Lake Powell** (pp68–9) near the city of Page.

Day 6

At **Wahweap Marina** (p69), take the 6-hour boat trip deep into the water-filled canyons of Lake Powell to the spectacular stone arch of the **Rainbow Bridge National Monument** (p68).

Day 7

The drive to **Grand Canyon North Rim** (p55) takes you through some of the most remote country on the Colorado Plateau. This quiet high-country destination offers some magnificent scenic drives to canyon overlooks as well as excellent hiking trails along the rim and into the canyon.

Prehistoric dinosaur exhibit at the Museum of Northern Arizona, Flagstaff

For practical information on traveling around Arizona and the Grand Canyon, see pp160–67

Seven Days in the Four Corners

- **Arriving** American Eagle arranges several flights a day to Flagstaff Pulliam from Phoenix (Sky Harbor International Airport). Most of the time, visitors to Flagstaff fly into Phoenix airport and rent a car for the 150-mile (241-km) drive to Flagstaff.

- **Transport** You can link this itinerary with the Grand Canyon itinerary above by driving 210 miles (337 km) to Sedona. The closest major airport to Canyon de Chelly is the Phoenix airport.

Day 1
Begin with a morning walk through the high country beauty of the Flagstaff Arboretum. At 7,200 ft (2,195 m), this giant wild garden show-cases the remarkable diversity of trees and plants of the Colorado Plateau. In the afternoon, explore the art, history, and culture of this region at the **Museum of Northern Arizona** *(p72)*.

Day 2
The scenic drive to **Monument Valley** *(pp108–9)* covers a rich variety of the striking Colorado Plateau landscapes. The famous stone buttes seen in a hundred Western movies begin to appear on the horizon. Start by driving the 17-mile (27-km) self-guided route through the valley. In the afternoon, take a Navajo-led jeep or horseback tour to explore more remote parts of the valley. Round off the day at **Gouldings Lodge** *(p109)* to see the Trading Post Museum.

Day 3
Arrive at the enigmatic **Hovenweep National Monument** *(p116)*. Eight centuries ago, Hovenweep was home to 2,500 people who lived in six villages scattered across this lonely, but beautiful high plateau.

Native American craft displayed at the Hubbell Trading Post, Ganado

Spend the day driving or walking the trails from one set of well-preserved ruins to another. Later, drive to the Mesa Verde National Park.

Day 4
Be prepared for a long couple of days as there is plenty to see at **Mesa Verde National Park** *(pp124–5)*. Start your trip at the visitors center, then take the guided tour of the Cliff House ruins. In the afternoon, drive to Chapin Mesa Archaeological Museum and then admire the Spruce Tree House ruins.

Day 5
Get a feel of the Puebloan way of life on the **Balcony House** *(p125)* tour, which requires climbing ladders. Wrap up your Mesa Verde trip with a short 1-mile (2-km) hike along the Soda Canyon trail near Balcony House.

The road to the Monument Valley rock formations

Day 6
Drive to **Chaco Culture National Historical Park** *(pp118–19)*. This shallow canyon is very remote, so it's a good idea to bring water and food and check National Park Service driving directions before starting out. The ruins here represent the apex of the Ancestral Puebloan culture. Start with the Nine Mile driving loop, visiting all the ruins dotting the valley. In the afternoon take the ranger-led tour of the large Chaco Canyon's Pueblo Bonito ruins. For adventure enthusiasts, round off the day by taking the Night Sky tour before driving to **Window Rock** *(p111)*, the nearest town with accommodations.

Day 7
From Window Rock drive to **Hubbell Trading Post** *(p111)*, a working trading post that dates back to 1878. Watch Navajo women weaving rugs and purchase excellent handcrafted Native jewelry, textiles, carvings, and other crafts here. In the afternoon, drive to Chinle and take the South Rim Trail along **Canyon de Chelly** *(pp112–13)* stopping to marvel at the overlooks. Only one trail into the canyon is open to visitors. The White House Trail is 2.5 miles (4 km) long and leads into and across the canyon, traversing through a shallow stream to a small cliff dwelling ruin. If the hike is too strenuous, arrange for a Navajo-led jeep or horseback excursions into the canyon.

Four Days in Phoenix

- **Arriving** Domestic and international flights land at Phoenix's Sky Harbor International Airport.

- **Transport** A rental car is the easiest and most practical way to get around and explore beyond the city limits. Public bus service exists, but is not efficient. There are also free shuttle services and an inexpensive light rail system. Numerous private tour companies offer bus tours throughout the Southwest departing from Phoenix. Other major airports are in Tucson and Las Vegas.

Shops on E Main Street in Old Town, Scottsdale

Day 1
The **Desert Botanical Garden** (p88) is one of the best places to see the variety of stunning desert landscapes found throughout the American Southwest. Morning is the best time for an outing here when birds and wildlife are active, and before the day warms up. In the afternoon, head to **Taliesin West** (p86), to explore the School of Architecture built by the famed architect Frank Lloyd Wright, which began as a winter school for his students.

Day 2
Start your day exploring the **Pueblo Grande Museum & Archaeological Park** (p87), which preserves the ruins of a large pueblo-style settlement built by the Hohokam people starting 1,500 years ago. The excellent museum showcases Hohokam art and culture, including several artifacts such as cooking utensils and pottery. In the afternoon, wander through the tree-lined streets of Old Town **Scottsdale** (p86) and the neighboring Arts District, where fine jewelry stores, art galleries, boutiques, and restaurants fill the historic buildings.

Day 3
If you are in the mood for outdoor adventure, hike up **Camelback Mountain** (p87)

with its 1,300-ft (396-m) vertical rise. The trails are challenging, so bring lots of water. For a more relaxing morning, visit the **Arizona Science Center** (pp82–3). In the afternoon, head to the **Heard Museum** (pp84–5), which features one of the world's most impressive collections of ancient and contemporary Native American art.

Day 4
Phoenix's **Pioneer Living History Village** (p89) features more than 20 historic buildings that represent Arizona's territorial period from 1863 to 1912. Visit the **Phoenix Art Museum** (p83) to enjoy one of the most impressive art collections in the American Southwest. In the afternoon, head to the **Challenger Space Center** (p89).

Exhibit at the Heard Museum, specializing in Indian American culture and art

For practical information on traveling around Arizona and the Grand Canyon see pp160–67

Seven Days in Phoenix and Southern Arizona

- **Arriving** Domestic and international flights land at Phoenix's Sky Harbor International Airport. From Bisbee, the nearest major airport is Tucson International Airport.

- **Transport** A rental car is a convenient option for getting around in Phoenix. Visitors can begin their tours by driving to Phoenix or the Grand Canyon Village.

Day 1
Spend the morning strolling among the beautiful landscapes of the **Desert Botanical Garden** (p88). Here, there are examples of all the desert ecosystems of the American Southwest. Spend the afternoon, exploring the remarkable collection of Native American art and artifacts at the **Heard Museum** (pp84–5).

Day 2
Devote the morning to appreciating the elaborate collection of American Western art as well as European, Latin American and contemporary artworks in the **Phoenix Art Museum** (p83). In the afternoon, discover the shops and galleries of **Scottsdale**'s (p86) Old Town and Arts District.

Day 3
Drive to **Boyce Thompson Arboretum** (p91) in the shadow of the **Superstition Mountains** (p90), which offers shady paths through lush native landscapes including rare desert riparian (riverside) ecosystems. Next, drive to the historic mining town of **Globe** (p91). Explore the town's historic district and visit the fascinating Gila County Historical Museum. From Globe, head to **Tucson** (pp94–101).

Day 4
Start your Tucson visit with a tour of the grandiose **San Xavier del Bac Mission** (pp98–9). Started in 1783, this elegant mission is the oldest intact

Interior detail of the San Xavier del Bac Mission near Tucson

European building in Arizona. It is operated by the Franciscan order and is considered one of the finest examples of Spanish Colonial architecture in America. Choose from three possible ways to spend your afternoon: explore the **Tucson Museum of Art & Historic Block** (p94); or head out of town to visit **Biosphere 2** (p100), or tour the **Titan Missile Museum** (p97).

Day 5
Saguaro National Park (p96) is named after the large multi-armed cactus (a symbol of the Southwest). The stunning Sonoran desert landscapes are home to a large variety of saguaro cacti. The park has an east and west section, one on each side of Tucson. Start in the east section, take the driving trip and stop at the visitors center. If you have time, hike one of the many trails. End your Tucson trip with a visit to the **Arizona-Sonora Desert Museum** (p96), which houses a botanical garden, a zoo, and

a museum all highlighting the flora, fauna, and ecology of this fascinating region.

Day 6
Start the day wandering through the **Tumacacori National Historical Park** (p103), situated an hour's drive away from Tucson. Located here are the well-preserved ruins of an old Franciscan mission and a museum with outdoor exhibits highlighting the mission era of the Southwest. In the afternoon, explore the historic western mining town of **Bisbee** (p103) Opt to take a guided jeep tour of the town or visit the famous Copper Queen Mine, one of the several local mines that produced millions of dollars worth of copper ore in its heyday.

Day 7
From Bisbee, drive to the famous Wild West town of **Tombstone** (p104). A walking tour of this city leads through the historic streets lined with buildings that have changed little since the 1880s, when wealth from silver mines turned Tombstone into a boom town of saloons and gambling halls. It was here that Wyatt Earp and his brothers, along with the notorious Doc Holliday, gunned down the Clanton gang at the OK Corral. In the afternoon, drive to **Kartchner Caverns State Park** (p105) for a cool underground tour of one of America's most impressive cave systems, or pay a visit to the **Amerind Foundation** (p105) to explore the superb museum filled with Native American archaeological and cultural artifacts.

Façade of Mission San Jose de Tumacacori at the Tumacacori National Historical Park

Putting Arizona on the Map

Arizona and the Four Corners area, which also takes in parts of Utah, Colorado, and New Mexico, lie in the southwest corner of the United States. Bordered by Mexico in the south, California in the west, and New Mexico in the east, Arizona covers around 113,000 sq miles (292,000 sq km). It is sparsely populated, with almost 80 per cent of its population of around 6.8 million living in the cities. Arizona's most famous sight is the magnificent Grand Canyon.

Hudson
Bay

Belcher Islands

Lac à l'Eau
Claire

Réservoir de
Caniapiscau

Smallwood
Reservoir

Labrador City

burchill

Nelson

ANITOBA

Radisson

Réservoir la
Grande Deux

Gagnon

Severn

ONTARIO

Réservoir
Opinaca

Lac Mistassini

Waskaganish
(Fort Rupert)

Godbout

Winnipeg
Winnipeg

1

11

Lake
Nipigon

11

Quebec City

117

MINNESOTA

61

Lake Superior

Montreal

11

94

35

2

WISCONSIN

Lake Huron

Lester B
Pearson
Toronto

NEW YORK

81

VT

Logan
Boston
MA

RI

Minneapolis
Minneapolis-
St Paul

St Paul

94

Lake Michigan

MICHIGAN

401

Buffalo

Lake Ontario

Detroit
Metropolitan
Detroit

75

Lake Erie

CT

Sioux
Falls

9

35

Mississippi

90

Milwaukee

Cleveland

90

New York

JFK

Des
Moines

IOWA

80

Chicago

80

INDIANA

OHIO

PENNSYLVANIA

Philadelphia

NJ

81

Philadelphia

Omaha

Chicago-
O'Hare

ILLINOIS

Indianapolis

Indianapolis

Pittsburgh

Pittsburgh

Baltimore

Dulles

DE

BWI Marshall

as City

Lambert-
St Louis

Cincinnati

WEST
VIRGINIA

Washington, DC

MD

St Louis

70

65

Louisville

75

Ohio

MERICA

MISSOURI

KENTUCKY

VIRGINIA

95

MA

Nashville

81

NORTH CAROLINA

homa

Arkansas

40

Little
Rock

40

TENNESSEE

24

Tennessee

Charlotte-
Douglas

Charlotte

allas

30

55

78

Memphis

59

85

SOUTH
CAROLINA

ARKANSAS

20

Birmingham

Atlanta

Hartsfield-Jackson

Jackson

ALABAMA

Alabama

GEORGIA

95

Atlantic

Ocean

45

MISSISSIPPI

Montgomery

75

Savannah

Red

65

10

Jacksonville

Jacksonville

LOUISIANA

Tallahassee

0 kilometers   300

on

10

New
Orleans

New
Orleans

Orlando

0 miles   300

Houston

Orlando

The Bahamas

pus
isti

FLORIDA

75

Miami

Miami

Key

☐ Arizona & the Four Corners

═ Interstate

— Railroad

▓ International border

-- Provincial border

For keys to symbols *see back flap*

A PORTRAIT OF ARIZONA

At the heart of all things Arizonan lies its landscape – stark and stunning, vast and magnificent. There is little in Arizona that is "normal" – from towering red rock buttes and deserts that secretly hoard explosions of life, to deep canyons that are encyclopedias of the planet's history. Everywhere there is a sense of grandeur, drama, and contrast.

Native American tribes have lived in this region for thousands of years. Their ancestors had flourishing civilizations that subsequently vanished, leaving mysterious and haunting ruins, which are today just a stone's throw from modern cities of glass and steel, towering above the ancient desert.

The Spanish, too, had a thriving culture here, a century before English colonists turned westward toward Arizona and the Southwest. When the Anglos finally reached the Southwest, their deeds and misdeeds gave rise to the legends of the Wild West.

Climate and Environment

Elevation, to a great extent, controls the environment in Arizona. For every 1,000 ft (300 m) in altitude, temperatures fall 3 to 5°F (1 to 2°C), and different flora and fauna dominate. In Arizona's southwest corner, the Sonoran Desert is often little more than 100 ft (30 m) above sea level. Here, days are searingly hot, nights are cold, and vegetation is sparse. Heading east, the land rises around 1,000 to 3,000 ft (300 to 1,000 m), and the desert often bursts into vibrant bloom after spring showers. The northern half of the state is dominated by the Colorado Plateau – a rock tableland covering a vast area of around 130,000 sq miles (336,700 sq km) and rising as high as 12,000 ft (3,660 m).

In southeastern Arizona, some mountains higher than 10,000 ft (3,050 m) are surrounded by desert, which has blocked the migration of plants and animals for millions of years, creating unique ecosystems called "Sky Islands." Here are found animals such as the Mount Graham red squirrel that exist nowhere else.

In this land of contrasts, an hour's drive can lead from arid, barren lands of

A sign for Flagstaff surrounded by a carpet of bright yellow flowers

◄ A hiker explores the famous Antelope Canyon in Page, Arizona

near-mystical silence, to mountains blanketed in lush and verdant forests fed by sparkling snow-melt streams.

Most parts of Arizona enjoy more than 300 days of sunshine a year, yet around 90 per cent of the land receives as little as 2 in (5 cm) and no more than 20 in (50 cm) of annual rainfall. Sudden summer rainstorms on the Colorado Plateau cause flash floods. Summer temperatures in the desert often reach more than 100°F (38°C), but can drop by up to 50°F (10°C) after sunset.

Mount Graham red squirrel in the Sky Islands

A Cultural Crossroads

Modern Arizona has been forged by the same three great cultures that have helped shape much of America: Native American, Hispanic, and Anglo-American. Spanish is the second language in Arizona, and throughout the Southwest. Everyday English is peppered with a range of Spanish phrases, reflecting a regional heritage stretching back to the 16th century. While US history usually focuses on developments in the east coast British colonies, Spanish explorers were in the Southwest in 1539 *(see p44)*, 80 years before the Pilgrims landed at Plymouth Rock. Native Americans have a far older relationship with Arizona. The Hopis and

Pueblos trace their ancestry to the ancient peoples *(see pp30–31)* who built the elaborate cliff dwellings at the sites of Mesa Verde, Canyon de Chelly, and Chaco Canyon. Today's Native populations have a hand in the government of their own lands and have employed a variety of ways to regenerate their economies – through casinos, tourism, coal production, and crafts such as pottery, basketry, and Hopi *kachina* dolls. Native American spiritual beliefs are complex, as each tribe has different practices, which are often tied to ancestors and the land. Most Native festivals and dances are open to visitors, although some are private affairs for spiritual reasons.

Politics and Economy

Today, Arizona is the country's fifth-largest state. Despite the fact that its population is increasing, Arizona remains one of the least populated of the United States, with an average density of just 60 people per square mile. However, there is intense urbanization in certain areas – Phoenix, Tucson, and Flagstaff account for around 50 per cent of the state's population. This has put an immense pressure on the

Native Americans performing a traditional dance during the Navajo Nation Fair at Window Rock

Downtown Tucson – the city's historical and cultural heart – at night

region's resources, particularly water, which has become one of the most pressing issues facing Arizona. In the 1930s, dam-building projects were initiated, starting with the Hoover Dam. The controversial Glen Canyon Dam, opened in 1963, flooded a vast area of natural beauty, as well as many sacred sites of the Native Americans. Today, many tribes have asserted ownership of the water on their lands. Water has also been channeled increasingly toward urban use as farmers in need of cash sell or lease their water rights.

Manufacturing, high technology, and the tourism industry have taken over from mining and ranching as the region's principal employers. However, mining and agriculture remain important elements of the economy.

Saxophone player, downtown Phoenix

Entertainment and the Arts

Arizona's canyons, deserts, mountains, rivers, and man-made lakes offer a plethora of hiking, watersports, skiing, and golfing opportunities. One of the best ways to experience the landscape is on a trail ride, while armchair cowboys can attend that great Southwestern event – the rodeo. The state's federally protected national parks, recreation areas, and monuments – such as Grand Canyon National Park, Glen Canyon National Recreation Area, and Saguaro National Park – are favorite haunts for hikers, rock climbers, and 4WD enthusiasts. Beside outdoor sport and activities, Arizona's red rock landscapes and light have always inspired artists, many of whom have settled in Sedona, Flagstaff, and Prescott. For culture lovers, there are orchestras, theaters, opera, and dance companies, who perform regularly in Phoenix and Tucson. Both cities also have a vibrant nightclub scene, featuring country, jazz, and alternate sounds. A flourishing Hispanic music scene livens up nightclubs, while Native American musicians such as Carlos R. Nakai mix traditional sounds with classical music and jazz.

The attractions of the stunning landscape and a romantic sense of the past combine to conjure up the legends of the "Wild West." For many, the Southwest offers the chance to indulge that bit of cowboy in their souls.

Landscapes of Arizona and the Four Corners

Arizona's colorful, beautiful, and varied landscape has been shaped by millions of years of volcanic eruption, uplift, and wind and water erosion. For much of the Paleozoic Era (between about 570 and 225 million years ago), the state was mostly covered by a vast inland sea that deposited over 10,000 ft (3,048 m) of sediment, which hardened into rock. Following the formation of the Rocky Mountains, some 80 million years ago, rivers and rainfall eroded the rock layers and formed the deep canyons and arches that distinguish Arizona's landscape.

The central geological feature of the region is the Colorado Plateau, which covers some 13,000 sq miles (34,000 sq km). It is cut through by many canyons, including the Grand Canyon *(see pp54–61)*.

Coral Pink Sand Dunes State Park's shimmering pink sand dunes cover more than 50 per cent of this 3,700-acre (1,500-ha) park.

The butte formations of Monument Valley *(see pp108–9)* are the result of erosion, and their tops mark the level of an ancient plain.

Arizona's mountains are part of the Rockies and were formed during volcanic activity and continental plate movement some 65 million years ago. Snow-covered peaks, forests of pine, juniper, spruce, and fir, and streams and small lakes fed by snowmelt, as well as alpine meadows are all found in this area.

Geographical Regions

Arizona's prominent features are the Colorado Plateau and the Sonoran Desert, which is divided into Colorado Desert and Arizona Upland. The High Country mountain ranges are surrounded by desert, creating the "Sky Islands" *(see p24)*.

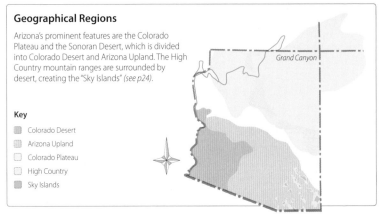

Grand Canyon

Key

- Colorado Desert
- Arizona Upland
- Colorado Plateau
- High Country
- Sky Islands

Lake Powell *(see pp68–9)* was formed by the damming of Glen Canyon in 1963. The creation of the 185-mile- (300-km-) long lake was reviled by environmentalists, and celebrated by watersport enthusiasts and parched farmers and city dwellers.

Antelope Canyon, in the Glen Canyon area, is the most famous of Arizona's narrow "slot" canyons. The canyon's rose-colored sandstone chambers, sculpted into sensual curves by centuries of flash floodwaters and desert winds, are a favorite subject for photographers.

The orange sand of Monument Valley's desert floor is dotted with plants such as sagebrush and cacti.

Mesas, Buttes, and Spires

Like canyons, mesas come in many sizes. Some large ones measure over 100 miles (160 km) across, and are often the result of land being forced up by geological forces. Other mesas, buttes, and spires are hard-rock remains left behind as a large plain cracked, and then eroded away.

The Colorado Plateau is crossed by river-forged canyons. Elevations here range from 2,000 ft (600 m) above sea level to around 13,000 ft (3,900 m). Dramatic variations in the landscape include desert, verdant river valleys, thickly forested peaks, and eroded bizarre sandstone formations.

Flora and Fauna

Despite the fact that over 70 per cent of Arizona is occupied by desert, it is not an arid, lifeless wasteland. Here, elevation, more than any other factor, determines the flora and fauna of a location.

The Sonoran Desert in the south is divided into the low elevation, arid Colorado Desert, and the comparatively higher and more verdant Arizona Upland. Covering much of the state's northern third is the 13,000 sq mile (34,000 sq km) Colorado Plateau. Above 7,000 ft (2,134 m) is High Country, where green pine forests, alpine meadows, and sparkling rivers abound. In the extreme southeast of the state, where the Sonoran Desert gives way to a part of the Chihuahuan Desert, the green-topped mountains of the High Country are surrounded by arid desert, creating special eco-zones called Sky Islands, where unique species have developed over the millennia.

The mountain lion, also known as a cougar or puma, is found in remote desert and mountain areas in Arizona. The males may be up to 8 ft (2.4 m) long and weigh 150 lbs (68 kg).

The Colorado Desert

Dry for most of the year, this vast, arid portion of the Sonoran Desert gets a small amount of winter rain that results in a display of wildflowers in spring. Other flora and fauna found here include creosote bush, cacti, yucca, jackrabbits, desert tortoises, and bighorn sheep.

The Arizona Upland

The summer "monsoon" and winter storms make the upland region – in the northeast of Arizona's Sonoran Desert – the greenest of the deserts. It is famous for its tall saguaro cactus (see p96), some of which attain heights of 50 ft (15 m), and provide a home for animals such as the gila woodpecker and the elf owl.

The blacktailed jackrabbit is born with a full coat of muted fur to camouflage it from predators such as the coyote.

Prickly pear cacti flower in spring and are among the largest of the many types of cacti that flourish in the Sonoran Desert.

The Joshua tree was named by Mormons who pictured the upraised arms of Joshua in its branches.

The desert tortoise can live for more than 50 years. It is now a protected species and is increasingly difficult to spot.

Dangers in the Desert

The danger of poisonous desert creatures has often been exaggerated. Although some desert creatures do, on rare occasions, bite or sting people, the bites are seldom fatal unless the victims are small children or have serious health problems. To avoid being hurt, never reach into dark spaces or overhead ledges where you can't see. Watch where you place your feet, and shake out clothes and shoes before putting them on. Never harass or handle a poisonous creature. If you are bitten, stay calm and seek medical help immediately.

The diamondback rattlesnake is found in Arizona's deserts and mountains. Its bite is venomous, but seldom deadly if treated. It usually strikes only when surprised.

The Arizona bark scorpion is golden in color. America's most venomous scorpion, it has a sting that requires prompt medical help.

The Colorado Plateau

Classically Western with canyons, cliffs, mesas, and buttes, the Colorado Plateau is dotted with cacti, sage, and mesquite in its lower reaches. At higher altitudes, the flora changes to piñon pines and junipers. Rattlesnakes, cougars, and coyotes are among the wildlife found on the plateau.

The High Country

At higher elevations, Arizona's plants and animals are similar to those of Canada. Black bears, mule deer, and elk are some of the fauna. Ponderosa pines are found at 6,000 to 9,000 ft (1,829 to 2,743 m), aspen forests at 8,000 to 11,000 ft (2,438 to 3,353 m), and alpine meadows at 11,000 to 13,000 ft (3,353 to 3,962 m).

Piñon pines are ball-shaped, less than 30 ft (9 m) tall, and are found between 4,000 and 6,000 ft (1,830 m).

Black bears inhabit Arizona's mountainous areas. Their diet consists of nuts, insects, and small mammals. They are shy, but may approach humans out of curiosity or if they smell food.

The coyote is a small, highly intelligent member of the dog family. It hunts both solo and in packs, and can often be heard howling at night.

Aspen trees are common at elevations over 8,000 ft (2,440 m). Their leaves turn a rich golden color in fall.

Art of Arizona

Arizona's qualities of light, open spaces, and colorful landscapes have inspired art and craft for centuries – from intricate baskets and pottery of the Native Americans to the religious art of the early Spanish missions. In the 1800s, Frederic Remington and Charles Russell painted romantic images of the Wild West. Later, in the 20th century, Ansel Adams photographed the beauty and physical drama of the land. Today, Arizona is a dynamic center for the arts, with vibrant art museums, busy galleries, and a lively community of artists.

Basketwork is associated with most Native tribes. Braided, twined, or coiled from willow or yucca leaves, the baskets are decorated differently by each tribe.

Anglo art developed as European settlers moved westward. Works by Frederic Remington *(see pp32–3)*, such as *Cowboy on a Horse* seen above, and by Thomas Moran captured cowboy life and the stunning landscapes of the West. Today, this trend continues with artists portraying traditional and contemporary life in the West.

Traditional Native Art

Five hundred years before Columbus arrived in the New World, Native tribes in Arizona were producing baskets, pottery, and jewelry of stunning delicacy and beauty. Thousands of artifacts recovered from Ancient Puebloan, Hohokam, and Mogollon sites are on display at major institutions. The Heard Museum *(see pp84–5)* has one of the world's most comprehensive collections of both ancient and contemporary Native art, and the Arizona State Museum *(see p95)* has a significant display that covers 2,000 years of Native history. The Museum of Northern Arizona in Flagstaff *(see p72)* features superb examples of Sinagua pottery and artifacts from early Navajo, Hopi, and Zuni tribal life. Native tribes still produce traditional art and crafts, and trading posts are an excellent place to see and purchase them *(see pp148–9)*.

Pottery
One of the oldest of all Native art form
exceptional pottery collections can be
seen at the Edge of Cedars State Park
(see p123).

Contemporary Sculpture

One of the most popular art forms in Arizona today, are excellent examples of contemporary sculpture such as the piece featured here – *Dineh* (1981). These can be seen in galleries throughout the state. *Dineh*, meaning "the people," is the word the Navajo use to describe themselves. This bronze displays clean lines and smooth surfaces that evoke the strength and dignity of the subjects.

Modern Native Artists

Native artists often blend traditional themes with modern styles. The Red-Tailed Hawk *(1986) by Daniel Namhinga reflects his Hopi-Tewa heritage in the stylized* kachina *and birdwing forms, boldly rendered in bright desert colors. It is part of the Native art collection at Heard Museum (see p85).*

Latin art first appeared in Arizona during the Spanish Colonial period, usually representing religious themes. Today, it depicts the Hispanic cultures of the American Southwest and Mexico. Exhibits featuring the works of renowned contemporary Latin artists can be found at major art museums.

Silver Jewelry
Made from silver and turquoise, the art of making jewelry was developed by the Navajo and Zuni tribes in the late 1800s.

Rugs
Weaving began in the mid-1800s. Today, a fine Navajo rug can sell for thousands of dollars.

Carvings
Kachina dolls represent Hopi spirits. They can be traced to the tribe's early history, and ancient ones are valued collector's items.

Architecture of Arizona

Arizona's distinctive architecture traces its influences to the Ancient Puebloan master-builders, whose stone and adobe cliff dwellings, such as Canyon de Chelly's Antelope House *(see p114)*, were suited to the region's harsh climate. Historic architecture can be seen in many old town districts, where adobes are arranged around a central plaza. But there are also other styles, from the Spanish Colonial of the 18th century to those of the 19th and early 20th century. Wooden storefronts, Victorian mansions, and miners' cottages all lend a rustic charm to the region's many mountain towns. Scottsdale *(see p86)* has an architecture school that was set up by Frank Lloyd Wright, one of the 20th century's most famous architects.

Immaculate Conception Church, Ajo

Traditional Adobe

Adobe ovens such as these were once used for baking

The traditional building material of the Southwest is adobe, a mixture of mud or clay and sand, with straw or grass as a binder. This is formed into bricks, which harden in the sun, then built into walls, cemented with a similar material, and plastered over with more mud. Adobe deteriorates quickly and must be replastered every few years. Modern adobe-style buildings are often made of cement and covered with lime cement stucco painted to look like adobe. Original dwellings had dirt floors and wooden beams *(vigas)* as ceiling supports. These structures also had adobe ovens that were used for baking.

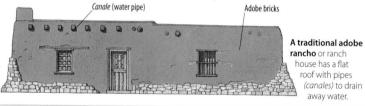
Canale (water pipe)

Adobe bricks

A traditional adobe rancho or ranch house has a flat roof with pipes *(canales)* to drain away water.

Spanish Colonial

In the 17th and 18th centuries, Spanish Colonial missions combined the Baroque style of Mexican and European religious architecture with Native design, using local materials and craftsmen. This style underwent a resurgence as Spanish Colonial Revival, from 1915 to the 1930s, and was incorporated into private homes and public buildings. Red-tiled roofs, ornamental terracotta, and stone or iron grille work were combined with white stucco walls. A fine example is Tucson's Pima County Courthouse *(see p94)*, with its dome adorned with colored tiles.

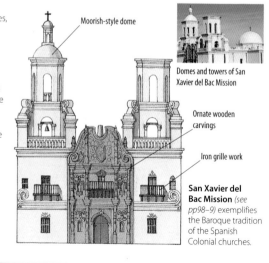

Moorish-style dome

Domes and towers of San Xavier del Bac Mission

Ornate wooden carvings

Iron grille work

San Xavier del Bac Mission *(see pp98–9)* exemplifies the Baroque tradition of the Spanish Colonial churches.

Mission Revival

Similar in spirit to Spanish Colonial trends, the early 20th-century Mission Revival style is characterized by stucco walls made of white lime cement, often with graceful arches, flat roofs, and courtyards, but with less ornamentation. A fine example of a Mission Revival-style bungalow is the J. Knox Corbett House in Tucson's El Presidio Historic District (see p94). Built of brick but plastered over in white to simulate adobe, it has a red-tile roof and a big screen porch at the back.

Façade of J. Knox Corbett House

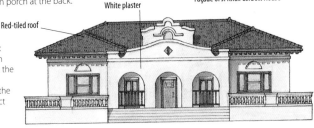
White plaster

Red-tiled roof

J. Knox Corbett House in Tucson was designed in the popular Mission Revival style by the Chicago architect David Holmes in 1906.

Contemporary Architecture

Arizona has inspired three of the 20th century's most prominent American architects. Frank Lloyd Wright (1867–1959) advocated "Organic Architecture" – the use of local materials and the importance of creating structures that blended with their settings. The architectural complex he built at Taliesin West in Scottsdale (see p86) includes a school, offices, and his home. Constructed from desert stone and sand, the expansive proportions of the complex reflect the vastness of the Arizona Desert. Mary Elizabeth Jane Colter (1870–1958) was one of the most influential architects in America at a time when women architects were virtually unknown. At the turn of the 20th century, the Santa Fe Railroad hired Colter to design several buildings in the Grand Canyon area. Colter was fascinated by Native American building styles and is credited with starting the architectural style called National Park Service Rustic. Her masterpiece is Hopi House (see p60), completed in 1904. In the 1940s, Italian Paolo Soleri (1919–2013) studied at Taliesin. In 1956, he established the Cosanti Foundation (see p87) devoted to what he termed "arcology." This synthesis of architecture and ecology minimizes energy waste, which is endemic in modern buildings and towns.

Interiors of the Frank Lloyd Wright-designed Taliesin West in Scottsdale, Phoenix

The visitor building at Arcosanti, designed by Paolo Soleri

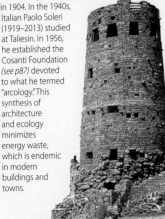
Desert View's stone watchtower designed by Mary Colter, at Grand Canyon South Rim

Native Cultures of Arizona

The Native peoples of Arizona have maintained many of their traditions, in spite of more than 400 years of armed conflict and brutal attempts at cultural assimilation since the arrival of the Spanish in 1539. Such hardships have forged their determination to retain cultural identities, though some have chosen to move between two worlds – living and working in the modern world while taking part in tribal life and traditional ceremonies. Since the mid-20th century, Native groups have led political campaigns for the restoration of homelands and compensation for past losses.

Today, there are 23 Native reservations in Arizona, the Navajo Reservation being the largest. Tourism and gambling have brought much-needed revenue, but battles over land rights and environmental issues continue.

Rodeo in session at the Apache reservation in Whiteriver, Arizona

The Apache

Despite their reputation as fierce warriors, reinforced by their legendary leaders Cochise and Geronimo (see p44), traditionally the Apache were mainly hunter-gatherers. They are thought to have roamed south from their Athabascan-speaking homelands in northern Canada during the 15th century.

The largest Apache reservations are the adjoining San Carlos and Fort Apache-White Mountain reservations in the east-central part of Arizona. Over 12,000 Apaches live on them, with the primary industries being tourism, timber, hunting, and cattle ranching. Successful management of their natural resources has ensured a small degree of economic stability. Visitors are welcome at the Apache reservations to watch rituals such as the *nah'ih'es* or Sunrise Ceremony, which marks a girl's transition to womanhood. Dances, festivals, and rodeos are also held on the reservations.

The Navajo

With a population of almost 200,000, the Navajo Nation is the largest reservation in southwestern USA, covering more than 25,000 sq miles (64,750 sq km) in Arizona, New Mexico, and southern Utah. The spiritual center of the Navajo Nation is Canyon de Chelly (see pp112–13), where Navajo farmers still live, tend to their sheep, and make rugs using the sheep wool. The Navajo are generally welcoming to visitors, and act as guides in Monument Valley and other sites on their land (see pp108–9). The Navajo economy is based on tourism and the sale of natural resources such as oil, coal, and uranium. However, in 2007, after years of debate, the Navajo decided to move forward with casino development to create much-needed jobs on the reservation.

While many Navajo now live off the reservation in cities and towns, the traditional dwelling, the *hogan*, remains an important focus of their cultural life. Today's *hogan* is an octagonal wood cabin, often fitted with electricity and other modern amenities, where family gatherings take place.

Navajo religious beliefs are still bound up with daily life, with farmers singing corn-growing songs and weavers incorporating a spirit thread into their rugs. Colorful and intricate sand paintings still play a part in healing ceremonies, which aim to restore *hozho*, or harmony, to ill or troubled individuals.

Navajo Indian woman shearing wool from a sheep

The Hopi

The predominant Pueblo tribe in Arizona is the Hopi, whose reservation is located in the center of the Navajo Reservation. They are one of 20 Pueblo tribes in the Southwest. Pueblo tribes share many of the same religious and cultural beliefs, though there are linguistic differences from tribe to tribe. Most Pueblo tribes trace their ancestry to the

Hopi Spirituality

Religion is a fundamental element of Hopi lifestyle. Their ceremonies focus on *kachina* (or *katsina*) – spirit figures that symbolize nature in all its forms. Familiar to visitors as the painted, carved wooden dolls available in many gift stores, the *kachina* lie at the heart of Hopi spirituality. During the growing season (December to July), these spirit figures are represented by *kachina* dancers who visit Hopi villages. During the rest of the year, the spirits are believed to reside in a shrine in the high San Francisco Peaks, north of Flagstaff. Hopi religious ceremonies are often held in the *kiva*, a round underground chamber, usually closed to visitors. Most celebrations are closed to non-Hopis, but some are open to the public. Photography of Pueblo villages and ceremonies is forbidden.

Young Hopi Rainbow dancer

Ancestral Puebloan people *(see pp42–3)*, who spread across the area from around 300 to 200 BC. The town of Walpi on the Hopi Reservation has been continuously occupied since AD 1100.

The oldest Hopi villages are on three mesa-tops, called First, Second, and Third mesas. The groups on each mesa are distinct, exceling at different crafts – pottery on First Mesa, jewelry on Second Mesa, and basketry on Third Mesa. All the settlements produce colorful *kachinas*.

The land occupied by the Hopi is among the starkest and most barren in all America. However, using the ancient irrigation techniques of their ancestors, the Hopi grow corn, beans, and squash. Each village holds sacred dances and ceremonies throughout the year.

The Tohono O'odham

Along with their close relatives, the Pima people, the Tohono O'odham live in South Arizona's Sonoran Desert. Due to the harsh environment here, neither tribe has ever been moved off its ancestral lands. These tribes are among the most anglicized in the region.

A member of the Tohono O'odham tribe at a ceremony at San Xavier del Bac Mission

The Tohono O'odham are mainly Christian. However, they still practice traditional ceremonies, such as the Saguaro Wine Festival and the Tcirkwena Dance, and are known for their fine basketwork.

The Havasupai and Hualapai

These two tribes occupy two separate reservations that stretch along the southern rim of the Grand Canyon. They trace their ancestry to the ancient Hohokam people and share similar languages. The only town on the Havasupai reservation is Supai, 8 miles (13 km) from the nearest road. At the heart of the reservation lie the beautiful Havasu Canyon and emerald green Havasu Falls *(see p54)*, a popular destination for hikers.

The Ute

This tribe once reigned over a vast territory, covering 85 per cent of Colorado until as late as the 1850s. Steady encroachment by settlers and mining interests eventually forced them to resettle. Today, the Ute welcome visitors to their two reservations along the southern Colorado border. The Ute Mountain Reservation is home to the little known but spectacular Ancestral Puebloan ruins of Ute Mountain Tribal Park *(see p116)*, and the southern Ute Reservation attracts thousands of visitors each year to the popular Sky Ute Casino Resort. The southern Utes also hold a colorful Bear Dance on Memorial Day weekend, and a sun dance in mid-summer.

Ute woman sewing moccasins with Mount Ute in the background

The Wild West

Romanticized in a thousand cowboy movies, the "Wild West" conjures up images of tough men herding cattle across the country before living it up in a saloon. But frontier life was far from romantic. Settlers arriving in this wilderness were caught up in a first-come-first-served battle for land and wealth, fighting Native Americans and each other for land. The rugged life of the prospectors and ranch cowboys helped to create the idea of the American West. Visitors can still see mining ghost towns such as Chloride (see p79) or enjoy re-enacted gunfights on the streets of Tombstone (see p104). In the late 19th century, however, the ability to shoot well was not only a survival skill, it often co-existed with a kill-or-be-killed ethos.

Women in the Wild West often had to step into the traditional roles of men. Calamity Jane, a woman scout, was known to be an excellent shot and horse rider.

A reward poster for William Bonney (better known as Billy the Kid), who was one of the Wild West's most notorious outlaws. He was eventually tracked and killed by Sheriff Pat Garrett at Fort Sumner, New Mexico, on July 14, 1881.

Deadwood Dick was the nickname of cowboy Nat Love, famed for his cattle-roping skills. Although there were around 5,000 black cowboys, there are no sights or museums commemorating them in Arizona today.

Cowboys were famous for their horsemanship and sense of camaraderie. The painting shows two friends attempting to save another.

The Conversation, or Dubious Company (1902) by Frederic Remington highlights the tensions between Natives and the US army, which had played a central role in removing tribes from their ancestral lands.

Cowboy fashion began to appear in advertisements in around 1900. The ever popular Levi Strauss denim clothing can be bought across the region *(see p144)*.

Guided trail rides are a great way to explore the Wild West and are part of the package of activities available at dude ranches *(see p154)*. These ranches offer visitors the opportunity to experience the contemporary cowboy lifestyle.

Horses were vividly depicted in Remington's dramatic action scenes. They were painted with astonishing realism, revealing a profound knowledge of their behavior and physique.

Southwestern Cowboys

New York-born artist Frederic Sackrider Remington (1861–1909) became well known for his epic portraits of cowboys, horses, soldiers, and Native Americans in the late 19th century. Featured above is Aiding a Comrade *(1890), one of his works that celebrates the bravery and loyalty of the cowboy, at a time when they and small-scale ranchers were being superceded by powerful mining companies and ranching corporations. Remington lamented the passing of these heroes: "Cowboys! There are no cowboys anymore!"*

The Gunfight at the OK Corral

One of the most famous tales of the Wild West is the "Gunfight at the OK Corral" in Tombstone, Arizona *(see p104)*. This struggle pitted two clans against each other, the Clantons and the Earps. The usual, often disputed, version features the Clantons as no-good outlaws and the Earps as the forces of law and order. In 1881 Virgil Earp was the town marshal, and his brothers Morgan and Wyatt were temporary deputies. The showdown on October 26 had the Earps and their ally Doc Holliday on one side and Billy Clanton and the McLaury brothers, Tom and Frank, on the other. Of the seven combatants, only Wyatt Earp emerged untouched by a bullet. Billy, Tom, and Frank were all killed. Wyatt Earp moved to Los Angeles, where he died in 1929.

Scene from the 1957 film *Gunfight at the OK Corral*, with Burt Lancaster and Kirk Douglas

Route 66 in Arizona

Route 66 is America's most famous road. Stretching for 2,448 miles (3,941 km), from Chicago to Los Angeles, it is part of the country's folklore, symbolizing the freedom of the open road and inextricably linked to the growth of automobile travel. Known also as "The Mother Road" and "America's Main Street," Route 66 was officially opened in 1926 after a 12-year construction process linked the main streets of hundreds of small towns that had been previously isolated. In the 1930s, a prolonged drought in Oklahoma deprived more than 200,000 farmers of their livelihoods and prompted their trek to California along Route 66. This was movingly depicted in John Steinbeck's novel *The Grapes of Wrath* (1939).

Seligman features several Route 66 stores and diners. Set among Arizona's Upland mountains, the road here passes through scenery that evokes the days of the westward pioneers.

Route 66 in Arizona passes through long stretches of wilderness bearing none of the trappings of the modern world. The state has the longest remaining stretch of the original road.

Key

🟫 Route 66

═ Other roads

-- State lines

0 kilometers 40

0 miles 40

Oatman is a former gold-mining boomtown. Today, its historic main street is lined with 19th-century buildings, shops and boardwalks. Gunfights are regularly staged here.

The Grand Canyon Caverns, discovered in 1927, are around 0.75 miles (1.2 km) below ground level. On a 45-minute guided tour visitors are led through football field-sized caverns adorned with stalagmites and seams of sparkling crystals.

The History of Route 66

In the 1940s and 1950s, as America's love affair with the car grew and more people moved west than ever before, hundreds of motels, restaurants, and tourist attractions appeared along Route 66, sporting a vibrant new style of architecture. The road's end as a major thoroughfare came in the 1970s with the building of a national network of multilane highways. Today, the road is a popular tourist destination in itself, and along the Arizona section, enthusiasts and conservationists have helped to ensure the preservation of many of its most evocative buildings and signs.

Locator Map
— Route 66
▨ Map area

A 1966 Ford Mustang Convertible arriving at the historic Delgadillo's Snow Cap Drive-In on Route 66

Holbrook was founded in 1882 and is another Route 66 landmark. It is famous for Wigwam Village, a restored 1950s motel, where visitors can stay in rooms that are designed to resemble Indian teepees.

Flagstaff is home to the famous Museum Club roadhouse, a large log cabin, built in 1931. It became a nightclub nicknamed "The Zoo," which was favored by country musicians traveling the road, including such stars as Willie Nelson.

Williams is known for its many nostalgic diners and motels. Twisters diner *(see p138)*, also known as The Route 66 Place, is crammed with road memorabilia, including the original 1950s soda fountain and bar stools.

ARIZONA THROUGH THE YEAR

The weather in the state of Arizona is well known for its extremes, ranging from the heat of the desert to the ice and snow of the mountains. Temperatures vary according to altitude, and so the higher the elevation of the land, the cooler the area will be. Because the climate can be unbearably hot during the summer months, particularly in the southern parts of the state, many people prefer to travel to Arizona during spring and fall. This part of the world is particularly beautiful in fall, with an astounding array of golds, reds, and yellows in the forests and national parks. Besides Arizona's natural beauty, visitors can experience many different kinds of festivals and celebrations, which are unique to the state and reflect its diverse mix of the three main Southwestern cultures – Native American, Hispanic, and European.

Spring

Everyone enjoys being outdoors in spring, and many festivals, events, and celebrations are held at this time throughout Arizona.

March

Cactus League Spring Training *(month long)* Greater Phoenix area. Major league baseball teams play in pre-season practice and exhibition games.
Guild Indian Fair & Market *(first weekend)* Phoenix. Held at the Heard Museum, the fair features Indian dancing, arts, crafts, and Native American food.
Midnight at the Oasis Festival *(early Mar)* Yuma. Cars and nostalgia, with over 800 restored and unusual cars on display.
St. Patrick's Day Parade *(mid-Mar)* Sedona. Annual parade celebrates the green, preceded by a 3-mile (5-km) race.

Rides at the Maricopa County fair held in Phoenix

Tucson Festival of Books *(mid-Mar)* Tucson. A university-sponsored event featuring talks and workshops by local and national authors, as well as displays by dozens of exhibitors.
Fourth Avenue Street Fair *(late Mar & early Dec)* Tucson. Artists from all over the US, food vendors, live music performances, sidewalk performers, and kids' entertainment.

April

Great Arizona Beer Festival *(Apr)* Mesa. A chance to sample more than 200 craft-brewed beers.
Phoenix Film Festival *(first or second week)* Phoenix. Week-long screenings of 130 carefully chosen films covering a wide range of subject matter.
Easter Pageant *(week preceding Easter)* Mesa. This extravagant annual outdoor theatrical production is held every night at the Mormon Mesa Arizona Temple with a cast of hundreds, in historical costumes.
Maricopa County Fair *(mid-Apr)* Phoenix. Carnival, entertainment, competitions, education, and fun times for all ages.
Tucson International Mariachi Conference *(mid–late Apr)* Tucson. Annual celebration of Mexican *mariachi* music and dancing.
Pima County Fair *(late Apr)* Tucson. Horses and cattle, gems and minerals, concerts, exhibits, rides, and food provide great family fun at this annual fair.
The Tucson Folk Festival *(late Apr–early May)* Tucson. Three big-name headline acts, over 120 local and regional acts on four stages, and food, folk art, and craft stalls feature at this festival.

Native dancer at the Guild Indian Fair and Market, Phoenix

Summer

Summer is warm and is the time for many open-air events, from carnivals and rodeos to cultural events. The weather in July and August, however, can be extreme, especially in Southern Arizona, which has very high temperatures and violent summer storms.

May

El Cinco de Mayo (May 5) Many Arizona towns. Festivities to mark the 1862 Mexican victory over the French include parades, dancing, and Mexican food.

Zuni Festival of Arts and Culture (late May) Flagstaff. A celebration of the culture and artistic traditions of Zuni Pueblo, with jewelry and ceramics.

Wyatt Earp Days (Memorial Day weekend) Tombstone. Mock gunfights, chili cook-off, "hangings," 1880s fashion show, street entertainment, and barbecue.

Phippen Western Art Show & Sale (Memorial Day weekend) Prescott. Western art and sculpture buyers, sellers, and admirers come for the juried fine arts show.

June

Sharlot Hall Museum Folk Arts Fair (first weekend) Prescott. Demonstrations of the arts, skills, and entertainments of the territorial years.

Flagstaff Pro Rodeo (mid-Jun) Flagstaff. Competitors

Folk arts fair at Sharlot Hall Museum, Prescott

take part in bronc and bull riding, roping, as well as barrel racing.

July

Hopi Festival of Arts and Culture (early Jul) Flagstaff. A celebration of Hopi culture featuring film, music, art, and dance.

Cowpunchers Reunion Rodeo (Jun or Jul) Williams. Watch cowboys in rodeo events, including bareback, team roping, calf roping, bull riding, and more.

Fourth of July (Jul 4) Most Arizona towns. Celebrations include parades, fireworks, rodeos, sports, music festivals, and Indian dances.

Frontier Days (first week) Prescott. The oldest professional rodeo in the world, featuring calf roping and wild horse racing.

Arizona Highland Celtic Festival (third Sat) Flagstaff.

Entertainment and activities for all ages with bagpipers, dances, athletic demonstrations, and food.

White Mountain Native American Art Festival & Indian Market (third weekend) Pinetop-Lakeside. Features the region's finest Native artists, demonstrations, performances, and foods.

Arizona Cardinals Training Camp (late Jul–mid-Aug) Flagstaff. Most practice sessions of this NFL team are open to the public.

August

Navajo Festival of Arts and Culture (first weekend) Flagstaff. Navajo artists and craftspeople display their work during a weekend of story-telling, dance, music, and art.

Payson Rodeo (third weekend) Payson. Sanctioned by the Professional Rodeo Cowboy Association (PRCA), the best of the best compete for sizeable prize money.

Arizona Cowboy Poets Gathering (Aug or Sep) Prescott. Blend of traditional and contemporary poems, songs and stories about the lives of working cowboys on the Arizona range.

Central Navajo Fair (late Aug) Chinle. Traditional celebration in the Navajo reservation.

Grand Canyon Music Festival (late Aug–early Sep) Grand Canyon Village. Fine chamber music, from Baroque to classical, jazz, fusion, and cross over.

Hispanic musicians or *mariachis* play at a Cinco de Mayo celebration

Fall

The autumnal forests and mountains of Arizona are striking, ablaze with brilliant yellows, reds, and golds. Fall is one of the best seasons for touring and sightseeing because the temperature is cooler and more comfortable.

September

Navajo Nation Fair & Rodeo (early Sep) Window Rock. Largest Native American fair in the US with a parade, a rodeo, traditional song and dance, and arts and crafts.

Coconino County Fair (Labor Day weekend) Flagstaff. Carnival rides, food, local arts and crafts exhibits, demolition derby and car shows, and live music.

Andy Devine Days (mid-Sep) Kingman. PRCA rodeo, parade and activities honor the town of Kingman and actor Andy Devine.

Sedona Winefest (late Sep) Sedona. Annual festival featuring more than 20 Arizona wineries, plus vendors, entertainment, live music, and food.

Flagstaff Festival of Science (late Sep–early Oct) Flagstaff. Ten days of events, including field trips, interactive exhibits, and open-houses at museums and observatories.

Apache County Fair (Sep) St. Johns. Horse racing, entertainment, and livestock shows and exhibits.

October

Sedona Arts Festival (early Oct) Sedona. This festival attracts artists from across the country (plus international guest artists) with KidZone art activities, a gourmet gallery, live music, and food.

Fort Verde Days (second weekend) Camp Verde. Annual event with parade, horse events, barbecue, cavalry drills, and art show.

Helldorado Days (third weekend) Tombstone. Features re-enactments, parades, a carnival, and music and street entertainment.

London Bridge Days (late Oct) Lake Havasu City. Annual celebration commemorates the dedication of the bridge with a parade, concerts, and samplings of some of the city's restaurants.

Celebraciones de la Gente (late Oct) Flagstaff. Crafts and culture festival honoring Arizona's Hispanic peoples.

Cowboy roping in a calf at a rodeo in the Southwest

Climate

The climate varies across the state. Phoenix and the southern areas have hot and dry summers and mild, sunny winters, whereas towns, such as Flagstaff, in the northern areas have snowy winters. These areas are colder due to their higher elevation.

GRAND CANYON (NORTH RIM)

°F/°C	Apr	Jul	Oct	Jan
Average daily maximum temperature	53/12	77/25	59/15	37/3
Average daily minimum temperature	29/-2	46/8	31/-1	16/-9
Average daily hours of sunshine	10 hrs	12 hrs	10 hrs	6 hrs
Average monthly rainfall	1.7 in	2.9 in	1.3 in	3.1 in

PHOENIX

°F/°C	Apr	Jul	Oct	Jan
Average daily maximum temperature	82/28	104/40	86/30	64/18
Average daily minimum temperature	54/12	77/25	55/13	39/4
Average daily hours of sunshine	12 hrs	13 hrs	10 hrs	8 hrs
Average monthly rainfall	0.3 in	1 in	0.3 in	0.8 in

GRAND CANYON (SOUTH RIM)

°F/°C	Apr	Jul	Oct	Jan
Average daily maximum temperature	61/16	84/29	64/18	41/5
Average daily minimum temperature	30/-1	54/12	37/3	19/-7
Average daily hours of sunshine	11 hrs	11 hrs	9 hrs	8 hrs
Average monthly rainfall	1.02 in	1.8 in	1.06 in	1.3 in

FLAGSTAFF

°F/°C	Apr	Jul	Oct	Jan
Average daily maximum temperature	58/14	82/28	64/18	42/6
Average daily minimum temperature	27/-3	50/10	31/-1	15/-9
Average daily hours of sunshine	11 hrs	12 hrs	9 hrs	7 hrs
Average monthly rainfall	1.5 in	2.8 in	1.6 in	2 in

TUCSON

°F/°C	Apr	Jul	Oct	Jan
Average daily maximum temperature	81/27	99/37	84/29	64/18
Average daily minimum temperature	51/11	74/23	57/14	39/4
Average daily hours of sunshine	12 hrs	12 hrs	10 hrs	9 hrs
Average monthly rainfall	0.3 in	2.4 in	1.1 in	0.9 in

Winter

Christmas in Arizona is celebrated in traditional American style, with lights decorating almost every building and tree. Much of the state – the low elevation areas – experiences mild, sunny winters. In areas above 7,000 ft (2,130 m), the ski season stretches from mid-December to early April.

November

El Tour de Tucson *(mid-Nov)* Tucson. Founded in 1983, this is America's largest perimeter cycling event, welcoming both professional racers and amateurs.

Yuma Colorado River Crossing Balloon Festival *(late Nov)* Yuma. More than 50 hot-air balloons fill the sky. Food, entertainment, and fireworks are part of the evening celebrations.

Christmas City *(late Nov–mid-Jan)* Prescott. Parades, bright lights, musical events, open houses, and shopping opportunities abound.

December

La Fiesta de Tumacacori *(first weekend)* Tumacacori. This festival is held on mission grounds to celebrate the Native American heritage of the upper Santa Cruz Valley.

Fourth Avenue Street Fair *(early Dec)* Tucson. Artists, food vendors, live music, sidewalk performers, kids' entertainment, and fun activities for all.

Festival of Lights *(second Sat)* Sedona. Take part in the lighting of 6,000 luminarias in Tlaquepaque's courtyards, and enjoy carolers, musicians, and dancers in this Spanish shopping center.

January

Fiesta Bowl Festival & Parade *(Dec 31 and New Year's Day)* Phoenix. Parade, street party, and college football at the University of Phoenix Stadium.

Tucson Area Square Dance Festival *(mid-Jan)* Tucson. The festival attracts thousands of dancers.

Saguaro cactus illuminated by lights during Christmas

Pow Wow – Gem & Mineral Show *(mid-Jan–early Feb)* Quartzsite. The largest of eight gem and mineral shows held during January and February.

Scottsdale Celebration of Fine Art *(mid-Jan–late Mar)* Scottsdale. Watch art being created as over 100 artists work in studios set up for the two-month-long event.

Tohono O'odham Nation Rodeo *(late Jan)* Sells. Arizona's longest-running Native rodeo, with games, events, and parades.

Waste Management Phoenix Open *(late Jan or Feb)* Scottsdale. PGA's annual golf tournament.

February

Tubac Festival of the Arts *(early Feb)* Tubac. This arts and crafts event is Arizona's longest-running festival.

Silver Spur Rodeo *(mid-Feb)* Yuma. Features numerous arts and crafts, rodeo, and Yuma's biggest parade.

Tucson Gem & Mineral Show *(mid-Feb)* Tucson. Open to visitors. One of the biggest gem and mineral shows in the US.

La Fiesta de los Vaqueros *(mid–late Feb)* Tucson. Rodeo and other cowboy events, plus the world's largest non-motorized parade.

Flagstaff Winterfest *(month long)* Flagstaff. Competitive Nordic and Alpine skiing, dog-sled races, stargazing and concerts, and family activities.

Sedona International Film Festival *(last weekend)* Sedona. Film fans gather to view films and attend workshops.

Skiers riding a chair lift outside Flagstaff

THE HISTORY OF ARIZONA

The story of Arizona's human history has been played out against a dramatic and hostile landscape. Despite the arid conditions, Native civilizations have lived here for thousands of years. Over the centuries, they have adjusted to the Hispanic colonizers of the 17th and 18th centuries, and the Anglo-Americans of the 19th and 20th. Each of these has molded the state's history.

Long before the appearance of the Spanish in the 1500s, the Southwest was inhabited by a variety of Native populations. Groups of hunters are believed to have walked to the region by crossing the Bering Straits over a land bridge that once joined Asia with North America around 25,000 to 35,000 years ago.

The first Native American peoples of this region are known as Paleo-Indians. Skilled hunters of mammoths and other large Pleistocene animals, the Paleo-Indians roamed the area in small groups between 10,000 and 8,000 BC. As the large mammals died out, they turned to hunting small game and gathering roots and berries. These hunter-gatherers are called the Archaic Indians. Anthropologists believe settled farming societies appeared gradually as the population grew, and that new crops and farming techniques were introduced by migrants and traders from Mexico around 800 BC, when corn first began to be cultivated in the region. Among the early farmers were the Basketmakers, named for the finely

wrought baskets they wove. Part of the early Ancestral Puebloan culture, these people are thought to have lived in extended family groups, in pithouse dwellings. By around AD 500, large villages, or pueblos, began to develop in the area. These usually centered around a big pithouse that was used for communal or religious purposes – the forerunner of the ceremonial *kiva (see pp42–3)*, which is still used today by the descendants of the Ancestral Puebloans to hold religious ceremonies.

By AD 700, there were three main cultures in the region: the Hohokam, Mogollon, and the Ancestral Puebloan. These were sophisticated agricultural societies that developed efficient and innovative techniques to utilize the desert's limited resources. The Mogollon were known for their pottery, and were one of the first groups to adjust to an agrarian lifestyle. The Hohokam farmed Central and Southern Arizona between 300 BC and AD 1350, and their irrigation systems enabled them to grow two crops a year.

6,000 BC Appearance of Archaic Indians, skilled small-game hunters and tool makers

Stone spear point

600 BC Corn arrives from Mexico. Start of agriculture, although the semi-nomadic quest for food predominates

200 BC Basket-makers in Four Corners region

10,000 BC	5,000 BC	1,000 BC	AD 1

10,000 BC Arrival of Paleo-Indians. A nomadic people, they hunted big game across the relatively temperate grasslands of Arizona

500 BC Beans and squash are grown, agriculture expands

300 BC Hohokam civilization in Central and Southern Arizona

Papago Indian woman from Pima County, Arizona, 1903

The Ancestral Puebloans

The hauntingly beautiful and elaborate ruins left behind by the Ancestral Puebloan people are a key factor in the hold that this prehistoric culture has over the public imagination. Also known as "Anasazi," a name coined by the Navajo meaning "Ancient Enemy Ancestor," today they are more accurately known as the Ancestral Puebloans, and are seen as the ancestors of today's Pueblo peoples.

The first Ancestral Puebloans are thought to have settled at Mesa Verde *(see pp124–25)* in around AD 550, where they lived in pithouses. By around AD 800 they had developed masonry skills and began building housing complexes using sandstone. From AD 1100 to 1300, impressive levels of craftsmanship were reached in weaving, pottery, jewelry, and tool-making.

Ceramics, such as this bowl, show the artistry of the Ancestral Puebloans. Pottery is just one of many ancient artifacts on show in museums in the region.

Kivas are round pit-like rooms dug into the ground and roofed with beams and earth.

Jackson Stairway in Chaco Canyon is evidence of the engineering skills of the Ancestral Puebloans. They also built networks of roads between their communities and extensive irrigation systems.

Tools of various types were skillfully shaped from stone, wood, and bone. The Ancestral Puebloans did not work metal, yet they managed to produce such beautiful artifacts as baskets, pottery, and jewelry.

Bone awl

Needle

Drills

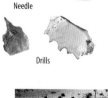

The blue corn growing on Hopi Reservation today is a similar plant to that grown by Ancestral Puebloans. They were also skilled at utilizing the medicinal properties of plants, including cottonwood bark, which contains a painkiller.

The kiva was the religious and ceremonial center of Ancestral Puebloan life. Still used by modern Pueblo Indians, a *kiva* usually had no windows and the only access was through a hole in the roof. Small *kivas* were used by a single family unit, while large *kivas* were designed to accommodate the whole community.

Where to Find Ancestral Puebloan Ruins

Navajo National Monument *(see p110)*; Canyon de Chelly National Monument *(see pp112–13)*; Hovenweep National Monument *(see p116)*; Chaco Culture National Historical Park *(see pp118–19)*; Mesa Verde National Park *(see pp124–25)*.

Petroglyphs were often used by Ancestral Puebloans as astronomical markers for the different seasons. This one was found at the Petrified Forest National Park *(see p73)*.

Pueblo Bonito features many examples of the masonry skills used by the Puebloan peoples.

Chaco Canyon's Pueblo Bonito

At Chaco Canyon (see pp118–19) the largest "great house" ever built was Pueblo Bonito with more than 600 rooms and 40 kivas. One current theory is that these structures did not house populations but were, in fact, public buildings for commerce and ceremonial gatherings. The lives of the Ancestral Puebloans were short, barely 35 years, and as harsh as the environment in which they lived. Their diet was poor, and arthritis and dental problems were common. Women often showed signs of osteoporosis or brittle bones as early as their first childbirth.

The Pueblo People

By AD 1300 the Ancestral Puebloans had abandoned many of their cities and migrated to areas where new centers emerged. Theories on why this occurred include a 50-year drought; the strain that a larger population placed on the desert's limited resources; and a lengthy period of social upheaval, perhaps stimulated by increasing trade with tribes as far away as central Mexico. The Ancestral Puebloans did not literally disappear, however, they live on today in Puebloan descendants who trace their origins to Mesa Verde, Chaco, and other sacred ancestral sites.

Painstaking excavation at an Ancestral Puebloan *kiva* in Chaco Canyon

Ancient Cultures

By around AD 800, the Ancestral Puebloans began to build elaborate ceremonial centers, such as Chaco Canyon *(see pp118–19)*, and to move pueblos off open mesa tops to cliff recesses in canyons such as Mesa Verde *(see pp124–25)*. Their numbers started diminishing around 1250. Chaco Canyon was abandoned about 1275, and Mesa Verde by 1300. By 1350, there was virtually no trace of the Ancestral Puebloans on the Colorado Plateau. Soon after, the Hohokam and the Mogollon became extinct. Experts theorize that a combination of a long drought and social unrest caused them to break up into smaller groups that were easier to sustain. However, these groups did not vanish entirely. Thus the Hopi, Zuni, and other modern tribes are the descendants of the Ancestral Puebloans, while the Pima and Tohono O'odham trace their ancestry to the Hohokam *(see pp30–31)*.

The Navajo and the Apache

The Navajo and Apache originated in the Athabascan culture of Canada and Alaska. The Navajo moved south between 1200 and 1400, while the Apache are thought to have arrived in the late 15th century. The Navajo were hunters who took to herding sheep brought by the Spanish. The Apache groups – Jicarilla, Mescalero, Chiricahua, and Western Apache – continued their nomadic lifestyle. They were skillful warriors, especially the Chiricahua of Southern Arizona, whose leaders Cochise and Geronimo fought Hispanic and Anglo settlers to deter them from colonization in the late 19th century.

The Arrival of the Spanish

In 1539, the Franciscan priest Fray Marcos de Niza led the first Spanish expedition into the Southwest. He was inspired by hopes of finding gold, and the desire to convert the Native inhabitants to Christianity. A year later, Francisco Vasquez de Coronado arrived with 330 soldiers, 1,000 Indian allies, and more than 1,000 heads of livestock. He conquered Zuni Pueblo, and spent two years traversing Arizona, New Mexico, Texas, and Kansas in search of the legendary city

Engraving by Norman Price of Coronado setting out to discover a legendary kingdom of gold in 1540

600 Earliest date for settlement of Acoma and Hopi mesas

1020 Chaco Canyon is at its height as a trading and cultural center

1300 Mesa Verde abandoned

1539 Fray Marcos de N heads first expedition the Southw

800

1000

1200

1400

800 Large pueblos such as Chaco Canyon under construction

1250 Ancient sites are mysteriously abandoned; new smaller pueblos are established along the Rio Grande

1400 Navajo and Apache migrate from Canada to the Southwest

1598 Juan de Oñate founds permanent colony in New Mexico

Illustration of the 1680 Pueblo Indian Revolt

the remaining 2,000 settlers driven south across the Rio Grande. In 1692, however, Don Diego de Vargas reclaimed Santa Fe, re-establishing Spanish control of the land. By the late 18th century, the Spanish were attempting to extend their power westward to California. Their first Arizona settlement was at Tubac, near Tucson, in 1752.

The beginning of the end of Spanish control came with the Louisiana Purchase of 1803. The French emperor, Napoleon, sold Louisiana, an enormous area of about 828,000 sq miles (2.2 million sq km) of land, to the recently formed United States. Land-hungry Americans began a rapid westward expansion toward the borders of Spanish-controlled Mexico. Compounding Spain's problems, Mexico's fight for independence began in 1810, but it was not until 1821 that independence was finally declared.

of gold, Cibola. His brutal treatment of the Pueblo people sowed the seeds for the Pueblo Revolt 140 years later.

The Colony of New Mexico

In 1598, Juan de Oñate arrived in the Southwest with 400 settlers, and set up a permanent colony called New Mexico. The colony included all of the present-day states of New Mexico and Arizona, as well as parts of Colorado, Utah, Nevada, and California.

Spanish attempts to conquer the Indian Pueblos led to hard and bloody battles but, despite the harsh conditions, more settlers, priests, and soldiers began to arrive in the area, determined to subdue the Natives, and to suppress their religious practices.

As the Spanish colonists spread out, they seized Pueblo farmlands and created huge ranches for themselves. A Pueblo uprising began on August 9, 1680, resulting in the deaths of 375 colonists and 21 priests, with

The Missions

In the late 17th century, Jesuit missionary Father Eusebio Kino lived alongside and established a rapport with the Pima people of Southern Arizona. He initiated the Jesuit practice of bringing gifts of livestock and seeds for new crops, including wheat. Those Natives involved in the missionary program escaped forced labor. Kino inspired the Natives living south of Tucson, at a place called Bac, to begin work on the first mission there, which later became the Southwest's most beautiful mission church, San Xavier del Bac (see pp98–9). When Kino died in 1711, there were around 20 missions across the region.

Father Eusebio Kino

1680 Pueblo Revolt drives Spanish out of the Southwest

Juan de Oñate

1711 Death of Father Kino; 20 missions in Southern Arizona

Anza

1775 Tucson founded. Juan Bautista de Anza reaches San Francisco

1783 Construction begins on Mission San Xavier del Bac

1650   1700   1750   1800

1691 Father Kino establishes first mission at Tumacacori, Arizona

1692 Diego de Vargas retakes Santa Fe

1752 First European settlement in Arizona set up at Tubac

1776 Two Franciscan priests are first to travel the Old Spanish Trail

1803 Louisiana Purchase extends US boundary to New Mexico border

A group of cowboys roping a steer, painted by C. M. Russell (1897)

The newly independent Mexicans were glad to do business with their Anglo-American neighbors, who brought much-needed trade.

The Arrival of Anglo-Americans

The first non-Spanish people of European descent, or Anglo-Americans, to arrive in the Southwest were "mountain men" and fur trappers in the early 1800s. They learned survival skills from Native tribes, married Native women, and usually spoke more than one Native language as well as Spanish.

While the Hispanic and the Natives were happy to trade with the Anglos, they were, at the same time, angered by the new settlers who built ranches and even towns on lands to which they had no legal right.

Land Disputes and the Indian Wars

After the Civil War (1861–65), reports of land and mineral wealth in the west filtered back east, and Anglo settlement in the west increased rapidly. By the 1840s, the US government had embarked on a vigorous expansion westward, with settlers accompanied by United States' soldiers. The primary problem they encountered were the constant raids by Natives, dubbed "the Indian problem." The US cavalry countered with raids and massacres of its own. In 1864, more than 8,000 Navajo were forced off their land, and made to march "The Long Walk" of 370 miles (595 km) east to a reservation at Bosque Redondo in New Mexico. Many died during harsh weather en route, and many more from disease at the reservation. In 1868, the Navajo were given 20,000 sq miles (51,800 sq km) across Arizona, New Mexico, and southern Utah.

In 1845, the US acquired Texas and, when Mexico resisted further moves, it set off the Mexican War. The Treaty of Guadalupe-Hidalgo ended the conflict in 1848, and gave the US the Mexican Cession (comprising California, Utah, Nevada, Northern Arizona, and parts of New Mexico, Wyoming, and Colorado) for $18.25 million. In 1854, the United States bought Southern Arizona through the Gadsden Purchase for $10 million. Finally, in 1863, the US government recognized Arizona as a separate territory,

Geronimo

Apache Warriors

The nomadic Apache lived in small communities in southeastern Arizona, and southern and northwestern New Mexico. Seeing them as a threat to the settlement of these territories, the US military was determined to wipe them out. The hanging of one of Chief Cochise's relatives in 1861 instigated a war that lasted more than a decade until Apache reservations were established in 1872. In 1877, a new leader, Victorio, launched a three-year guerrilla war against the settlers that ended only with his death. The most famous Apache leader, Geronimo, led a campaign against the Mexicans and Anglos from 1851 until he surrendered in 1886. He was sent to a reservation in Florida.

Apache leader Geronimo, in a fierce pose in this picture from 1886

and drew the state line that exists between it and New Mexico today.

In the 1870s, vast areas of Arizona became huge cattle and sheep ranches, and by the 1880s, four major railroads crossed the region. These became a catalyst for new industries in the region. Arizona was granted statehood in 1912, and in the years leading up to and following World War I, the state experienced an economic boom because of its rich mineral resources.

The Demand for Water

As the region's population expanded, the supply of water became one of the most pressing issues, and a series of enormous dams were constructed. Dam- and road-building projects, in turn, benefited the region's economy and attracted even more settlers.

The Hoover Dam was constructed between 1931 and 1936, but by the 1960s even that had proven inadequate. Glen Canyon Dam was completed in 1963, flooding an area of great beauty to create the huge reservoir known as Lake Powell, and destroying many ancient native ruins.

The issue of water continues to be a serious problem in the Southwest, and projects to harness water from available sources are under debate.

The Southwest Today

Arizona's economy continues to prosper, and its population is still growing, augmented by thousands of winter residents from the north, or "snowbirds." An ever-increasing number of tourists visit the state's scenic and historic wonders, preserved in national parks, monuments, and recreational areas. Set up in the early 20th century, the parks highlight conservation issues and Native cultures, all of which will help guard Arizona's precious heritage for generations to come.

Mining boom prospector

Glen Canyon Dam

1925	1950	1975	2000	2025

1931–36 Hoover Dam constructed

1974 Central Arizona Project initiated to harvest water from the Colorado River for thirsty Phoenix

2000–2003 Forest fires devastate large tracts of timber in Eastern and Northern Arizona

2015 Grand Canyon West receives a record 1 million visitors

1963 Opening of the Glen Canyon Dam

1996 Bill Clinton signs Navajo-Hopi Land Dispute Settlement Act, ending violent conflicts between tribes

2012 Arizona celebrates its 100th year of statehood

2007 The Grand Canyon Skywalk opens

ARIZONA & THE FOUR CORNERS AREA BY AREA

Introducing Arizona & the Four Corners

This is a region of vast expanses and stunning natural beauty. In Arizona's southwest corner lies the hostile, but eerily beautiful, Sonoran Desert. Its boundaries are marked by the important cities of Tucson and Phoenix. To the north the landscape rises through the red rock canyonlands around Sedona to green mountain towns such as Flagstaff and Payson. Beyond lies the enormous Colorado Plateau, cut by the almost unimaginable depth and beauty of the Grand Canyon *(see pp54–67)*. In the east, the Four Corners area is the only place in the USA where four states – Utah, Colorado, Arizona, and New Mexico – meet at a single point. It is dominated by dramatic canyonlands such as Monument Valley and ancient ruins that stand as haunting epitaphs in a lonely but captivating landscape.

One of the Mittens in Monument Valley

Lake Powell in Glen Canyon National Recreation Area

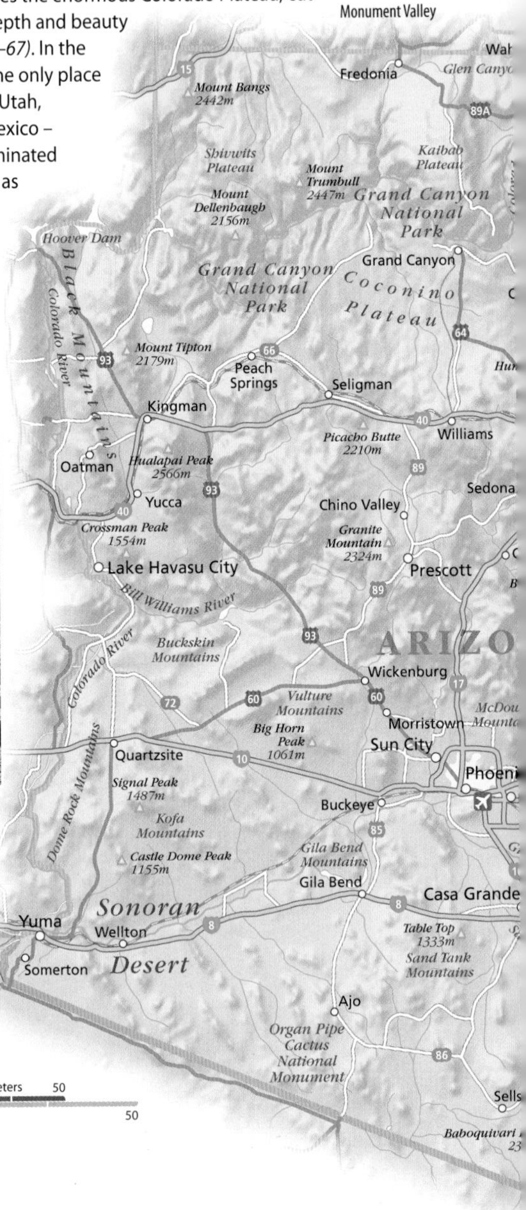

Map labels

Wal
Fredonia
Glen Canyo
Mount Bangs 2442m
89A
Shivwits Plateau
Kaibab Plateau
Mount Trumbull 2447m
Grand Canyon National Park
Mount Dellenbaugh 2156m
Hoover Dam
Grand Canyon National Park
Grand Canyon
Coconino Plateau
Mount Tipton 2179m
Peach Springs
66
Seligman
40
Kingman
Picacho Butte 2210m
Williams
Oatman
Hualapai Peak 2566m
93
89
Sedona
Yucca
Chino Valley
Crossman Peak 1554m
Granite Mountain 2324m
Prescott
Lake Havasu City
Bill Williams River
89
Buckskin Mountains
ARIZO
Colorado River
93
Wickenburg
17
72
Vulture Mountains
60
McDou
Mounta
Big Horn Peak 1061m
Morristown
60
Quartzsite
10
Sun City
Signal Peak 1487m
Buckeye
Phoeni
Kofa Mountains
85
Castle Dome Peak 1155m
Gila Bend Mountains
Gila Bend
Casa Grande
8
Sonoran
Yuma
Wellton
8
Table Top 1333m
Sand Tank Mountains
Somerton
Desert
Ajo
Organ Pipe Cactus National Monument
86
Sells
Baboquivari 23

Key

- ▬ Interstate
- ▬ Major highway
- ▪▪▪ State boundary
- ---- Minor road
- △ Summit

0 kilometers 50
0 miles 50

◀ Scenic landscape of Monument Valley Navajo Tribal Park, located along the Arizona-Utah border

Getting Around

Phoenix is a major hub for international and domestic flights, but many airlines fly directly to Tucson as well. The region is serviced by Amtrak train services and regular Greyhound buses. Driving, however, is the preferred option and the area has a network of well-maintained highways. Northern Arizona is bisected by I-40 and I-10 cuts across the south; I-17 is the main north–south artery. A private car is essential for getting around the Four Corners; a high-clearance 4WD vehicle is recommended for traveling many interesting, unpaved regional roads.

Skyscrapers dominating the skyline of downtown Phoenix

For keys to symbols *see back flap*

GRAND CANYON & NORTHERN ARIZONA

For most people, Northern Arizona is famous as the location of the Grand Canyon, a gorge of breathtaking proportions carved out of rock by the Colorado River. Northern Arizona's other attractions include the high desert landscape of the Colorado Plateau, with its sagebrush and yucca, punctuated by the forested foothills of the San Francisco Peaks. The Kaibab, Prescott, and Coconino National Forests cover large areas, and provide the setting for the lively city of Flagstaff as well as for the charming towns of Sedona and Jerome. The region is dotted with fascinating mining ghost towns such as Oatman, a reminder that Arizona won its nickname, the Copper State, from the mineral mining boom of the first half of the 20th century.

More than 25 per cent of Arizona is Native American reservation land. The state is also home to several Puebloan ruins, most notably the hilltop village of Tuzigoot and the hillside remains of Montezuma Castle.

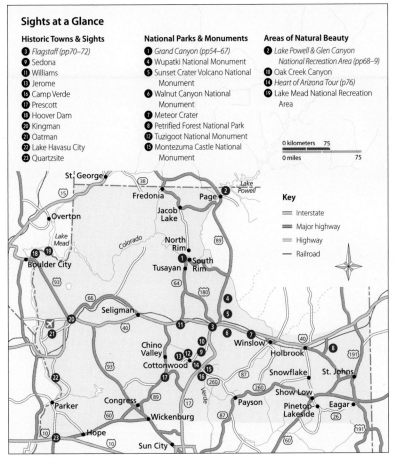

Sights at a Glance

Historic Towns & Sights
❸ Flagstaff (pp70–72)
❾ Sedona
⓫ Williams
⓭ Jerome
⓰ Camp Verde
⓱ Prescott
⓲ Hoover Dam
⓴ Kingman
㉑ Oatman
㉒ Lake Havasu City
㉓ Quartzsite

National Parks & Monuments
❶ Grand Canyon (pp54–67)
❹ Wupatki National Monument
❺ Sunset Crater Volcano National Monument
❻ Walnut Canyon National Monument
❼ Meteor Crater
❽ Petrified Forest National Park
⓬ Tuzigoot National Monument
⓯ Montezuma Castle National Monument

Areas of Natural Beauty
❷ Lake Powell & Glen Canyon National Recreation Area (pp68–9)
❿ Oak Creek Canyon
⓮ Heart of Arizona Tour (p76)
⓳ Lake Mead National Recreation Area

0 kilometers 75
0 miles 75

Key
▭▭▭ Interstate
▬▬▬ Major highway
═══ Highway
— Railroad

◀ Cathedral Rock from Oak Creek in Sedona, Arizona

For keys to symbols *see back flap*

❶ Grand Canyon

Grand Canyon is one of the world's great natural wonders and an instantly recognizable symbol of the Southwest. The canyon runs through Grand Canyon National Park *(see pp56–7)*, which is one of the most visited national parks in the US, and is 277 miles (446 km) long, an average of 10 miles (16 km) wide, and around 5,000 ft (1,500 m) deep. It was formed over a period of six million years by the Colorado River, whose fast-flowing waters sliced their way through the Colorado Plateau *(see p23)*, which includes the gorge and most of Northern Arizona and the Four Corners region. The plateau's geological vagaries have defined the river's twisted course, and exposed vast cliffs and pinnacles ringed by rocks of different colors, variegated hues of limestone, sandstone, and shale *(see pp58–9)*. The canyon is spectacular by any standard, but its beauty is in the ever-shifting light patterns, and the colors that the rocks take on – bleached white at midday, but red and ocher at sunset.

Mule Trips
Mule rides, which must be booked months in advance, are a popular way to explore the canyon's narrow trails *(see p65)*.

Havasu Canyon
The 10-mile (16-km) trail to the beautiful Havasu Falls is a popular hike. The land is owned by the Havasupai tribe, who offer horseback rides and guided tours into the canyon.

Grandview Point
At 7,400 ft (2,250 m), Grandview Point is one of the highest places on the South Rim, the canyon's southern edge. It is one of the stops along Desert View Drive *(see p57)*. The point is thought to be the spot from where the Spanish had their first glimpse of the canyon in 1540.

North Rim

The North Rim receives roughly one tenth the number of visitors of the South Rim. While less accessible, it is a more peaceful destination offering a sense of unexplored wilderness. It has a range of hikes, such as the North Kaibab Trail, a steep descent down to Phantom Ranch on the canyon floor *(see p61)*.

Grand Canyon Skywalk

This horseshoe-shaped glass walkway is suspended 4,000 ft (1,200 m) above the Colorado River. Some 450 tons of steel were used in the construction of this spectacular structure *(see p67)*.

Yavapai Point at the South Rim

Situated 5 miles (8 km) north of the canyon's South Entrance, along a stretch of the Rim Trail, is Yavapai Point. Its observation station offers spectacular views of the canyon, and a viewing panel identifies several of the central canyon's landmarks.

Bright Angel Trail

Used by both Native Americans and early settlers, the Bright Angel Trail follows a natural route along one of the canyon's enormous fault lines. It is an appealing option for day hikers because, unlike some other trails in the area, it offers some shade and several seasonal water sources *(see p61)*.

Grand Canyon National Park

A World Heritage Site, Grand Canyon National Park is located entirely within the state of Arizona. The park covers 1,904 sq miles (4,930 sq km), and is made up of the canyon itself, which starts where the Paria River empties into the Colorado, and stretches from Lees Ferry to Lake Mead *(see p78)* and adjoining lands. The area won protective status as a National Monument in 1908 after Theodore Roosevelt visited in 1903, observing that it should be kept intact for future generations as "… the one great sight which every American … should see." The National Park was created in 1919.

The park has two main entrances, on the North and South Rims of the canyon. However, the southern section of the park receives the most visitors and can become very congested during the summer season *(see pp60–61)*.

North Rim Entrance Station

Point Sublime

Crystal Creek

Bright Angel Po

Shiva Temple

Colorado River

Isis Temple

Havasu Canyon

Diana Temple

Bright Angel

①

Hopi Point

Yavapai Point

Hermits Rest

②

Grand Canyo Village

Yaki

Flagstaff, Williams

Tusayan

Grand Canyon Lodge
Perched above the canyon at Bright Angel Point, the Grand Canyon Lodge has rooms and a number of dining options *(see p61, p130 & p136).*

| 0 kilometers | 5 |
| 0 miles | 5 |

Hermit Road
A free shuttle bus runs along this route to the Hermits Rest viewpoint during the summer. It is closed to private vehicles March to November *(see p60).*

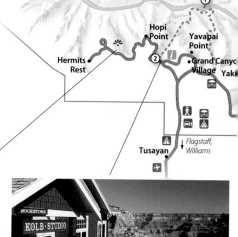

Kolb Studio
Built in 1904 by brothers Emery and Ellsworth Kolb, who photographed the canyon extensively, the Kolb Studio is now a National Historic Site and book store.

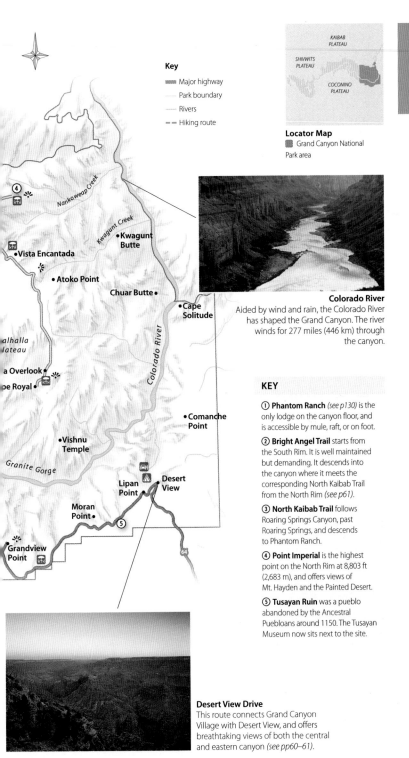

Key

▬ Major highway
— Park boundary
— Rivers
-- Hiking route

Locator Map
▦ Grand Canyon National
Park area

KAIBAB
PLATEAU
SHIVWITS
PLATEAU
COCONINO
PLATEAU

④
Nankoweap Creek

Kwagunt Creek
• **Kwagunt Butte**

▣ • **Vista Encantada**

• **Atoko Point**

Chuar Butte •

Colorado River

•**Cape Solitude**

alhalla
lateau

a Overlook •
pe Royal •

•**Comanche Point**

•**Vishnu Temple**

Granite Gorge

Lipan Point •   **Desert View**

Moran Point •

⑤

Grandview Point

64

Colorado River
Aided by wind and rain, the Colorado River has shaped the Grand Canyon. The river winds for 277 miles (446 km) through the canyon.

KEY

① **Phantom Ranch** (see p130) is the only lodge on the canyon floor, and is accessible by mule, raft, or on foot.

② **Bright Angel Trail** starts from the South Rim. It is well maintained but demanding. It descends into the canyon where it meets the corresponding North Kaibab Trail from the North Rim (see p61).

③ **North Kaibab Trail** follows Roaring Springs Canyon, past Roaring Springs, and descends to Phantom Ranch.

④ **Point Imperial** is the highest point on the North Rim at 8,803 ft (2,683 m), and offers views of Mt. Hayden and the Painted Desert.

⑤ **Tusayan Ruin** was a pueblo abandoned by the Ancestral Puebloans around 1150. The Tusayan Museum now sits next to the site.

Desert View Drive
This route connects Grand Canyon Village with Desert View, and offers breathtaking views of both the central and eastern canyon (see pp60–61).

For keys to symbols see back flap

The Geology of the Grand Canyon

Grand Canyon's multicolored layers of rock provide the best record of the Earth's formation anywhere in the world. Each stratum of rock reveals a different period in the Earth's geological history beginning with the earliest, the Precambrian Era, which covers geological time up to 570 million years ago. Almost two billion years of history have been recorded in the canyon, although the most dramatic changes took place relatively recently, five to six million years ago, when the Colorado River began to carve its path through the canyon walls. The sloping nature of the Kaibab Plateau has led to increased erosion in some parts of the canyon.

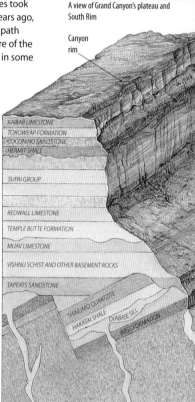

A view of Grand Canyon's plateau and South Rim

Canyon rim

KAIBAB LIMESTONE
TOROWEAP FORMATION
COCONINO SANDSTONE
HERMIT SHALE

SUPAI GROUP

REDWALL LIMESTONE

TEMPLE BUTTE FORMATION

MUAV LIMESTONE

VISHNU SCHIST AND OTHER BASEMENT ROCKS

TAPEATS SANDSTONE

SHINUMO QUARTZITE

HAKATAI SHALE

DIABASE SILL

BASS FORMATION

The canyon's size is awe-inspiring, attracting millions of visitors every year. Pictured here is the North Rim.

Record of Life

The fossils found in each layer tell the story of the development of life on Earth. The oldest layer, the Elves Chasm Pluton, was formed in the Proterozoic era, when the first bacteria and algae were just emerging. Later layers were created by billions of small marine creatures whose hard shells eventually built up into thick layers of limestone.

An asymmetrical canyon, the Grand Canyon's North Rim is more eroded than the South Rim. The entire Kaibab Plateau slopes to the south, so rain falling at the North Rim flows toward the canyon and over the rim, creating deep side canyons and a wide space between the rim and the river.

The Surprise Canyon formation, a layer that formed 320 million years ago was first classified by geologists in 1985. It is visible only in remote parts of the Grand Canyon, but can be seen at its most dramatic in Antelope Canyon, near Page.

The Colorado River changed its course about 5 million years ago. It is thought that it was encompassed by another, smaller river that flowed through the Kaibab Plateau. The force of the combined waters carved out the deep Grand Canyon.

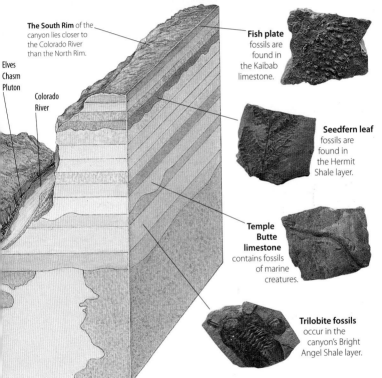

The South Rim of the canyon lies closer to the Colorado River than the North Rim.

Elves Chasm Pluton

Colorado River

Fish plate fossils are found in the Kaibab limestone.

Seedfern leaf fossils are found in the Hermit Shale layer.

Temple Butte limestone contains fossils of marine creatures.

Trilobite fossils occur in the canyon's Bright Angel Shale layer.

How the Canyon was Formed

While the Colorado River accounts for the canyon's depth, its width and formations are the work of even greater forces. Wind rushing through the canyon erodes the limestone and sandstone a few grains at a time. Rain pouring over the canyon rim cuts deep side canyons through the softer rock. Perhaps the greatest canyon-building force is ice. Water from rain and snowmelt works into cracks in the rock. When frozen, it expands, forcing the rock away from the canyon walls. The layers vary in hardness. Soft layers erode quickly into sloped faces. Harder rock resists erosion, leaving sheer vertical faces.

Crack formed by ice and water erosion

Exploring Grand Canyon National Park

The Grand Canyon offers awe-inspiring beauty on a vast scale. The magnificent rock formations with towers, cliffs, steep walls, and buttes recede as far as the eye can see, their bands of colored rock varying in shade as light changes through the day. The park's main roads, Hermit Road and Desert View Drive, both accessible from the South Entrance, overlook the canyon. Grand Canyon Village is located on the South Rim and offers a range of facilities. Visitors can also enter the park from the north, although this route (Hwy 67) is closed during winter. Walking trails along the North and South Rims offer staggering views but, to experience the canyon at its most fascinating, the trails that go down toward the canyon floor should be explored.

The Bright Angel Trail on the South Rim, and the North Kaibab Trail on the North Rim, descend to the canyon floor, and are tough hikes involving an overnight stop.

Adobe pueblo-style architecture of Hopi House, Grand Canyon Village

▦ Grand Canyon Village

Grand Canyon National Park.
Tel (928) 638-7888. ♿ partial.
Grand Canyon Village has its roots in the late 19th century. The extensive building of visitor accommodations started after the Santa Fe Railroad opened a branch line here from Williams in 1901, though some hotels had been built in the late 1890s. The Fred Harvey Company constructed a clutch of well-designed, attractive buildings. The most prominent is **El Tovar Hotel** (see p130 and p136). Opened in 1905, it is named for a Spanish explorer who reached the gorge in 1540. The **Hopi House** also opened in 1905 – a rendition of a traditional Hopi dwelling, where locals could sell their craftwork as souvenirs. It was built by Hopi craftsmen and

designed by Mary E. J. Colter. An ex-schoolteacher and trained architect, Colter drew on Southwestern influences, mixing both Native American and Hispanic styles (see p29). She is responsible for many of the historic structures that now grace the South Rim, including the 1914 **Lookout Studio** and **Hermits Rest**, and the rustic 1922 **Phantom Ranch** (see p130 and p136) on the canyon floor.

Today, Grand Canyon Village has a wide range of hotels, restaurants, and stores. It is surprisingly easy to get lost here since the buildings are spread out and discreetly placed among wooded areas. The village is not only the starting point for most of the mule trips through the canyon, but also the terminus for the Grand Canyon Railway.

South Rim

Most of the Grand Canyon's 6 million annual visitors come to the South Rim, since, unlike the North Rim, it is open year-round and is easily accessible along Highway 180/64 from Flagstaff (see pp70–72) or Williams.
Hermit Road and **Desert View Drive** (Hwy 64) start at Grand Canyon Village and encompass a selection of the choicest views of the gorge. Hermit Road is closed to private vehicles from March to November each year but there are free shuttle buses. Desert View Drive is open all year.

From the village, Hermit Road meanders west along the South Rim, extending for 8 miles (13 km). Its first viewpoint is **Trailview Overlook**, which provides an overview of the canyon and the winding course of the Bright Angel Trail. Moving on, **Maricopa Point** offers especially panoramic views of the canyon but not of the Colorado River, which is more apparent from nearby **Hopi Point**. At the end of Hermit Road lies Hermits Rest, where a gift shop, decorated in rustic style, is located in yet another Mary Colter-designed building.

The longer Desert View Drive runs in the opposite direction, east, and covers 26 miles (42 km). It winds for 12 miles (20 km) before reaching **Grandview Point**, where the Spaniards may have had their first glimpse of the canyon in 1540. About 10 miles (16 km) farther on lie the pueblo remains of **Tusayan Ruin**, where there is a small museum with exhibits on Ancestral Puebloan life. The

The interior of the Hermits Rest gift store with crafts for sale lining the walls

Desert View's stone watchtower, on Desert View Drive

California Condors

America's largest bird, the California condor, has a wingspan of over 9 ft (2.7 m). Nearly extinct in the 1980s, the last 22 condors were captured for breeding in captivity. In 1996, the first captive-bred birds were released in Northern Arizona. Today, more than 70 condors fly the skies over Northern Arizona. They are frequent visitors to the South Rim, though visitors should not approach or attempt to feed them.

A pair of California condors

road continues on to the stunning overlook of **Desert View**. The watchtower here was Colter's most fanciful creation, its upper floor decorated with early 20th-century Hopi murals.

Just east of Grand Canyon Village is **Yavapai Point** from where it is possible to see Phantom Ranch *(see p130)*. This is the only roofed accommodation available on the canyon floor, across the Colorado River.

North Rim

Standing at about 8,000 ft (2,400 m), the North Rim is higher, cooler, and greener than the South Rim, with dense forests of ponderosa pine, aspen, and Douglas fir. Visitors are most likely to spot wildlife such as the mule deer, Kaibab squirrel, and wild turkey on the North Rim.

The Rim can be reached via Highway 67, off Highway 89A, ending at **Grand Canyon Lodge** *(see p130 and p136)*, where there are visitor services, a campground, a gas station, a restaurant, and a general store. Nearby, the North Rim Visitor Center offers maps of the area. Facilities on the North Rim are closed mid-October to mid-May, while the road access is blocked by snow for most of the winter. The North Rim is twice as far from the river as the South Rim, and the canyon really stretches out from the overlooks giving a sense of its 10-mile (16-km) width. There are about 30 miles (45 km) of scenic roads along

the North Rim, as well as hiking trails to high viewpoints or down to the canyon floor, particularly the **North Kaibab Trail** that links to the South Rim's Bright Angel Trail. The picturesque **Cape Royal Drive** starts north of Grand Canyon Lodge and travels 23 miles (37 km) to Cape Royal on the Walhalla Plateau. From here, several famous buttes and peaks can be seen, including Wotans Throne and Vishnu Temple. There are also several short walking trails around Cape Royal. A 3-mile (5-km) detour leads to **Point Imperial**, the highest point on the canyon rim, while along the way the **Vista Encantada** has delightful views and picnic tables overlooking the gorge.

Mule deer on the canyon's North Rim

Bright Angel Trail

This is the most popular of all Grand Canyon hiking trails. The Bright Angel trailhead is at Grand Canyon Village on the South Rim. The trail begins near the **Kolb Studio** *(see p56)* at the western end of the village. It then switches dramatically down the side of the canyon for 9 miles (14 km). The trail crosses the river over a suspension bridge, ending a little further on at Phantom Ranch. There are two resthouses and a fully equipped campground along the way. Do not attempt to walk all the way to the river and back in one day. Many walk from the South Rim to one of the rest stops and then return up to the Rim. Temperatures at the bottom of the canyon can reach 110°F (43°C) or higher during the summer. It's essential for day hikers to carry a quart (just over a liter) of water per person per hour for summer hiking, as well as plenty of salty snacks. Carrying a first-aid kit is also recommended.

Hikers on a zigzagging trail in Grand Canyon National Park

Sunset vista of Grand Canyon National Park ▶

Grand Canyon Adventures

The Grand Canyon's beauty and grandeur, the diversity of activities it offers, and the availability of top-notch tours and outfitters have made it one of the most popular outdoor adventure sites in the world. Many of the classic Grand Canyon experiences, such as mule and helicopter tours, Rim-to-Rim hikes and whitewater raft trips, rate as once-in-a-lifetime adventures for many people. But not all Grand Canyon adventures involve white-knuckle thrills. There are activities geared for every interest and physical ability, from birdwatching to ranger-led interpretive walks along the North and South Rims, to a host of educational programs lasting an hour or a week. If there is anything to stymie the would-be adventurer, it is only the sheer number of experiences to choose from.

Hikers studying a map of the Grand Canyon

Canyon Hiking Tips

Over 400 people require medical evacuations from the canyon each year. Most are healthy people under 40 who are dehydrated or exhausted. It is essential that you:

- Drink plenty of water and/or electrolyte liquids as you hike, even if you don't feel thirsty.
- Eat often, even while you are hiking. High-carb and salty foods are good.
- Wear a hat, sun-protective clothing, and sunscreen.
- Do not attempt to hike to the bottom of the canyon and back in a single day.

Backcountry Camping

In the Grand Canyon Park, backcountry camping exists primarily to facilitate multi-day hikes into the canyon. In fact, demand far outpaces supply, so visitors should try and reserve camp spaces early if they are contemplating spending a few nights in the canyon. Reservations can be made up to four months in advance. If no camp spaces are available for the time of your visit, it is possible to sign up for a guided hike with companies that pre-book campsites. **Wildland Trekking** and **Discovery Treks** are two of the many tour companies

Hiking

The most popular day hikes in the park involve a descent into the canyon and a fairly strenuous climb back up, on well-maintained trails, such as Bright Angel and Hermits Rest (see pp54–61). Once below the Rim, these trails offer ever changing views of the canyon on the way down, sometimes passing by steep overlooks and a few shaded rest areas. Visitors are strongly advised to carry water on these hikes.

For those wanting an easier stroll, there are relatively level trails that follow the edge of the canyon. At the South Rim, the 13-mile- (21-km-) long Rim Trail can be crowded where it passes through the Grand Canyon Village, but provides wonderful solitude and stunning vistas just a mile away. At the North Rim, the Transept Trail is an easy 1-mile (2-km) hike that winds through thick woods to come out at various points along the canyon's edge. Try to head out early to avoid the crowds.

Many hikers consider a Rim-to-Rim hike (descending from one Rim and hiking up to the other Rim) to be the ultimate canyon hiking experience, but it is also extremely demanding, with more than 10,000 ft (3,050 m) of a vertical descent and ascent over 22 miles (35 km). Bright Angel to North Kaibab, or the reverse, is the most popular Rim-to-Rim route, as it offers the only accessible river crossing. Most Rim-to-Rim hikers spend one or two nights at the Bright Angel campground (advance reservations required).

Camping out in the Grand Canyon National Park

Cyclists on the Rim Trail at Grand Canyon National Park

in the Grand Canyon that offer three- to seven-day hikes, both for beginners and for experienced hikers.

Mountain Biking

Although mountain bikes are not allowed on hiking trails within the National Park, there are several scenic roads on which they are permitted. At the North Rim, just outside the park, the Kaibab National Forest offers mountain bikers the 18-mile- (29-km-) long Rainbow Rim Trail and the Arizona Trail, both of which follow the Rim and offer superb views of the canyon. Both trails have varied sections ranked easy to difficult. **Escape Adventures** offers four- and five-day bike adventures on the North Rim.

At the South Rim, a paved, multi-purpose trail follows the rim itself from Monument Creek Vista to Hermits Rest and offers panoramic views.

Birdwatching

Birdwatching is a popular pastime at the Grand Canyon for both serious and casual birders. Hawks and bald eagles can be seen gliding silently above the canyon. Other species, such as canyon wrens, pygmy nuthatches, mountain chickadees, and red crossbills, are quite tame, and can be seen along the tourist trails. Also, many people visit the South Rim for a glimpse of the rare

California condors (see p61). For those who want a more in-depth experience, bird-watching is a major component of many of the outdoor programs offered by the **Grand Canyon Field Institute**.

Educational Tours

The Grand Canyon is a natural classroom for the study of desert and canyon ecology, history, archaeology, geology, and natural history. One of the most accessible sources of short educational courses are ranger-led day-programs offered by the National Park. More in-depth, single and multi-day programs are offered by the renowned **Grand Canyon Field Institute**. Begun in 1993, the institute's programs include wilderness studies, ecology, and photography. The **Museum of Northern Arizona** also offers a variety of educational tours,

as do numerous commercial hiking tour operators such as **Discovery Treks**.

Mule Trips

Since their inception in 1904, mule rides have been one of the most popular of all Grand Canyon adventures. Although thousands of people undertake these trips each year, they should not be taken lightly – this is a demanding adventure. Run by **Xanterra Parks & Resorts**, the trips fill early and may be booked up to two years in advance. The trip takes two days, descending Bright Angel Trail, with an overnight stay and hearty steak dinner at Phantom Ranch (see p130 and p136). The ride offers ever-changing panoramas of the canyon in both directions. Guides stop frequently to ensure everyone is drinking water, as dehydration is a common and sometimes serious problem. Riders must be at least 4.7 ft (1.38 m) tall, weigh less than 200 lbs (91 kg), understand fluent English, and be unafraid of heights. One-day trips that go only halfway into the canyon are also available.

Those wanting a tamer adventure can opt for short trail rides on horseback, which are offered by **Apache Stables** at the South Rim, just outside the park's boundary. For a longer horseback adventure, contact the **Arizona Outback Adventures**, which offers one-day and multi-day adventures into the beautiful Havasu Canyon (see p54).

Mule rides into Grand Canyon National Park – a popular adventure

A helicopter conducts an aerial tour of the Grand Canyon, offering breathtaking views

Air Tours

An airplane trip over the Grand Canyon offers a unique opportunity to view the vastness of the canyon, and is a particularly good option for visitors with limited mobility. Regular tours leave from Grand Canyon Airport in Tusayan, immediately south of the South Rim. **Grand Canyon Airlines** offers tours in larger twin-Engine aircraft that seat 17.

Helicopters, which fly at just 500 ft (150 m), compared to 900 ft (275 m) for airplanes, offer an even more intimate look at the canyon. Several operators, such as **Maverick Helicopters** and **Papillon Grand Canyon Helicopters**, offer 25- to 50-minute tours over the canyon from Grand Canyon Airport. Note that flights have to follow set figure-of-eight routes over the National Park, and that helicopters are forbidden to descend into the North and South Rims of the canyon.

Almost all airplane and helicopter tours from Las Vegas go to the North and South Rims of the National Park, as well as to the much nearer Grand Canyon West, site of the Skywalk, where helicopters are permitted to land beside the river. **The Tour Exchange** provides various air tour options departing from Las Vegas at discounted prices.

River Trips

Perhaps no adventure puts visitors in touch with the beauty of the canyon as much as a paddling trip down the Colorado River. The classic river trip, offered by outfits such as **Canyon Explorations**, **Arizona River Runners**, **OARS**, and **Arizona Raft Adventures** is undertaken in moderate-sized rubber rafts that seat four to seven people, and are powered by a highly trained guide at the oars. Several rafts usually make the run together, with one or two reserved for provisions. A full-river trip starts at Lees Ferry and covers 280 miles (450 km) over 14 to 16 days, taking out at Diamond Creek. Stretches of quiet water are interspersed with 49 of America's most impressive whitewater runs. The rafts stop every night to pitch camp and most tour operators pride themselves on providing excellent meals. They also offer hikes into the canyons on the sides, so tourists can view the flora and fauna,

and waterfalls in the area. Also available are half-river trips lasting five to nine days that begin or end at Phantom Ranch and require hiking in or out of the canyon. Some tour companies, such as **Hatch River Expeditions**, offer trips in larger, motorized rafts that seat 15, and can run the canyon in just seven days.

Dory Trips and Kayak Support Trips

Dories were the first type of boat used to run the Colorado River. Although similar in many ways to rubber rafts, dories are smaller, and many paddlers feel they offer a simpler and more intimate river experience. Several tour operators, including **OARS** and **Grand Canyon Expeditions**, offer 7- to 14-day dory trips through the canyon.

Dory running on the Specter Rapids, Colorado River

Many skilled watersports enthusiasts may long for the opportunity to challenge the river under their own power, in a whitewater kayak. However, they should be aware that waiting lists for solo permits are extremely long. A suitable alternative might be to sign up for a kayak support trip; operators provide groups of paddlers with supplies, camping gear, and food, which follows along in a support raft. Full and half-river trips are available through several outfitters, including **Canyon Explorations**.

Grand Canyon Skywalk

This horseshoe-shaped bridge outside the National Park at Grand Canyon West on the **Hualapai Reservation**, allows thrill-seekers to walk 70 ft (21 m) beyond the canyon rim on a glass-floored walkway that's suspended 4,000 ft (1,200 m) above the canyon floor. Cameras are not allowed on the walkway. As it is a very long and remote drive from the nearest highway, almost all visitors arrive on air tours from Las Vegas.

Spectacular views on the Grand Canyon Skywalk

DIRECTORY

Backcountry Camping

Discovery Treks
21001 N Tatum Blvd, 1630-522 Phoenix, AZ 85050.
Tel (888) 256-8731.
w discoverytreks.com

Wildland Trekking
4025 E Huntington, Suite 150, Flagstaff AZ 86004.
Tel (800) 715-4453.
w wildlandtrekking. com

Mountain Biking

Escape Adventures
10575 Discovery Dr, Las Vegas, NV 89135.
Tel (800) 596-2953, (702) 596-2953.
w escapeadventures. com

Birdwatching

Grand Canyon Field Institute
PO Box 399, Grand Canyon, AZ 86023.
Tel (866) 471-4435.
w grandcanyon.org/ fieldinstitute

Educational Tours

Discovery Treks
See Backcountry Camping.

Grand Canyon Field Institute
See Birdwatching.

Museum of Northern Arizona
3101 N Fort Valley Rd, Flagstaff, AZ 86001.
Tel (928) 774-5213.
w musnaz.org

Mule Trips

Apache Stables
PO Box 158, Grand Canyon, AZ 86023.
Tel (928) 638-2891.
w apachestables.com

Arizona Outback Adventures
16447 N 91st St, Suite 101, Scottsdale, AZ 85260.
Tel (866) 455-1601, (480) 945-2881.
w aoa-adventures.com

Xanterra Parks & Resorts
PO Box 699, 10 Albright, Grand Canyon, AZ 86023.
Tel (888) 297-2757.
w grandcanyonlodges. com

Air Tours

Grand Canyon Airlines
Grand Canyon National Airport, Highway 64, Grand Canyon, AZ 86023.
Tel (866) 235-9422.
w grandcanyon airlines.com

Maverick Helicopters
Grand Canyon National Airport, Highway 64, Grand Canyon, AZ 86023.
Tel (928) 638-2622.
w maverickhelicopter. com

Papillon Grand Canyon Helicopters
PO Box 455, Grand Canyon, AZ 86023.
Tel (888) 635-7272, (928) 638-2419.
w papillon.com

The Tour Exchange
2350 S Jones Blvd, Suite 101, Las Vegas, NV 89146.
Tel (844) 868-7392.
w thetourexchange. com

River Trips

Arizona Raft Adventures
4050 E Huntington Dr, Flagstaff, AZ 86004.
Tel (800) 786-7238, (928) 526-8200.
w azraft.com

Arizona River Runners
PO Box 47788, Phoenix, AZ 85068.
Tel (800) 477-7238.
w raftarizona.com

Canyon Explorations
PO Box 310, Flagstaff, AZ 86002.
Tel (800) 654-0723, (928) 774-4559.
w canyonx.com

Hatch River Expeditions
5348 E Burris Lane, Flagstaff, AZ 86004.
Tel (800) 856-8966.
w hatchriver expeditions.com

OARS
PO Box 67, Angels Camp, CA 95222.
Tel (800) 346-6277.
w oars.com

Dory Trips and Kayak Support Trips

Canyon Explorations
See River Trips.

Grand Canyon Expeditions
PO Box 0 Kanab, UT 84741.
Tel (800) 544-2691.
w gcex.com

OARS
See River Trips

Grand Canyon Skywalk

Hualapai Reservation
Tel (888) 868-9378, (928) 769-2636.
w grandcanyonwest. com

❷ Lake Powell & Glen Canyon National Recreation Area

The building of Glen Canyon Dam in 1963 created the 185-mile- (298-km-) long Lake Powell. Originally intended as a reservoir for drinking and irrigation water, in 1972 the Glen Canyon National Recreation Area (NRA) was opened to allow public access. Covering more than one million acres of desert and canyon country, mostly along the Utah side of Lake Powell, the area is a popular hiking and 4WD destination. Initially built for dam workers, the town of Page is now the starting point for exploring Lake Powell and the NRA. Along the lake shore, the Wahweap and Bullfrog marinas hum with activity, and watersports are popular. In recent years, prolonged drought has lowered lake levels by approximately 40 per cent.

Rainbow Bridge National Monument
Rising 290 ft (88 m) above Lake Powell, this natural bridge is accessible by boat from Wahweap or Bullfrog marinas, then a mile- (2-km-) long walk.

View of Lake Powell
The blue waters of the man-made Lake Powell are encircled by colorful sandstone coves – once Glen Canyon's side canyons – and dramatic buttes and mesas.

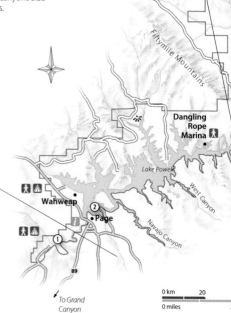

Escalante River

Fiftymile Mountains

Dangling Rope Marina

Lake Powell

West Canyon

Wahweap

Page

Navajo Canyon

89

To Grand Canyon

0 km   20

0 miles   20

Antelope Canyon
Bands of sandstone curve sinuously together, sometimes just a few feet apart, in this famously deep "slot" canyon.

For hotels and restaurants see pp130–31 and pp136–8

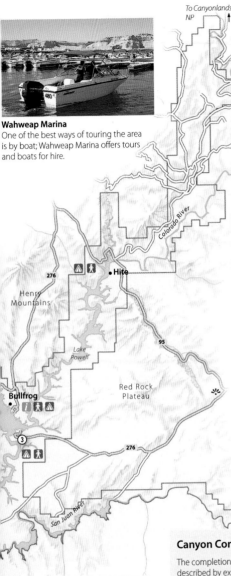

To Canyonlands NP

Wahweap Marina
One of the best ways of touring the area is by boat; Wahweap Marina offers tours and boats for hire.

276

Henry Mountains

• Hite

Colorado River

Lake Powell

95

Bullfrog

3

Red Rock Plateau

276

San Juan River

Boating on Lake Powell
On summer weekends, the lake is a busy place as powerboats, waterskiers, houseboat parties, jetskis, and catamarans explore its myriad sandstone side canyons. Colorado River float trips, available below Glen Canyon dam, are a special attraction.

Key

═══ Highway

═══ Unpaved road

KEY

① **Lees Ferry** was a Mormon settlement in the 19th century. Today, this outpost offers tourist facilities, including a ranger station and campground.

② **Glen Canyon Dam** was completed in 1963 and rises 710 ft (213 m) above the bedrock of the Colorado River.

③ **Halls Crossing** has a marina and is the starting point for the regular ferry service to Bullfrog Bay.

Canyon Controversy

The completion of Glen Canyon Dam flooded the area described by explorer John Wesley Powell as "a curious ensemble of wonderful features." Controversial from the start, the project spurred the environmentalist Sierra Club to campaign against the original plans. Today, they continue to argue for the restoration of Glen Canyon, believing that ancient ecosystems are being ruined. Pro-dam advocates point out the value of the dam's ability to store water, generate power, and provide recreation.

Lake Powell behind the vast Glen Canyon Dam

❸ Flagstaff

Nestling among the pine forests of Northern Arizona's San Francisco Peaks, Flagstaff is one of the region's most attractive towns. It is a lively, easy-going place with a good selection of bars and restaurants among the maze of old red-brick buildings that make up its compact downtown. Flagstaff's first Anglo settlers were sheep ranchers who arrived in 1876. The railroad came in 1882, and the town developed as a lumber center.

Flagstaff is the home of Northern Arizona University, which has two appealing art galleries, and is a good base for visiting Grand Canyon's South Rim, just under 2 hours' drive away. The surrounding mountains attract hikers in summer and skiers in winter.

The town of Flagstaff with the San Francisco Peaks as a backdrop

Exploring Flagstaff

Flagstaff's center is narrow and slender, channeling north toward the Museum of Northern Arizona and south to the university. At its heart is a pocket-sized historic district, an attractive ensemble of red-brick buildings, which houses the best restaurants and bars. Lowell Observatory is located on Mars Hill, a short distance from downtown, and the popular Arizona Snowbowl ski resort is an enjoyable 10-minute drive to the north of the town.

🏛 Lowell Observatory

1400 W Mars Hill Rd. **Tel** (928) 774-3358. **Open** 10am–10pm Mon–Sat, 10am–5pm Sun. **Closed** Jan 1, Thanksgiving, Dec 24 & 25. 🅿 🅰 📷
W lowell.edu

Tucked away on a hill about a mile northwest of the town center, the Lowell Observatory was founded in 1894 and named for its benefactor, Percival Lowell, a member of one of Boston's wealthiest families. He financed the observatory to look for life on Mars and chose the town because of its high altitude and clear mountain air. The observatory went on to establish an international reputation with its documented evidence of an expanding universe, data that was disclosed to the public in 1912. One of the observatory's famous astronomers, Clyde

The 1930 Pluto dome, Flagstaff Lowell Observatory

Tombaugh, discovered the planet Pluto on February 18, 1930 (Pluto has now been reclassified as a dwarf planet).

Visitors have access to the main rotunda, exhibit halls, and the John Vickers McAllister Space Theater, which shows presentations on the night sky and current research at Lowell. Campus tours are available daily, and telescope viewings nightly.

🏛 Historic Downtown District

Just 10 minutes' walk from end to end, Flagstaff's historic downtown dates mainly from the 1890s. Many buildings sport decorative stone and stucco friezes, and are now occupied by cafés, bars, and stores. Architecturally, several buildings stand out, particularly the restored Babbitt Building and the 1926 train station that today houses the visitor center. Perhaps the most attractive building is the Weatherford Hotel, which was opened on January 1, 1900. It was named for its owner, Texan entrepreneur John W. Weatherford, and was much admired for its grand two-story wraparound veranda and its sunroom.

🏛 Northern Arizona University

624 S Knoles Dr. **Tel** (928) 523-9011. **Open** times vary; call in advance.
W nau.edu

Flagstaff's lively café society owes much to the 29,000 students of Northern Arizona University. The main entrance point to the campus is located on Knoles Drive. Green lawns, stately trees, and several historic buildings make this a pleasant place to visit. Of particular note are two campus art galleries: the Beasley Gallery in the School of Art Building, which features temporary exhibitions and student work, and the Northern Arizona University Art Museum housed in Old Main Building, the university's oldest. This features the permanent Weiss Collection, which includes works by the famous Mexican artist Diego Rivera.

Arts and Crafts swinging settee at Riordan Mansion

🏛 Riordan Mansion State Historic Park

409 W Riordan Rd. **Tel** (928) 779-4395. **Open** May–Oct: 9:30am–5pm; Nov–Apr: call for opening hours. **Closed** Dec 25. 🚻 ♿ 🆆 azstateparks.com

In the mid-1880s, Michael and Timothy Riordan established a lumber company that quickly made them a fortune. The brothers then built a house of grandiose proportions, a 40-room log mansion with two wings, one for each of them. Completed in 1904 and now preserved as a State Historic Park, the house has a rustic exterior, and Arts and Crafts furniture inside.

🏛 Pioneer Museum

2340 N Fort Valley Rd. **Tel** (928) 774-6272. **Open** 9am–5pm Mon–Sat, 10am–4pm Sun (Sep–May: 10am–4pm Mon–Sat). **Closed** public hols. 🚻 🆆 arizonahistoricalsociety.org

This museum occupies an elegant stone building that was originally erected as a hospital in 1908. It opened in 1960 and incorporates the Ben Doney homestead cabin. On display in the grounds are a steam locomotive of 1929 and a Santa Fe Railroad caboose. Inside, a particular highlight is a selection of Grand Canyon photographs taken in the early 1900s by Ellsworth and Emery Kolb.

Arizona Snowbowl

Snowbowl Rd, off Hwy 180. **Tel** (928) 779-1951. Flagstaff Snow Report: (928) 779-4577. **Open** Dec–mid-Apr. 🆆 arizonasnowbowl.com

Downhill skiing can be enjoyed at Arizona Snowbowl just 7 miles (11 km) north of town. The mountains here are the San Francisco Peaks, which receive an average of 260 in (660 cm) of snow annually, enough to supply the various ski runs that pattern the lower slopes of the 12,356-ft- (3,707-m-) high Agassiz Peak. Facilities include five chairlifts, and a ski school for beginners. In summer, there is a hiking trail up to the peak, while the Arizona Scenic Chairlift (10am–4pm Fri–Sun) is an open chairlift that offers spectacular views of the scenery.

🏛 Museum of Northern Arizona

See p72.

VISITORS' CHECKLIST

Practical Information
Road map C3. 🔼 70,000. ℹ️ Flagstaff Visitor's Center, at Amtrak depot, 1 E Rte 66, Flagstaff. **Tel** (928) 774-9541. **Open** 8am–5pm Mon–Sat, 9am–4pm Sun. **Closed** Jan 1, Thanksgiving, Dec 25. 🆆 flagstaffarizona.org

Transport
✈️ Pulliam Airport, 4 miles (6 km) south of town. 🚆 Amtrak Flagstaff Station, 1 E Rte 66. 🚌 Flagstaff bus station, 880 E Butler Ave.

Flagstaff

1. Lowell Observatory
2. Historic Downtown District
3. Northern Arizona University
4. Riordan Mansion State Historic Park

Pulliam Airport
6 km (4 miles) ✈️

For keys to symbols *see back flap*

Flagstaff: Museum of Northern Arizona

The Museum of Northern Arizona holds one of the Southwest's most comprehensive collections of archeological artifacts, as well as fine art and natural science exhibits. The collections are arranged in galleries around a central courtyard. The Archaeology Gallery gives an introduction to the historic cultures. The Ethnology Gallery documents 12,000 years of tribal cultures on the Colorado Plateau, while the Babbitt Gallery showcases traditional and modern pottery of the Hopi people. The museum shop sells contemporary native fine arts and the bookstore specializes in native arts and crafts.

VISITORS' CHECKLIST

Practical Information
3101 N Fort Valley Rd. **Tel** (928) 774-5213. **Open** 10am–5pm daily (from noon Sun). **Closed** Jan 1, Thanksgiving, Dec 25. ♿ ♿ 📷
W musnaz.org

★ **Ethnology Gallery**
This gallery highlights the living cultures of the Hopi, Navajo, Pai, and Zuni people.

The historic courtyard has exhibits that focus on the variety of plants and animals found on the Colorado Plateau through the ages.

The Kiva Gallery replicates the inside of a *kiva* (see pp42–3).

Babbitt Gallery

Entrance

Archaeology Gallery

Geology Gallery
A lifesize skeletal model of a Dilophosaurus is ringed by dioramas of ancient Arizona desert scenes.

Key
- Archaeology Gallery
- Ethnology Gallery
- Babbitt Gallery
- Geology Gallery
- Historic courtyard
- Changing Exhibition Gallery
- Non-exhibition space

Museum Façade
Built in 1935, the museum has a stone façade and is listed on the National Register of Historic Places.

❹ Wupatki National Monument

Road map C3. Forest Service Rd 545, Sunset Crater/Wupatki Loop Rd. **Tel** (928) 679-2365. 🚌 Flagstaff. 🚆 Flagstaff. **Open** 9am–5pm daily. **Closed** Dec 25. 🅿 ♿ partial. 🌐 **nps.gov/wupa**

Covering more than 55 sq miles (142 sq km) of sun-scorched wilderness to the north of Flagstaff, the Wupatki National Monument incorporates about 2,700 historic sites once inhabited by the ancestors of the Hopi people. The area was first settled after the eruption of Sunset Crater in 1064. The Sinagua people and their Ancestral Puebloan cousins (*see pp42–3*) realized that the volcanic ash had made the soil more fertile and consequently favourable for farming. The power of the volcanic eruption may also have appealed to their spirituality. They left the region in the early 13th century, but no one really knows why.

The largest site here is the Wupatki Pueblo, built in the 12th century and once a four-story pueblo complex of 100 rooms, housing more than 100 Sinagua. The structures rise from their rocky outcrop overlooking the desert. A trail from the visitor center explores the remains of the complex, whose most unusual feature is its ballcourt. Here the Sinagua may have played at dropping a ball through a stone ring without using their hands or feet.

❺ Sunset Crater Volcano National Monument

Road map C3. Hwy 545 off Hwy 89, Sunset Crater/Wupatki Loop Rd. **Tel** (928) 526-0502. 🚌 Flagstaff. 🚆 Flagstaff. **Open** Jun–Oct: 8am–5pm; Nov–May: 9am–5pm. **Closed** Dec 25. 🅿 ♿ 🌐 **nps.gov/sucr**

Volcanic eruptions between 1040 and 1100 formed the 400-ft- (120-m-) deep Sunset Crater, leaving a cinder cone that is 1,000 ft (300 m) high. The cone is black at the base and tinged with reds and oranges farther up. The 1-mile (2-km) Lava Trail offers an easy stroll around the ashy landscape with its lava tubes, bubbles, and vents.

❻ Walnut Canyon National Monument

Road map C3. Hwy 40 exit 204. **Tel** (928) 526-3367. 🚌 Flagstaff. 🚆 Flagstaff. **Open** Jun–Oct: 8am–5pm; Nov–May: 9am–5pm. **Closed** Dec 25. 🅿 ♿ partial. 🌐 **nps.gov/waca**

Located about 10 miles (16 km) east of Flagstaff, off Interstate Highway 40, the Walnut Canyon National Monument houses a collection of single-story cliff dwellings. These were inhabited by the Sinagua people in the 12th and 13th centuries.

Today, visitors to Walnut Canyon can tour the 25 cliff dwellings huddled underneath the natural overhangs of its eroded sandstone and limestone walls. Sinagua artifacts are on display in the Walnut Canyon Visitor Center, which also houses a small museum.

❼ Meteor Crater

Road map C3. South 6 miles off Hwy 40 exit 233. **Tel** (928) 289-2362. 🚌 Flagstaff. 🚆 Flagstaff. **Open** Jun–Aug: 7am–7pm; Sep–May: 8am–5pm. **Closed** Dec 25. 🅿 ♿ partial. 🌐 **meteorcrater.com**

Petroglyph from Walnut Canyon

This meteorite impact crater so closely resembles a moon crater that NASA astronauts trained here in the 1960s. It was formed nearly 50,000 years ago and is 550 ft (168 m) deep and 2.4 miles (3.8 km) in circumference. The informative visitor center has exhibits and a film.

❽ Petrified Forest National Park

Road map D3. Off Hwy I-40. **Tel** (928) 524-6228. **Open** times vary; see website for details. **Closed** Dec 25. 🅿 ♿ partial. 🌐 **nps.gov/pefo**

Millions of years ago rivers swept trees downstream into a vast swamp. Groundwater transported silica dioxide, eventually turning the timber into the quartz stone logs seen today, with colored crystals preserving the trees' shape and structure. Running the length of the forest is the famous Painted Desert, an area of colored bands of sand and rock that change from blues to reds as the shifting light catches the different mineral deposits.

From here, a 28-mile (45-km) scenic road has nine overlooks. Near the south end of the road is the **Rainbow Forest Museum**.

🏛 **Rainbow Forest Museum**
Off Hwy 180 (S entrance). **Tel** (928) 524-6228. **Open** as Petrified Forest National Park (above). **Closed** Dec 25. 🅿

Ruins of a 12th-century pueblo building at Wupatki National Monument

❾ Sedona

Founded by Theodore Schnelby in 1902, and named for his wife, Sedona was a quiet town until 1981. That year, author and renowned psychic Page Bryant claimed to have located seven "vortexes" emanating powerful spiritual energy in and around this beautiful town, and declared it the "heart-chakra of the planet." Since then, New Agers have developed Sedona as a spiritual, artistic, and outdoor-oriented resort town. Today, artists of all kinds sell their works in a growing number of galleries, such as those in Tlaquepaque, a superbly rendered village of artists, craftspeople, and imaginative shops.

VISITORS' CHECKLIST

Practical Information
Road map B3. 🅰 10,000.
ℹ 331 Forest Road, (800) 288-7336. **Open** 8:30am–5pm daily. Spas: Mii Amo at Enchantment Resort, (888) 749-2137; Los Abrigados Resort & Spa, (800) 418-6499. Art Shopping: Tlaquepaque Art Village, (928) 282-4838. 🎷 Red Rocks Music Festival (Jan & late Aug–early Sep). 🆆 visitsedona.com

Transport
✈ Pulliam Airport, Flagstaff (no commercial flights to Sedona Airport).

Cathedral Rock

One of Sedona's seven "energy vortexes," Cathedral Rock is revered in Native American mythology as the birthplace of the "First Man" and "First Woman." It is a popular place for sunrise and sunset hikes, and the view of Cathedral Rock overlooking Oak Creek is one of the most photographed scenes in Arizona.

Havasupai Storyteller
Native American themes and traditions are often components of many of the programs offered in and around Sedona.

Crystal Therapy
Sedona's New Age centers offer a dazzling array of alternative therapies.

Spa Resorts
Sedona's natural desert beauty and reputed healing energies have made it a premier center for spas and resorts.

Tlaquepaque Art Village
Sedona has attracted many artists and craftspeople, whose creations are on display in fine shops and galleries.

⑩ Oak Creek Canyon

Road map B3. 🅸 (928) 282-4119.

Just south of Flagstaff, Highway 89A weaves a charming route through Oak Creek Canyon on its way to Sedona. In the canyon, dense woods shadow the road, and the steep cliffs are colored in bands of red and yellow sandstone, pale limestone, and black basalt. The canyon is a popular summer vacation area with many day-hiking trails, such as the East Pocket Trail, a steep, wooded climb to the canyon rim. One of the prettiest and easiest hikes in Oak Creek is along the 3-mile (5-km) West Fork Trail, which follows a stream past abandoned apple orchards and into a narrow red rock canyon. At nearby Slide Rock State Park, swimmers enjoy sliding over the rocks that form a natural water chute.

⑪ Williams

Road map B3. 🅰 3,000. 🚉 🅸 200 W Railroad Ave, (928) 635-1418. 🅦 **experiencewilliams.com**

This distinctive little town was named in 1851 for Bill Williams (1787–1849), a legendary mountain man and trapper who lived for a time with the Osage Indians in Missouri. The town grew around the railroad that came in the 1880s, and when this was followed by a spur track to Grand Canyon's South Rim in 1901, Williams became established as a tourist center. By the late 1920s, it was also a popular rest stop on Route 66 (*see pp34–5*).

The town has retained its frontier atmosphere, complete with Stetson-wearing locals. Most hotels and diners are located on a loop that follows Route 66 on one side, and Interstate Highway 40 on the other. Diners evoke the 1950s, and are filled with Route 66 memorabilia, including original soda fountains and posters.

Picturesque Oak Creek Canyon – a popular summer destination

⑫ Tuzigoot National Monument

Road map B3. Follow signs from Hwy 89A. **Tel** (928) 634-5564. **Open** 8am–4pm daily. **Closed** Dec 25. 🅿 🅦 **nps.gov/tuzi**

Perched on a solitary limestone ridge, the ruins of Tuzigoot National Monument offer fine views of the Verde River Valley. The pueblo was built by the Sinagua people between the 12th and 15th centuries and, at its peak, had a population of around 300. It was abandoned in the early 15th century, when the Sinagua are believed to have migrated north.

Tuzigoot was partly rebuilt by a local and federally funded program during the Depression in the 1930s. This emphasized one of the most unusual features of pueblo building, the lack of doorways. The normal pueblo room was entered by ladder through a hatchway in the roof. Sinaguan artifacts and art are on display at the visitor center here.

⑬ Jerome

Road map B3. 🅰 500. 🅸 Box K, Jerome. 🅦 **jeromechamber.com**

Approached from the east along Highway 89A, Jerome is easy to spot, with its old brick buildings high above the valley. Silver mining began here in the 1870s, but the town's big break came in 1912 when prospectors struck substantial copper. World War I sent the price of copper sky-high, and Jerome boomed. In the Wall Street Crash of 1929, however, copper prices tumbled, and the boom times were over. Jerome was a ghost town by the early 1960s, but its fortunes have now been revived by an influx of artists and artisans.

Façade of an early 20th-century store on Jerome's historic Main Street

⑭ Heart of Arizona Tour

The Verde River passes through the wooded hills and fertile meadows of Central Arizona, before opening into a wide, green valley between Flagstaff and Phoenix. The heart of Arizona is full of charming towns such as Sedona, hidden away among stunning scenery, and the former mining town of Jerome. Over the hills lies Prescott, once state capital and now a busy, likable little town with a center full of dignified Victorian buildings. The area's ancient history can be seen in its two beautiful pueblo ruins, Montezuma Castle and Tuzigoot.

Tips for Drivers

Recommended route: From Sedona, take Hwy 89A to Tuzigoot, Jerome, and Prescott. Hwy 69 runs east from Prescott to Interstate Hwy 17, which connects to Camp Verde, Fort Verde, and Montezuma Castle.
Tour length: 85 miles (137 km).
When to go: Spring and fall are delightful; summer is very hot.

① **Sedona**
Set among dramatic red rock hills, Sedona *(see p74)* is a popular resort, known for its New Age stores and galleries, as well as for its friendly ambience.

② **Tuzigoot National Monument**
Stunning views of Verde River Valley are seen at this ruined pueblo *(see p75)*, occupied until 1425.

Key

▨▨ Tour route
═ Other roads

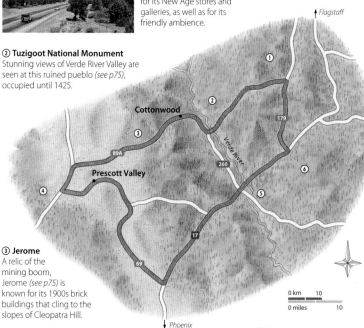

③ **Jerome**
A relic of the mining boom, Jerome *(see p75)* is known for its 1900s brick buildings that cling to the slopes of Cleopatra Hill.

④ **Prescott**
This charming historic town is set among the rugged peaks and lush woods of Prescott National Forest, making it a popular center for many outdoor activities.

⑥ **Montezuma Castle National Monument**
The Ancestral Puebloan ruins here date from the 1100s and occupy one of the loveliest sites in the Southwest.

⑤ **Camp Verde**
A highlight of this little town is Fort Verde. Built by the US Army in 1865, the fort is manned by costumed guides.

❶ Montezuma Castle National Monument

Road map B3. Hwy I-17 exit 289. **Tel**
(928) 567-3322. **Open** 8am–5pm daily.
Closed Dec 25. 🅿 W nps.gov/moca

Dating from the 1100s, the
pueblo remains that make up
Montezuma Castle occupy an
idyllic location, built into the
limestone cliffs high above
Beaver Creek, a couple of
miles to the east of Interstate
Highway 17. Once home to
the Sinagua people, this cliff
dwelling originally contained
20 rooms on five floors.
Montezuma Castle was declared
a National Monument in 1906
to preserve its excellent
condition. The visitor center
has a display on Sinaguan life,
and is found at the start of an
easy trail along Beaver Creek.
The National Monument also
incorporates Montezuma
Well, situated about
11 miles (18 km) to
the northeast. This
natural sinkhole,
50 ft (15 m) deep
and 470 ft (140 m)
in diameter, had
religious significance
for Native Americans,
who believed it
was the site of the
Creation. Over 1,000
gallons (3,790 liters)
of water flow through
the sinkhole every
minute, an inexhaustible supply
that has long been used for
irrigation. A narrow trail leads
around the rim before twisting
its way down to the water's edge.

Pueblo remains of Montezuma Castle, built into limestone cliffs

❶ Camp Verde

Road map B3. 🄰 10,000.
🄸 435 S Main St, (928) 554-0851.
🄰 W visitcampverde.com

Farmers founded the small
settlement of Camp Verde in
the heart of the Verde River
Valley in the 1860s. It was a risky
enterprise as the Apache lived
nearby, but the US Army quickly
moved in to protect the settlers,
building **Fort Verde** in 1865.
Today, Camp Verde remains

Costumed guides at Fort
Verde State Historic Park

at the center of a large and
prosperous farming and
ranching community. It was
from Fort Verde that the army
orchestrated a series of brutal
campaigns against the Apache,
which ended with the Battle
of the Big Dry Wash in 1882.
Once the Apache had been sent
to reservations, Fort Verde was
no longer needed and it was
decommissioned
in 1891. Four of its
original buildings
have survived.
The former army
administration
building contains a
collection of exhibits
on army life. The
interiors of the other
three houses, on
Officers' Row, have
been restored. At
times, volunteers
dressed in period
costume act as guides and
re-enact scenes from the fort's
daily life. Call ahead for a
schedule of such events.

🏛 **Fort Verde State Historic Park**
Off Hwy I-17, Camp Verde. **Tel** (928)
567-3275. **Open** 9am–5pm daily.
W azstateparks.com/parks/fove

❶ Prescott

Road map B3. 🄰 40,000. ✈ 🚌 🚇
🄸 117 W Goodwin St, (928) 445-
2000. W prescott.org

Surrounded by high-country
and lakes, this attractive
Victorian town gives little
evidence of its early days as
a hard-drinking frontier area.

Perhaps the three years spent
as the early capital of the
Arizona Territories gave it some
respectability. Palace Saloon
is the only structure left from
"Whiskey Row," where over
20 saloons once stood. The
Governor's Mansion – really
just a large log cabin – is part
of the **Sharlot Hall Museum**.
This exceptional museum is
named for Sharlot Hall, a
pioneer, writer, and early
activist who served as Arizona's
first salaried historian. Her
paintings and photographs
form the core of a collection
that fills nine buildings.

Fans of Native history should
visit **Smoki Museum**. Located
in a replica of a Hopi pueblo,
the museum contains over
2,000 Native artifacts from
prehistoric to modern. The
museum's basket collection
is said to be one of the best in
the United States. Also of note
is the **Phippen Museum**, which
has an impressive collection of
historic and contemporary
Western art.

🏛 **Sharlot Hall Museum**
415 W Gurly St. **Tel** (928) 445- 3122.
Open May–Sep: 10am–5pm Mon–Sat,
noon–4pm Sun; Oct–Apr: 10am–4pm
Mon–Sat, noon– 4pm Sun. 🅿
W sharlot.org

🏛 **Smoki Museum**
147 N Arizona St. **Tel** (928) 445-1230.
Open 10am–4pm Mon–Sat; 1–4pm
Sun. 🅿 W smokimuseum.org

🏛 **Phippen Museum**
4701 Hwy 89 N. **Tel** (928) 778-1385.
Open 10am–4pm Tue–Sat, 1–4pm
Sun. **Closed** Thanksgiving, Dec 25.
🅿 W phippenartmuseum.org

⓲ Hoover Dam

Road map A2. ℹ️ Hoover Dam Visitor Center, Hoover Dam, Boulder City, (702) 494-2517. **Open** 9am–4:15pm (5:15pm summer) for start of last tour. **Closed** Thanksgiving, Dec 25. 🚻 ♿ 🅦 **usbr.gov/lc/hooverdam**

Named for Herbert Hoover, the 31st president, the historic Hoover Dam sits at Arizona's border with Nevada, 30 miles (48 km) east of Las Vegas. Built between 1931 and 1935 across the Colorado River's Black Canyon, the dam gave this desert region a reliable water supply and provided inexpensive electricity. Today, it supplies water and electricity to the three states of Nevada, Arizona, and California, and has created Lake Mead – a popular tourist center. Visitors to the dam can take the 30-minute Powerplant Tour, which includes a guided tour of the power plant and admission to the Visitor Center, or the 60-minute Dam Tour, which also includes a guided tour of the passageways within the dam itself.

Eight miles (13 km) west of Hoover Dam is **Boulder City**, built as a model community to house dam construction workers. With its neat yards and suburban streets, it is one of Nevada's most attractive and well-ordered towns. Its Christian

Lake Mead, a popular tourist destination for watersports

founders banned casinos, and there are none here today. Several of its original 1930s buildings remain, including the restored 1933 Boulder Dam Hotel, which houses the **Hoover Dam Museum**.

The museum tells the history and development of Boulder City, Hoover Dam, Lake Mead, and the Lower Colorado River region through 3-D interactive displays and exhibits. Several artifacts and photographs, which highlight the lives of the workers who built the dam, provide a sense of the complexity and the immense scale of the Hoover Dam project.

🏛 Hoover Dam Museum
1305 Arizona St, Boulder City. **Tel** (702) 294-1988. **Open** 10am–5pm daily. **Closed** Jan 1, Thanksgiving, Dec 25. 🚻 ♿ 🅦 **bcmha.org**

⓳ Lake Mead National Recreation Area

Road map A2. 🚌 Las Vegas. Alan Bible Visitor Center: **Tel** (702) 293-8990. **Open** 9am–4:30pm. **Closed** Jan 1, Thanksgiving, Dec 25. 🚻 ♿ limited. ⛺ 🅦 **nps.gov/lame**

After the completion of the Hoover Dam, the waters of the Colorado River filled the deep canyons that once towered above the river to create a huge reservoir – the largest artificial lake in America. This lake, with its 700 miles (1,130 km) of shoreline, is the centerpiece of Lake Mead National Recreation Area, a 2,345-sq-mile (6,075-sq-km) tract of land. The focus is on watersports, especially sailing, waterskiing, and fishing. Striped bass and rainbow trout are popular catches. There are also several campgrounds and marinas.

⓴ Kingman

Road map A3. 🚗 35,000. 🚆 🚌 🚐 ℹ️ 120 W Andy Devine Ave, (928) 753-6106. **Open** 8am–5pm daily. 🅦 **gokingman.com**

Located in the middle of the desert, Kingman was founded by the Santa Fe Railroad as a construction camp in 1882. In the 1920s, the town became an important stop on Route 66 (see pp34–5), and during the 1930s depression it was crowded with migrants fleeing the Midwest. Today, Kingman's claim to fame is being situated on the longest remaining stretch of Route 66. Renewed interest in the road has resulted in the renovation

The Construction of the Hoover Dam

Hoover Dam sign

More than 1,400 miles (2,250 km) in length, the Colorado River flows through seven states from the Rocky Mountains to the Gulf of California. A treacherous, unpredictable river, it used to be a raging torrent in spring and a trickle in the heat of summer. As a source of water it was therefore unreliable and, in 1928, the seven states it served signed the Boulder Canyon Project Act to define how much water each state could siphon off. The agreement paved the way for the Hoover Dam, and its construction began in 1931. It was a mammoth task, and more than 5,000 men toiled day and night to build what was, at 726 ft (218 m), the world's tallest dam. The dam contains 17 hydroelectric generating units.

View of the Hoover Dam

of many of Kingman's Route 66 diners, motels, and tourist stops. The visitor center, housed in the "Powerhouse," which was built in 1907, features a replica Route 66 diner and the Route 66 Museum, which traces the road's journey from its origins.

Chloride, a former mining town, is an enjoyable day trip from Kingman. A boomtown during the late 19th century, it still has many of its original structures, including a raised wooden sidewalk, and some shops and galleries.

Oatman – a boomtown of the early 20th century

❹ Oatman

Road map A3. 🅰 100. 🅸 PO Box 423, Oatman, (928) 768-6222. 🆆 **oatmangoldroad.org**

Prospectors struck gold in 1904 in the Black Mountains, and Oatman became their main supply center. Today, it is popular with visitors wanting a taste of its boomtown past, such as the 1920s Oatman Hotel (*see p137*), where Carole Lombard and Clark Gable honeymooned in 1939. Oatman is inhabited by several wild burros, which are tame and used to being fed by visitors.

❷ Lake Havasu City

Road map A3. 🅰 54,000. ✈ 🚌 🅸 314 London Bridge Rd, (928) 453-3444. 🆆 **golakehavasu.com**

California businessman Robert McCulloch founded Lake Havasu City in 1964. The resort city he built on the Colorado River was popular with the landlocked citizens of Arizona. His real brainwave, however, came four years later when he bought the historic London Bridge and transported it all the way from England to Lake Havasu.

Some people mocked McCulloch, suggesting that he had thought he was buying London's Gothic Tower Bridge, not this much more ordinary one. There was more hilarity when it appeared that there was nothing in Havasu City for the bridge to span. Undaunted, McCulloch simply created the waterway he needed by dredging a mile-long channel through the area. Today, Lake Havasu City is one of the most visited outdoor recreation areas in Arizona, attracting families and sports enthusiasts alike. The town is always busy with visitors enjoying the shops and restaurants. There are also watersports of every kind, from powerboating and houseboating to jetskiing and kayaking. Golf, hiking, and 4WD adventures are also very popular.

❷ Quartzsite

Road map A4. 🅰 3,700. 🚌 🅸 Quartzsite Chamber of Commerce, 100 W Main, (928) 927-9321. 🆆 **quartzsitebusiness chamber.com**

This quiet village, located in the low desert, 10 miles (16 km) east of the Colorado River, has long been a favorite collecting site for rockhounds. In the 1970s, the winter population began to swell as escapees from the northern cold arrived in droves to park their RVs for a modest sum on government land. Many were rockhounds, and they started Quartzsite's first gem and mineral show.

Today, over a million people visit the town every winter, and eight major gem and mineral shows take place in January and February. Everything from antiques and collectibles to solar panels and eyeglasses can be purchased in what must be the most curious and diverse flea market in America.

London Bridge spanning a man-made waterway in Lake Havasu City

PHOENIX & SOUTHERN ARIZONA

Mountain ranges and sun-bleached plateaus sculpt the wide landscapes of Southern Arizona, a spectacular region dominated by pristine tracts of desert, parts of which are protected within the Saguaro National Park and the Organ Pipe Cactus National Monument. This land was first farmed around 400 BC by the Hohokam people *(see p41)*, who carefully used the meager water supplies to irrigate their crops. When the Spanish settled here in the 18th century, they built fortified outposts throughout the region. This Hispanic heritage is recalled by the beautiful mission churches of San Xavier del Bac and Tumacacori, and in the popular historic city of Tucson that grew up around the 1776 Spanish fort.

When silver was discovered nearby in the 1870s, the scene was set for a decade of rowdy frontier life. Today, towns such as Tombstone, famous for the "Gunfight at the OK Corral," re-create this Wild West era. The influx of miners also spurred the growth of Phoenix, a farming town established on the banks of the Salt River in the 1860s. Phoenix is now the largest city in the Southwest, known for its warm winter climate and recreational facilities.

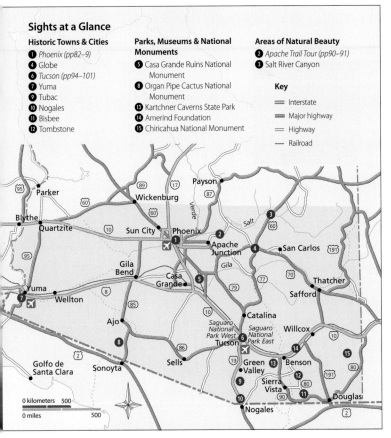

Sights at a Glance

Historic Towns & Cities
1. Phoenix (pp82–9)
4. Globe
6. Tucson (pp94–101)
7. Yuma
9. Tubac
10. Nogales
11. Bisbee
12. Tombstone

Parks, Museums & National Monuments
5. Casa Grande Ruins National Monument
8. Organ Pipe Cactus National Monument
13. Kartchner Caverns State Park
14. Amerind Foundation
15. Chiricahua National Monument

Areas of Natural Beauty
2. Apache Trail Tour (pp90–91)
3. Salt River Canyon

Key
— Interstate
— Major highway
— Highway
— Railroad

◀ San Xavier del Bac Mission, the oldest mission church in the American Southwest

For keys to symbols *see back flap*

❶ Phoenix

Phoenix is a huge metropolis, stretching across the Salt River Valley. Farmers and ranchers settled here in the 1860s. By 1912, the city had developed into the political and economic focus of Arizona and was the state capital. As it grew, it absorbed surrounding towns, although each district still maintains its identity. Downtown Phoenix is now being reinvigorated and is home to many historic attractions. These include restored Victorian houses in Heritage Square, the Phoenix Art Museum, and the Heard Museum *(see pp84–5)* with its excellent collection of Native American artifacts.

The 1900 façade of the Arizona State Capitol Building

Exploring Downtown Phoenix

Downtown Phoenix, where the city began in the 19th century, is centered on Washington and Jefferson Streets, which run east to west between 7th Street and 19th Avenue. Central Avenue is the main north–south axis: to its east, parallel roads are labeled as "Streets," while roads to the west are "Avenues." City sights are too far apart to see on foot, but the Metro Light Rail system connects Downtown sights in its 20-mile- (32-km-) run from Camelback Road in the north to Tempa and Mesa in the southwest.

🏛 Arizona State Capitol Museum

1700 W Washington St. **Tel** (602) 926-3620. **Open** Sep–May: 9am–4pm Mon–Fri; 10am–2pm Sat. **Closed** public hols. 📷 ♿ 🌐 lib.az.us/museum

Completed in 1900, the Arizona State Capitol housed the state legislature until they moved into new premises in 1960. The handsome building is topped by a copper dome. The interior is now a museum; guided tours include both original legislative chambers, which have been carefully restored, and a series of sepia photographs that document the history of Phoenix.

🏛 Heritage Square

115 N 6th St. ♿ partial. Rosson House: **Tel** (602) 262-5070.
🌐 rossonhousemuseum.org

Phoenix is a thoroughly modern Sunbelt city, which mushroomed at an extraordinary rate after World War II. Many of its older buildings did not survive this intensive expansion – it's hard to imagine now that this was originally a settlement of adobe ranches. However, a number of late 19th- and early 20th-century buildings still survive in its downtown core. The most interesting of these are found on tree-lined Heritage Square, where several have become museums, restaurants, and tearooms, and the whole ensemble is pleasant for a stroll.

The showpiece Rosson House, on Monroe Street, was built for Dr. and Mrs. Roland Lee Rosson in the Queen Anne style, in 1895. A handsome wooden mansion, kitted out with appropriate Victorian furnishings, it features a wraparound veranda and a distinctive hexagonal turret. Visitors can explore it from top to bottom, and learn about its Territorial-era history, on hour-long guided tours. Buy tickets online or in the Burgess Carriage House next door, which was constructed in an expansive Colonial-style rare in the Southwest. The 1900 Silva House nearby is a Neo Classical bungalow that is occupied by a restaurant.

🏛 Arizona Science Center

600 E Washington St. **Tel** (602) 716-2000. **Open** 10am–5pm daily. **Closed** Thanksgiving, Dec 25.
📷 ♿ 🌐 azscience.org

This ultra-modern facility, a somewhat incongruous presence right next to Heritage Square, holds more than 300 interactive science exhibits spread over four levels, and covers everything from physics and energy to the human body. In the popular "All About Me" gallery on Level One, which focuses on human biology, visitors can walk through a colossal "working" stomach, complete with authentic smells. Also on Level One, "The W.O.N.D.E.R. Center" is an exploration of the human brain and

Arizona State Capitol Museum

| 0 meters | 500 |
| 0 yards | 500 |

here is a "Flight Zone," in which kids get to design and try out new kinds of helicopters, and climb into a genuine airplane fuselage.

Level Three has "My Digital World," where visitors explore the science and technology behind digital communications, how ideas and information are shared, and experiment with

augmented reality. Also on this level is the "Forces of Nature" exhibit, which is devoted to the world's weather systems as well as natural phenomena ranging from volcanoes to tornadoes.

While the Science Center is primarily targeted at children, for whom a half-day visit seems to fly by, there's something here for everyone, including a five-story IMAX theater and a planetarium.

🏛 Phoenix Art Museum

1625 N Central Ave. **Tel** (602) 257-1222. **Open** 10am–9pm Wed; 10am–5pm Thu–Sat; noon–5pm Sun. **Closed** public hols. 🅿 🅰 🖥 🏛
W phxart.org

Housed in a dramatic and ever-expanding modern complex not far south of the Heard Museum, Phoenix's

acclaimed Art Museum is home to Arizona's finest collection of American and European art, with particular emphasis on changing depictions of the Southwest. It also boasts a fascinating

array of Asian art and artifacts, both ancient and contemporary, and has a reputation for its consistently high quality temporary exhibitions.

Along with paintings by such great names of the American West as Frederic Remington (1861–1909) *(see pp32–3)*, there's some first-rate work from the Taos art colony of the 1900s, including four canvases by Georgia O'Keeffe (1887–1986), the most distinguished member of the group. Among other featured artists are Gilbert Stuart (1755–1828), whose celebrated *Portrait of George Washington* (1796) is seen on every dollar bill, while European works range from Claude Monet's *Flowering Arches* to Anish Kapoor's mysterious, large-scale sculpture from 2003, *Upside Down Inside Out*. The stunning Katz Wing houses a permanent collection of contemporary fashion design and photographic works.

Visitors who are tempted to linger at the museum for most of the day can pause for lunch at the museum's highly recommended restaurant.

Sights at a Glance

① Arizona State Capitol Museum
② Heritage Square
③ Arizona Science Center
④ Phoenix Art Museum
⑤ Heard Museum

Modern exterior of the Arizona Science Center

Phoenix: Heard Museum

The Heard Museum was founded in 1929 by Dwight Heard, a wealthy rancher and businessman who, with his wife, Maie, assembled an extraordinary collection of Southwest Native American art in the 1920s. Several benefactors later added to the collection; they included Senator Barry Goldwater of Arizona and the Fred Harvey Company, who donated their *kachina* dolls *(see p27)*. The museum exhibits more than 40,000 works, but its star attraction is their display of more than 500 dolls. Additionally, the museum showcases baskets, pottery, textiles, and fine art, as well as sumptuous silverwork by the Navajo, Zuni, and Hopi peoples.

The Indian Boarding School Exhibit
This exhibit depicts the mandate that forced American Indian children to attend residential boarding schools far from their homes and families.

Gallery Guide

The first floor is anchored by a grass amphitheater, four courtyards, seven galleries, the world's largest collection of kachina *dolls, two restaurants, an outdoor sculpture garden, and the Native People in the Southwest exhibit. The second level features the Billie Jane Baguley Library and Archives, with a comprehensive collection of photographs and the Indian Boarding School exhibit.*

Second floor

First floor

Ullman Learning Center features interactive exhibits related to Native American life in Arizona.

Key

- Kitchell Gallery
- Lyon Family Gallery
- Sandra Day O'Connor Gallery
- Ullman Learning Center
- Freeman Gallery
- Home: Native People in the Southwest
- Lincoln Gallery
- Jacobson Gallery of Indian Art
- Nichols Sculpture Garden
- Berlin Mezzanine
- Billie Jane Baguley Library and Archives
- Indian Boarding School exhibit
- Jack Steele Parker Gallery
- Non-exhibition space

Acceptance
The Nichols Sculpture Garden is an outdoor gallery with native trees and a garden atmosphere. *Acceptance* (1997) by Retha Walden Gambaro is representative of the fine sculptures on display in the changing exhibitions.

VISITORS' CHECKLIST

Practical Information
2301 N Central Ave. **Tel** (602) 252-8840, (602) 252-8848.
Open 9:30am–5pm Mon–Sat, 11am–5pm Sun. **Closed** Dec 25.
♿ ⬇ 🎒 📷 ∅
Ⓦ heard.org

Transport
🚌 Phoenix Greyhound Station.

★ **Home: Native People in the Southwest**
This award-winning collection of over 2,000 Native artifacts spans 14 centuries, and includes jewelry, basketry, textiles, pottery, and one of the West's best collections of *kachina* dolls.

Red-Tailed Hawk (1986)
Dan Namingha's impressionistic view of a Hopi *kachina* in hawk form is displayed as part of the Heard's fine art collection.

The Kitchell Gallery
explores the traditions of Native art.

Main entrance

Red Totem (1980)
George Morrison's sculpture reflects the fusion of traditional and contemporary styles in the Native American Fine Art Movement.

Exploring Metropolitan Phoenix

Phoenix is one of North America's largest cities. In addition to its city population of well over one million, Phoenix has a burgeoning number of residents in its metropolitan area, totaling more than four million. The city fills the Salt River Valley, occupying more than 2,000 sq miles (5,200 sq km) of the Sonoran Desert. It is famous for winter temperatures of 60 to 70°F (16 to 21°C) and around 300 days of sunshine a year. This makes Phoenix a popular destination with both tourists and "snowbirds," visitors who spend their winters here.

Metropolitan Phoenix includes the former town of Scottsdale, 12 miles (19 km) northeast of downtown. With air-conditioned malls, designer stores, hotels, and restaurants, it is a good base for visiting Taliesin West and Papago Park, and is famous for its world-class golf courses (see pp156–7). Tempe, 6 miles (10 km) east of downtown, is home to Arizona State University, while Mesa has the Arizona Temple, a large Mormon church built in 1927.

Sights at a Glance

❶ Scottsdale
❷ Taliesin West
❸ Cosanti Foundation
❹ Camelback Mountain
❺ Pueblo Grande Museum & Archaeological Park
❻ Papago Park
❼ Mystery Castle
❽ Challenger Space Center
❾ Musical Instrument Museum
❿ Pioneer Living History Village

Key

▦ Downtown Phoenix
▬ Interstate
▭ Major highway
═ Highway
— Railroad

0 kilometers 15
0 miles   15

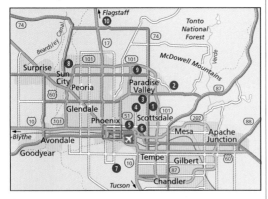

Scottsdale

12 miles (19 km) northeast of Phoenix. Founded in the late 1800s, Scottsdale was named after its developer, army chaplain Winfield Scott (1837–1910), whose religious scruples helped keep the early settlement free from saloons and gambling.

Scottsdale's quiet, tree-lined streets and desert setting attracted the architect Frank Lloyd Wright (see p29), who established Taliesin West here. The area still attracts artists and designers, but it is best known for its golf courses – there are more than 200 in and around

Scottsdale. At the center of the district, to either side of Scottsdale Road between 2nd Street and Indian School Road, the streets are lined with low, brightly painted adobe buildings, which house many of the city's most fashionable restaurants as well as bars, antiques stores, and art galleries. The vibrant heart of it all, well suited to a pleasant half-day's browsing, is Scottsdale Downtown, where the arts shopping district takes in Main Street, Marshall Way, Old Town, and Fifth Avenue. The El Pedregal Festival Marketplace is further north. Scottsdale also holds Phoenix's most popular shopping mall, Fashion Square, with its array of designer stores and excellent restaurants (see p146).

Scottsdale's elegant shopping mall, Fashion Square

🏛 Taliesin West

Cactus Rd at Frank Lloyd Wright Blvd, Scottsdale. **Tel** (480) 860-2700. **Open** 9am–4pm daily. **Closed** Easter, Thanksgiving, Dec 25. 🅿 ♿ 🄫
🆆 **franklloydwright.org**

Generally regarded as the greatest American architect of all time, Frank Lloyd Wright (1867–1959) established the 600-acre (240-ha) Taliesin West complex as a winter school for his students in 1937. Wright had come to prominence in Chicago during the 1890s with a series of strikingly original houses that featured an elegant open-plan style. Although noted for his use of local materials such as desert rocks and earth, he also pioneered the use of pre-cast

Innovative design of the Cosanti Foundation gift shop

concrete. Today, Taleisin West is home to the Frank Lloyd Wright School of Architecture, where students live and work for up to five years. The students also work as guides to the complex. There are a variety of tours, from 1 to 3 hours. Ninety-minute tours begin every hour from 9am to 3pm.

Taleisin West is approached along a winding desert road. The muted tones of the low-lying buildings reflect Wright's enthusiasm for the desert setting. He was careful to enhance, rather than dominate, the landscape.

🏛 Cosanti Foundation

6433 Doubletree Ranch Rd, Paradise Valley. **Tel** (480) 948-7135. **Open** 9am–5pm daily. **Closed** Jan 1, Easter Sun, Thanksgiving, Dec 25. 🚹 donation requested. 🚻 ⓦ **arcosanti.org**

In 1947, Italian architect Paolo Soleri (1919–2013) came to study at Taliesin West. He set up the Cosanti Foundation in Scottsdale nine years later to further his investigations into what he termed "arcology": a combination of architecture and ecology to create new urban habitats *(see p29).*

Today, the Cosanti site consists of simple, low structures housing studios, a gallery, and workshops. This is where the employees make and sell their trademark windbells. Guided visits can be arranged with advance notice.

Visitors can also take an interesting tour of Soleri's main project, Arcosanti, which lies 60 miles (100 km) north of Phoenix on Interstate Highway 17. The educational project began in 1970 as a way to test the "arcology concept", with its aim of reducing human impact on the environment while improving quality of life. Structures combine work and leisure space, and accommodations.

🏔 Camelback Mountain

Named for its humped shape, this mountain rises high above its suburban surroundings just 7 miles (11 km) northeast of downtown Phoenix. A distinctive landmark, the mountain is a granite and sandstone outcrop formed by prehistoric volcanic forces. It is best approached from the north via the marked turn off McDonald Drive near the junction of Tatum Boulevard. From the parking lot, a well-marked path leads to the summit, a steep climb that covers 1,300 ft (390 m) in the space of a mile.

Camelback Mountain is adjacent to the Echo Canyon Recreation Area, a lovely enclave with a choice of shaded picnic sites.

🏛 Pueblo Grande Museum & Archaeological Park

4619 E Washington St. **Tel** (602) 495-0900. **Open** 9am–4:45pm Mon–Sat; 1–4:45pm Sun. **Closed** public hols; May–Sep: Sun & Mon. 🚹 🚻 ⓦ **pueblogrande.com**

Located 5 miles (8 km) east of downtown Phoenix, the Pueblo Grande Museum displays a Hohokam ruin and many artifacts, including cooking utensils and pottery. Many of these pieces come from the adjacent Archaeological Park, the site of a Hohokam settlement from the 8th to 14th centuries. The site was originally excavated in 1887, and today has a path through the ruins. Informative signs point out the many irrigation canals once used by the Hohokam to water their crops.

Taliesin West façade, designed by Frank Lloyd Wright to blend with the desert landscape

For hotels and restaurants see pp131–2 and pp138–41

Cacti in the Desert Botanical Garden at Papago Park

🔲 Papago Park

Galvin Parkway & Van Buren St.
Tel (602) 261-8318. **W** phoenix.gov

Papago Park is situated 6 miles (10 km) east of downtown Phoenix, and is a popular place to unwind, with a number of hiking and cycling trails, picnic areas, and fishing ponds. Many of Phoenix's top attractions are located within the rambling boundaries of Papago Park. The most famous of these is the award-winning **Desert Botanical Garden**. Covering over 145 acres (59 ha), the park displays more than 20,000 cacti and desert flora from around the world. The most popular part of the garden is the paved Desert Discovery Trail, which winds past half the known species of cacti in the world. Some of the rarer and more fragile specimens can be found in the nearby Cactus House and Succulent House. Of particular interest are the Sybil B. Harrington Galleries, which display examples of the remarkable varieties of cacti and succulents found around the world. The garden is prettiest in spring, when many species flower. Guided tours explain the extraordinary life cycles of the desert plants seen here. The rolling hills and lakes of **Phoenix Zoo** also occupy a large area of the Papago Park. A series of natural habitats, including the Arizona-Sonora Desert and a tropical rainforest, have been reproduced at the zoo. It is

home to more than 1,400 animals from around the world; the animals' movements are controlled by banks and canals rather than fences. The Arizona Trail area of the zoo gives visitors a chance to encounter rarely seen animals that are native to Arizona's deserts and mountains. A Safari Train provides a narrated tour of the zoo.

Also in Papago Park is the **Hall of Flame Museum**, which houses an exceptional collection of fire engines and firefighting equipment, dating from 1725. The museum traces the history of organized fire-fighting, displaying over 130 wheeled pieces and thousands of smaller items. Arranged chronologically, the first gallery features hand- and horse-drawn fire equipment from the 18th and 19th centuries. The second gallery contains over 27 motorized fire engines from the early 20th century, while those dating from 1930 to the present are showcased in the third and fourth galleries.

Also part of the museum is the National Firefighting Hall of Heroes, which honors firefighters who have died in the line of duty, or been decorated for heroic service. The Wildland Firefighting Gallery is the only museum in the US dedicated to the hotshot, smoke jumper, and helitack firefighters.

🔲 Desert Botanical Garden

1201 N Galvin Pkwy. **Tel** (480) 941-1225. **Open** 8am–8pm (May–Sep: from 7am). **Closed** major public hols.
🅿️ ♿ 📷 **W** dbg.org

ⓧ Phoenix Zoo

455 N Galvin Pkwy. **Tel** (602) 286-3800.
Open Jan 9–May 31 & Sep–Oct: 9am–5pm; Jun–Aug: 7am–2pm; Nov–Jan 8: 9am–4pm. **Closed** Dec 25. 🅿️ ♿
W phoenixzoo.org

🏛 Hall of Flame Museum

6101 E Van Buren St, Phoenix.
Tel (602) 275-3473. **Open** 9am–5pm Mon–Sat; noon–4pm Sun.
Closed Jan 1, Thanksgiving, Dec 25.
🅿️ **W** hallofflame.org

ⓧ Mystery Castle

800 E Mineral Rd. **Tel** (602) 268-1581.
Open Oct–May: 11am–3:30pm Thu–Sun. 🅿️ 📷 **W** mymystery castle.com

Mystery Castle is possibly Phoenix's most eccentric attraction. In 1927, a certain Boyce Luther Gulley came to the city hoping that the warm climate would improve his ailing health. His young daughter, Mary Lou Gulley, loved building sandcastles on the beach and, since Phoenix was so far away from the ocean, Gulley set about creating a real-life fairy-tale sandcastle for her.

He started work in 1930 and continued for 15 years, until his death in 1945. Discarded bricks, desert rock, railroad refuse, and an assortment of scrapyard junk, including old car parts, have been used to build the structure. The 18-room interior has 13 fireplaces, and can be seen on a guided tour, which explores the quirky building and its eclectic collection of antiques and furniture from around the world.

Exterior of Phoenix's unusual Mystery Castle

Entrance to the Challenger Space Center

🏛 Challenger Space Center

21170 N 83rd Ave, Peoria. **Tel** (623) 322-2001. **Open** noon–4pm Mon–Fri, 10am–4pm Sat. **Closed** major hols. Public programs: call ahead for a schedule of events. 🏛 ✅
W **azchallenger.org**

Named in honor of the *Challenger* shuttle crew that lost their lives in the 1986 disaster, the center's mission is "to inspire, excite, and educate people of all ages about the mysteries and wonders of space, science, and the universe in which we live." Their main objective is to provide educational programs for school children. The same 2-hour programs are run on Saturdays for the public, and are geared for both adults and children.

Utilizing the center's simulated space station and mission control center, the programs integrate teamwork, math, science, and leadership skills into exciting programs that replicate voyages to Mars or to a comet hurtling through space. There are also daily tours of the facility that include an introduction to the center's ongoing programs, and a wide variety of displays and exhibits. One of the highlights of the tour is a stroll along a floating balcony to view "A Tour of the Universe" – a breathtaking six-story tall, 27,000 sq ft (2,508 sq m) mural by official NASA space artist, Robert McCall. The mural, which depicts man's quest in space, wraps 360 degrees around the inside of the center's vast rotunda. The center also hosts star gazing and other fun, educational family programs throughout the year.

🏛 Musical Instrument Museum (MIM)

4725 E Mayo Blvd. **Tel** (480) 478-6000. **Open** 9am–5pm daily (Dec 25: from 11am). **Closed** Thanksgiving. ♿ accessible seating in the theater, plus assistive listening system available on request. **W** **mim.org**

This museum houses a vast collection of instruments from around the world and a gallery where visitors can touch, play, and hear an array of instruments from many different cultures. Those in tune with history will appreciate the Mechanical Gallery, which features a selection of musical instruments from the late 19th and early 20th centuries, such as player pianos, mechanical zithers, and cylinder music boxes that "play themselves." The Geographic Gallery displays instruments and artifacts from five major regions: Africa and the Middle East, Asia and Oceania, Europe, Latin America, and the United States and Canada. Included in the admission price is a guided

The Orientation Gallery in the Musical Instrument Museum (MIM)

tour of instruments on display. Concerts are held in a 300-seat theater three to four days a week, and they feature artists performing jazz, classical, bluegrass, and other musical genres. To fit in with the international theme, the Café Allegro consists of stations serving global cuisine, as well as local and regional dishes.

🏛 Pioneer Living History Village

3901 W Pioneer Rd. **Tel** (623) 465-1052. **Open** Jun 1–Sep 5: 7am–11am Wed–Sun; Sep 6–May 31: 9am–4pm Wed–Sun. **Closed** Jan 1, Easter, Thanksgiving, Dec 25. 🏛
W **pioneeraz.org**

Unlike some of Arizona's Hollywood-inspired Wild West towns, Arizona Pioneer Historical Village puts historical accuracy and education at the forefront of the experience. That doesn't stop them from staging a gunfight in the street, but at least it is a historically accurate gunfight. The village, with the help of several costumed re-enactors, re-creates a frontier town from Arizona's territorial heyday circa 1860 to 1912. There are 29 buildings, 24 of which are originals moved here from other parts of Arizona. The remaining buildings are replicas of buildings that once stood in the territory. The blacksmith's shop, for example, is a duplicate of the shop that stood in Globe in the 1870s. Also of note are the bank, sheriff's office, a ranch complex, and even an opera house that once hosted the legendary actress Lillie Langtry.

❷ Apache Trail Tour

The towering rocky spires and canyons of the Superstition Mountains are the setting for this loop-trail that weaves together desert beauty and Western legends. Starting at Apache Junction, the route climbs to the Tonto National Monument and the Lost Dutchman State Park. The road turns to gravel as it rises past three cool, man-made lakes, and continues to Globe. Descending, the road offers stunning views as it winds through red rock canyons to the town of Superior, and the lovely gardens and shady trails of Boyce Thompson Arboretum.

Tips for Drivers

Tour length: 120 miles (193 km).
Tour route: Drive this route clockwise starting north on Route 88, from Lost Dutchman State Park to Roosevelt Dam.
When to go: Spring and fall are the most pleasant. Summer can be very hot, and winter can be cold with occasional snow.

③ **Tonto National Monument**
These cliff dwellings were occupied by the Salado Indians from the 13th to the 15th centuries. The museum here contains fine examples of their pottery and textiles.

② **Lost Dutchman State Park**
Named after the mystery mine, the park offers hiking trails through a high Sonoran Desert landscape, and great views of the surrounding mountains.

Goldfield

Tortilla Flat

Roosevelt Lake ③
④

Roosevelt Dam

Tonto Nati Monument

88

② ①

Apache Junction

60

Florence Junction

⑥ ⑤

Lost Dutchman Mine Mystery

In the 1870s, Prussian immigrant Jacob Waltz left his home in Phoenix, returning with high-grade gold ore. Drinking and spending lavishly, he often spoke of a rich mine in the Superstition Mountains. Years later, on his deathbed, he purportedly told his caregiver the location of the mine. She and countless others have since tried to find the "Lost Dutchman Mine" without success. It remains one of the most captivating mysteries of the Wild West.

Weaver's Needle peak, fabled location of the mystery mine

① **Superstition Mountains**
Rising over 6,000 ft (1,829 m), this wild and rocky mountain range i 40 miles (64 km) from Phoenix. Prospectors have long sought wealth here.

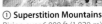

Roosevelt Dam
Completed in 1911, it supplies water to Phoenix. The lake here is a favorite with boaters and fishermen.

Superior
Settled in 1870, the town has the world's smallest museum, which houses the largest Apache Tear gemstone on earth.

Boyce Thompson Arboretum
Dedicated to propagating desert species, the arboretum is very beautiful when the spring flowers bloom.

Key

- Tour route
- Other roads

❸ Salt River Canyon

Road map C4. ℹ Tonto Basin Ranger District, Hwy 188, near Roosevelt, (928) 467-3200.

The Apaches used this deep, wild canyon as a refuge from US troops in the 1800s. Today, the Salt River marks the border between the San Carlos Apache Reservation and the White Mountain Apache Reservation. The 9-mile (15-km) rim-to-rim drive on Highway 60 is truly awe-inspiring as the road drops almost 2,000 ft (610 m) in a series of hairpin turns to cross the river on a narrow bridge. Occasionally a driver forgets to pay attention, or loses control on the descent, and the resulting twisted wreckage sometimes stays for weeks at the bottom of the gorge as a visual warning to others. Numerous pullouts exist along the road for those who want to stop and admire the view. At the bottom, near the bridge, there is a parking area with interpretive signage. Several companies offer single and multi-day whitewater rafting tours (see p153), which provide tremendous views of the 50 sq mile (130 sq km) wilderness that surrounds the river.

The beautiful and dramatic wilderness of Salt River Canyon

❹ Globe

Road map C4. 🚹 7,500. 🚌 ℹ Globe Chamber of Commerce, 1360 N Broad St, (928) 425 4495. 🚠 🅦 **globemiamichamber.com**

The mining town of Globe lies about 100 miles (160 km) east of Phoenix in the wooded Dripping Spring and Pinal Mountains. In 1875, prospectors struck silver here, in what was then part of an Apache reservation. The silver-bearing hills were annexed from the reservation, and Globe was founded as a mining town. It was named for a massive nugget of silver, shaped like a globe, which was unearthed in the hills nearby. The silver was quickly exhausted, but copper mining thrived until 1931, and continues today. Globe has an attractive historic district, and its history is outlined in the **Gila County Historical Museum**. On the south side of town are the Besh-Ba-Gowah Ruins, home of the Salado people in the 13th and 14th centuries.

🏛 **Gila County Historical Museum**
1330 N Broad St. **Tel** (928) 425-7385. **Open** 10am–4pm Mon–Fri; 11am–3pm Sat. **Closed** Jan 1, Dec 25. 🅦 **gilahistorical.com**

❺ Casa Grande Ruins National Monument

Road map C4. **Tel** (520) 723-3172. **Open** 9am–5pm. **Closed** Thanksgiving, Dec 25. 🚠 ♿ 🅦 **nps.gov/cagr**

From around 200 BC until the middle of the 15th century, the Hohokam people farmed the Gila River Valley to the southeast of Phoenix. Among the few Hohokam sites that remain, the fortresslike structure that makes up the Casa Grande National Monument is one of the most distinctive. Built in the early decades of the 14th century, and named the "Big House" by a passing Jesuit missionary in 1694, this sturdy four-story structure has walls up to 4-ft (1.2-m) thick. The interior is out of bounds, but visitors can stroll around the exterior. The visitor center has a small museum with some interesting exhibits on Hohokam history and culture. Casa Grande is located 15 miles (24 km) east of Interstate Highway 10 (I-10) on the outskirts of Coolidge. It should not be confused with the town of Casa Grande, found to the west of I-10.

❻ Tucson

Arizona's second-largest city, Tucson has a friendly, welcoming atmosphere and a variety of interesting attractions to entertain the increasing number of visitors it receives each year. The city is located on the northern boundary of the Sonoran Desert in Southern Arizona, in a basin surrounded by five mountain ranges.

When the Spanish colonizers arrived in the early 18th century they were determined to seize land from the local Tohono O'odham and Pima Native tribes, who put up strong resistance. This led the Spanish to move their regional fortress, or presidio, from Tubac to Tucson in the 1770s. The city was officially founded by Irish explorer Hugh O'Connor in 1775. Tucson's pride in its history is reflected in the careful preservation of 19th-century downtown buildings in the Barrio Historic District.

Contemporary glass skyscrapers in downtown Tucson

Exploring Tucson

Tucson's major art galleries and museums are clustered around two central areas: the University of Arizona (UA) campus, lying between Speedway Blvd, E Sixth Street, Park and Campbell avenues, and the downtown area, which includes the Barrio and El Presidio historic districts. The latter contains many of the city's oldest buildings, and is best explored on foot, as is the Barrio Historic District, south of Cushing Street.

🏛 Tucson Museum of Art & Historic Block

140 N Main Ave. **Tel** (520) 624-2333. **Open** 10am–5pm Tue–Sat (to 8pm 1st Thu of month), noon–5pm Sun. **Closed** Jan 1, Easter Sun, Jul 4, Thanksgiving, Dec 25. 🎫 (free 5–8pm on 1st Thu of month). ♿ 📷
🌐 tucsonmuseumofart.org

The Tucson Museum of Art opened in 1975 and is located on the Historic Block, which also contains five of El Presidio's

oldest dwellings – all of which are at least 100 years old. These historic buildings form part of the art museum and house different parts of its extensive collection. The museum's sculpture gardens and courtyards also form part of the Historic Block complex.

The art museum itself displays contemporary and 20th-century European and American works. In the adobe Stevens House (1866), the museum has its collection of pre-Columbian tribal artifacts, some of which are 2,000 years old. There is the Spanish Colonial collection with some stunning pieces of religious art. The 1850s **Casa Cordova** houses *El Nacimiento*, a Nativity scene with more than 300 earthenware figurines, on display from November to March. The **J. Knox Corbett House**, built in 1907, has Arts and Crafts Movement pieces such as a Morris chair.

Both guided and self-guided walking tours of this district are available from the Tucson Museum of Art.

🏛 Pima County Courthouse

115 N Church Ave.

The courthouse's pretty tiled dome is a downtown landmark. It was built in 1927, replacing its predecessor, a one-story adobe building dating from 1869. The position of the original presidio wall is marked out in the courtyard, and a section of the wall, 3-ft- (1-m-) thick and 12-ft- (4-m-) high, can still be seen inside the building.

🏚 El Presidio Historic District

The El Presidio Historic District occupies the area where the original Spanish presidio, San Agustin del Tucson, was built in 1775. More than 70 of the houses here were constructed during the Territorial period, before Arizona became a state in 1912. Today, these historic buildings are largely occupied by shops, restaurants, and office. However, archaeological excavations in the area have found artifacts from much earlier residents, the Hohokam Indians.

🏠 St. Augustine Cathedral

192 S Stone Ave. **Tel** (520) 623-6351. **Open** Services only; call for times.
🌐 cathedral-staugustine.org

St. Augustine Cathedral was begun in 1896 and modeled after the Spanish Colonial style of the Cathedral of Querétaro in central Mexico. This gleaming white building features an imposing sandstone façade with intricate carvings of the yucca, the saguaro, and the horned toad – three symbols of the Sonoran Desert – while a bronze statue of St. Augustine, the city's patron saint, stands above the main door.

🏚 Barrio Historic District

This area was Tucson's business district in the late 19th century. Today, its streets are quiet and lined with original adobe houses painted in bright colors. On nearby Main Street is the "wishing shrine" of **El Tiradito**,

One of many 19th-century adobe houses in the Barrio Historic District

which marks the spot where a young man was killed as a result of a lovers' triangle. Local people light candles here for his soul, and still believe that if their candles burn for a whole night, their wishes will come true.

🏛 University of Arizona

ℹ Visitors' Center, 811 N Euclid Ave. **Tel** (520) 621-5130. **Open** 9am–5pm Mon–Fri. **Closed** UA holidays.
Ⓦ **arizona.edu/visit**

Several museums are located on or near the UA campus, about a mile (2 km) east of downtown. The **Arizona History Museum** traces Arizona's history from the arrival of the Spanish in 1539 to modern times. The **University of Arizona Museum of Art** focuses on European and American fine art from the Renaissance to the 20th century. Opposite the museum is the **Center for Creative Photography**, which contains the work of more than 60 of the 20th century's greatest American photographers. Visitors can also view the archives. The **Flandrau Science Center** features a range of interactive exhibits that are child-friendly.

One of the most renowned collections of artifacts, covering 2,000 years of Native history, is displayed by the **Arizona State Museum**, which was founded in 1893 and is the oldest anthropology museum in the region.

Downtown Tucson

① Tucson Museum of Art & Historic Block
② Pima County Courthouse
③ El Presidio Historic District
④ St. Augustine Cathedral
⑤ Barrio Historic District

0 meters 100
0 yards 100

For keys to symbols see back flap

Exploring Around Tucson

Beyond downtown, Metropolitan Tucson extends north to the Santa Catalina Mountains, the foothills of which are the start of a scenic drive to the top of Mount Lemmon. To the west are the Tucson Mountains, which frame the western portion of Saguaro National Park, the other half of which lies east of the city. To the south lies the beautiful mission church of San Xavier del Bac, which stands out from the flat, desert landscape of the Tohono O'odham Indian Reservation.

Vistas of tall saguaro cacti in Saguaro National Park

Sights at a Glance

1. Saguaro National Park (East & West)
2. Arizona-Sonora Desert Museum
3. Old Tucson Studios
4. San Xavier del Bac Mission
   See pp98–9
5. Pima Air & Space Museum
6. Sabino Canyon Tours
7. Mount Lemmon

Key

- Downtown Tucson
- Interstate
- Major highway
- Highway
- Railroad

0 kilometers 7
0 miles 7

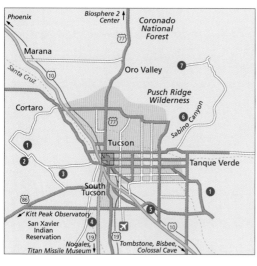

🏛 Arizona-Sonora Desert Museum

2021 N Kinney Rd. **Tel** (520) 883-2702. **Open** Mar–May & Sep: 7:30am–5pm daily; Jun–Aug: 7:30am–5pm Sun–Fri, 7:30am–10pm Sat; Oct–Feb: 8:30am–5pm daily. 🅿 ♿ ⓦ desert museum.org

This museum covers more than 21 acres (8.5 ha), and includes a botanical garden, zoo, and natural history museum, where displays describe the history, geology, and flora and fauna of the region. Outside, a walkway passes more than 1,200 varieties of plants, which provide the setting for a range of creatures, including hummingbirds, wildcats, and Mexican wolves.

One of many flowering cacti at the Arizona-Sonora Desert Museum

🎬 Old Tucson Studios

201 S Kinney Rd. **Tel** (520) 883-0100. **Open** hours vary; visit the website for details. **Closed** Thanksgiving, Dec 24 & 25. 🅿 ♿ ⓦ oldtucson.com

Modeled on a Western town of the 1860s, the studio was built as a set for a Western movie in 1939. Since then, Old Tucson Studios has formed the backdrop for some of Hollywood's most famous Westerns, such as *Gunfight at*

🌵 Saguaro National Park

3693 S Old Spanish Trail. **Tel** (520) 733-5153. **Open** 24 hrs. Visitor Centers: 9am–5pm daily. **Closed** Dec 25. 🅿 ♿ ⓦ nps.gov/sagu

The saguaro (pronounced sa-wah-ro) cactus is unique to the Sonoran Desert. The largest cactus species in the US, it has a life span of up to 200 years. Those specimens that survive into old age may reach heights of up to 50 ft (16 m) and weigh more than 8 tons (7 kg).

The park comprises two tracts of land on the eastern and western flanks of Tucson, that together cover more than 142 sq miles (368 sq km). The 6-mile (10-km) Bajada Loop Drive runs deep into the park on a gravel road, past hiking trails and picnic areas. One of these trails leads to Hohokam petroglyphs carved into volcanic rock. The eastern park has the oldest saguaros, which can be seen along the 8-mile (13-km) Cactus Forest Drive. There are also more than 100 miles (160 km) of hiking trails here. The park offers guided walks during the winter season.

Map labels:
Phoenix
Biosphere 2 Center
Coronado National Forest
Marana
77
Oro Valley
Santa Cruz
10
Pusch Ridge Wilderness
Cortaro
77
Sabino Canyon
Tucson
Tanque Verde
South Tucson
86
Kitt Peak Observatory
San Xavier Indian Reservation
19
19
Nogales, Titan Missile Museum
Tombstone, Bisbee, Colossal Cave
10

he OK Corral (1957) and *Rio Bravo* (1958). The popular 1970s TV series *Little House on the Prairie* was also filmed here. More recently, movies such as *Tombstone* (1993) and *To Kill a Memory* (2011) were partly shot here.

Main Street's 1860s frontier atmosphere provides an authentic setting for performers in period costume, who entertain visitors with stunt shows, mock gunfights, and stagecoach rides. Visitors can also take part in such activities as panning for gold.

Gunfight staged outside the mission at Old Tucson Studios

🏠 San Xavier del Bac Mission
See pp98–9.

🏛 Titan Missile Museum
1580 W Duval Mine Rd, Sahuarita. **Tel** (520) 625-7736. **Open** 9:45am–4pm Sun–Fri, 8:45am–5pm Sat. **Closed** Thanksgiving, Dec 25. 🅿 ♿ 📷 9am–4pm. 🌐 **titanmissilemuseum.org**

This remote site, 25 miles (40 km) south of Tucson, is a great place to get in touch with the potential horror of the Cold War years. Built in 1963, this is one of 18 Titan II silos constructed around the Tucson area (out of 54 in the United States). This station and its single, multiple-warhead nuclear missile – the

largest ever built in the US – stood ready to launch within minutes for over 20 years. Today, it is one of only two remaining Titan II missiles and launch sites left, as all the others were decommissioned by 1987. The museum tour includes a walk through the buildings and a peek down into the silo, followed by a visit to the below-ground missile launch facility and a look at the missile from within the silo.

🏛 Pima Air & Space Museum
6000 E Valencia Rd. **Tel** (520) 574-0462. **Open** 9am–5pm. **Closed** Thanksgiving, Dec 25. 🅿 ♿ 📷 call for times. 🌐 **pimaair.org**

Located 9 miles (14 km) southeast of downtown Tucson, this museum contains one of the largest collections of aircraft in the world. Visitors are met with the astonishing sight of more than 300 vintage aircraft lined up across the desert.

Three presidential aircraft are displayed – Eisenhower's, Kennedy's, and Johnson's –

For hotels and restaurants see pp131–2 and pp138–41

as well as a replica of the Wright brothers' famous 1903 aircraft. Tours around the adjacent Davis-Monthan Air Force Base boneyard feature B-29s, supersonic bombers, and other planes.

🏛 Colossal Cave
Colossal Cave Mountain Park, PO Box 70, 16721 E Old Spanish Trail, Vail. **Tel** (520) 647-7275. **Open** 8am–5pm daily. **Closed** Thanksgiving, Dec 25. 🅿 📷 🌐 **colossalcave.com**

The first European to discover Colossal Cave was Solomon Lick in 1879, but he was a relative latecomer. The cave was used by the Sobaipuri people as early as 1450, and later by the Hohokam. Although opened for tours in 1923, it has never been fully explored – it took over two years to map the first two miles of the cave's estimated 39 miles (63 km) length.

Visitors today take a 50-minute guided tour that descends six stories into spaces draped in stalactites and stalagmites. The tour is only half a mile in length, but requires descending and climbing 363 stairs. There are longer, more energetic tours available on Saturdays.

Colossal is a "dry cave" – it is no longer being shaped by water, and its ample air supply keeps the inside temperature at a comfortable 70°F (21°C). The cave is on the grounds of La Posta Quemada (Burned Station) Ranch, named for a Southern Pacific stagecoach station, which was destroyed by a fire in 1875.

Birdwatching in the Canyons of Southern Arizona

The landscape of Southern Arizona may seem dry, but this high desert environment gets about 11 in (280 mm) of rain annually. This enables vegetation to flourish which, in turn, attracts a variety of birds. In fact, the area is one of the top five birdwatching locations in the US. Just off I-19, near Green Valley, Madera Canyon plays host to some 400 bird species. Along with the more common varieties of hummingbirds, flycatchers, and warblers, many rare species, such as the brown-crested flycatcher and the black-and-white warbler, are often sighted here. Farther afield, Ramsey Canyon in the Huachuca Mountains is the country's hummingbird capital with 14 varieties of these tiny, delicate creatures.

Broad-billed hummingbird

John Fitzgerald Kennedy's presidential plane at the Pima Air & Space Museum

Tucson: San Xavier del Bac Mission

San Xavier del Bac is the oldest and best-preserved mission church in the Southwest. An imposing landmark as it rises out of the stark, flat landscape of the surrounding Tohono O'odham reservation, its white walls dazzle in the desert sun. A mission was first established here by the Jesuit priest Father Eusebio Kino in 1700 *(see p45)*. The complex seen today was completed in 1797 by Franciscan missionaries.

The Hill of the Cross, to the east of the mission, offering fine views

Built of adobe brick, the mission is considered to be the finest example of Spanish Colonial architecture in the US *(see p28)*. The church also incorporates other styles, including several Baroque flourishes. In the 1990s its interior was extensively renovated, and five *retablos* (altarpieces) have been restored to their original glory.

★ **Façade of the Church**
The ornate Baroque façade is decorated with the carved figures of saints (although some are much eroded) including a headless St. Cecilia and an unidentifiable St. Francis, now a simple sand cone.

Stonework Detail
It was long thought that St. Catherine of Siena and St. Barbara were the identities of the carved statues to the left of the entrance, however they have now been identified as St. Agatha of Catania and St. Agnes of Rome.

KEY

① **The mortuary chapel** contains a statue of the Virgin Mary, surrounded by candles.

② **The bell tower's** elegant, white dome reflects the Moorish styles that are incorporated into San Xavier's Spanish Colonial architecture.

③ **The patio** is closed to the public but can be seen from the museum.

④ **The museum** includes a sheepskin psalter and photographs of other historic missions on the Tohono O'odham reservation.

Painted Ceiling
On entering the church, visitors are struck by the dome's ceiling with its glorious paintings of religious figures. Vivid pigments of vermilion and blue were used to contrast with the stark white stone background.

★ Main Altar
The spectacular gold and red
retablo mayor is decorated in
Mexican Baroque style with
elaborate columns. More
than 50 statues were carved
in Mexico, then brought to
San Xavier where artists
gilded and painted them
with brightly colored glazes.

VISITORS' CHECKLIST

Practical Information
Road map C5.
1950 W San Xavier Rd, 10 miles
(16 km) south of Tucson on I-19.
Tel (520) 294-2624. **Open** 7am–
5pm. booths selling
Native American fry bread.
W sanxaviermission.org

Altar Dome
The dome and
high transepts are
filled with painted
wooden statuary and
covered with murals
depicting scenes
from the Gospels.

The shop
entrance

Chapel of Our Lady
This statue is one of the
church's three sculptures of
Mary. Here she is shown as La
Dolorosa or Sorrowing Mother.

Sabino Canyon Tours

5700 N Sabino Canyon Rd.
Tel (520) 749-2861. **Open** 8:30am–
4:30pm. Tram Tours: Jul–mid-Dec:
9am–4pm daily (to 4:30pm Sat & Sun);
mid-Dec–Jun: 9am–4:30pm daily.
sabinocanyon.com

Sabino Creek began carving its
way through Mount Lemmon,
13 miles (21 km) northeast of
Tucson, five million years ago.
The result was the lovely Sabino
Canyon, with its towering rock
walls and sparkling streams lined
with cottonwood trees. Today,
motorized trams take visitors on
a 45-minute narrated trip into
the canyon. Tourists can get off
at one of several stops to hike
on trails that range from easy to
moderately difficult. Evening
tram tours are also available at
various times of the year.

Mount Lemmon

(520) 749-8700.
The highest peak in the
Santa Catalina Mountains,
standing at 9,157 ft
(2,790 m), Mount
Lemmon is located in
the Coronado National
Forest. During summer,
thousands of visitors
drive up on the weekends for
rock climbing, hiking, camping,
and fishing. A 1-hour drive,
beginning in the Tucson city
limits and connecting to the
Mount Lemmon Highway,
takes visitors to the summit.
The highway affords splendid
vistas of the Tucson valley.
There are around 150 miles

Radio telescope
at Kitt Peak

(240 km) of hiking trails here,
while a side road leads to
the quaint resort village
of Summerhaven, with
shops and restaurants.
At the top, the Ski
Valley lift operates
for a small fee most
of the year, offering
magnificent views.

Biosphere 2

5 miles (8 km) NE of jct of
Hwys 77 & 79. **Tel** (520) 838-
6200. **Open** 9am–4pm.
Closed Thanksgiving, Dec 25.
b2science.org

Biosphere 2 is a unique research
facility that was set up in 1991.
Eight people were sealed within
a futuristic structure of glass and
white steel furnished with five
of the Earth's habitats: rainforest,
desert, savanna, marsh, and
an ocean with a living coral

Space Age buildings of the Biosphere 2, north of Tucson

reef. Over a period of two
years, the effect of the people
on the environment as well as
the effect of their environment
on them were studied.

Today, there are no people
living in the Biosphere, which
is being used to explore and
address issues of global environmental change. Visitors can take
a 2-hour guided tour of the
facility, which consists of about
150 stairs, and a 1-mile (2-km)
round-trip walk.

Kitt Peak Observatory

Rte 86 to 386. **Tel** (520) 318-8726.
Open 9am–3:45pm daily. **Closed** Jan 1
Thanksgiving, Dec 25. donation
requested. (fee) 10am, 11:30am,
1:30pm. **noao.edu/kpno**

Located 56 miles (90 km)
southwest of Tucson, Kitt
Peak boasts one of the largest
and most diverse collections

Observatories at Kitt Peak in Southern Arizona

For hotels and restaurants see pp131–2 and pp138–41

of astronomical observatories on the planet. It was established as a scientific center for the study of astronomy in 1952. Visitors can take a guided tour of the facility and get a close-up look at (but not through) several of the largest and most famous telescopes. To actually view the cosmos, you have to sign up and pay (up to a month in advance) for nightly programs that allow you to scan the heavens through telescopes at the visitors' observatory. The guided program (Sep–mid-Jul) is very popular. Warm clothing is recommended.

❼ Yuma

Road map A4. 🚹 93,000. 🚉 Amtrak, 2815 Gila St. 🚌 Greyhound, 170 E 17th Place. 🚹 Yuma Convention & Visitors' Bureau, 201 N 4th Ave, (800) 293-0071. **Open** Jun–Sep: 9am–5pm Tue–Sun; Oct–May: 9am–5pm daily.
🌐 **visityuma.com**

Yuma occupies a strategic position at the confluence of the Colorado and Gila rivers in Arizona's far southwestern corner. Though noted by Spanish explorers in the 16th century, it was not until the 1850s that the town rose to prominence, when the river crossing became the gateway to California for thousands of gold seekers. Later, Yuma was a supply depot as riverboats steamed up and down the Colorado to link with the Sea of Cortez. In the early 20th century, Yuma was an important stop on the first ocean-to-ocean transcontinental road that ended in San Diego. Sadly, however, for much of the 20th century, Yuma was a dusty, bypassed border town.

Yuma's hot, sunny winter climate has made it a magnet for "snowbirds" escaping the northern cold. Their swelling numbers have brought about a renaissance, as the town adds attractions, hotels, restaurants, and services.

The town's first major construction project was Yuma Territorial Prison in 1876. Arizonans were more than

Boats and watersports in the picturesque setting of Lake Yuma

delighted to finally have a place to put away the growing numbers of train robbers, polygamists, murderers, and outlaws. Criminals, on the other hand, were less than thrilled, as Yuma Prison had a notorious reputation for stifling heat and brutal conditions. The prison's most famous inmate was John Swilling, sometimes called the "Father of Phoenix," who made big money selling real estate. He later tried robbing a stagecoach after falling on hard times. Visitors to the **Yuma Territorial Prison State Historic Park** can see the grounds and, in winter, take a guided tour to hear stories of the prison's famous and infamous inhabitants, guards, riots, and escapes.

Yuma's history as a crossroads is highlighted at the **Yuma**

Crossing State Historic Park. It features several buildings reconstructed to their 1870s appearance, including a telegraph office and the Commanding Officer's quarters, which dates back to 1855. As the town became an important junction for supplies, the military took an interest, and built Fort Yuma in 1851, now owned by the Quechan Indians.

Environs
About 40 miles (64 km) northeast of Yuma, the **Castle Dome Museum** contains the remnants of a mining town barely changed from 1864. The mills still house the original boiler, stamp mill, and elevator. Other weather-beaten buildings include a church, schoolhouse, blacksmith shop and saloons – all laden with period artifacts.

🏛 **Yuma Territorial Prison State Historic Park**
1 Prison Hill Rd. **Tel** (928) 783-4771. **Open** 9am–5pm daily. 🚫 ♿ 🅿
🌐 azstateparks.com/parks/yute

🏛 **Yuma Crossing State Historic Park**
201 North 4th Ave. **Tel** (928) 329-0471. **Open** Jun–Sep: 9am–5pm Tue–Sun; Oct–May daily. 🚫 ♿ 🌐 azstate parks.com/parks/yuqu

🏛 **Castle Dome Museum**
Castle Dome Mine Rd. **Tel** (928) 920-3062. **Open** 10am–5pm daily. 🚫
🌐 castledomemuseum.org

Cell blocks at the historic, territorial prison in Yuma

Rare cacti at the Organ Pipe Cactus National Monument

❽ Organ Pipe Cactus National Monument

Road map B5. **Tel** (520) 387-6849.
Visitor Center: **Open** 8:30am–5pm
daily. **Closed** Thanksgiving, Dec 25.
🅿 ♿ 📷 🅰 🆆 nps.gov/orpi

The organ pipe is a Sonoran Desert species of cactus, which is a cousin to the saguaro (see p96) but with multiple arms branching up from the base, as its name suggests. The organ pipe is rare in the United States, growing almost exclusively in this large and remote area of land along the Mexican border in southwest Arizona. Many other plant and animal species flourish in this unspoiled desert wilderness, although a lot of animals, such as snakes, jackrabbits, and kangaroo rats, emerge only in the cool of the night. Other cacti such as the saguaro, the Engelmann prickly pear, and the teddybear cholla are best seen in the early summertime when they give their glorious displays of floral color.

There are two scenic drives through the park: the 21-mile (34-km) **Ajo Mountain Drive** and the shorter 5-mile (8-km) **Puerto Blanco Drive**. The mostly gravel Ajo Mountain Drive takes 2 hours and

Orange flowers of the barrel cactus

winds through startling desert landscapes in the foothills of the mountains. The paved Puerto Blanco Drive leads to a half-hour trail into Red Tanks Tinaja and the picnic area near Pinkley Peak. A variety of hiking trails in the park range in difficulty from paved, wheelchair-accessible paths to wilderness walks. A visitor center offers exhibits on the park's flora and fauna, as well as maps and camping permits, and there are guided walks in winter. Be aware that the park is a good 2.5- to 3-hour drive from Tucson one way. If you want to explore this environment in any detail, plan to camp overnight. Ajo, 34 miles (55 km) to the north, has motels and services.

❾ Tubac

Road map C5. 🏔 1,200. 🛈 Tubac Chamber of Commerce, (520) 398-2704. 🆆 **tubacaz.com**

The Royal Presidio (fortress) of San Ignacio de Tubac was built in 1752 to protect the local Spanish-owned ranches and mines, as well as the nearby missions of Tumacacori and San Xavier, from attacks by local Pima Indians. Tubac was also the first stopover on the famous overland expedition to colonize the San Francisco Bay area in 1776. The trek was led by the fort's captain, Juan Bautista de Anza. Following his return, the garrison moved north to Tucson, and for the next 100 years, Tubac declined. Today, the town is one of Arizona's largest art communities, with attractive shops, galleries, and restaurants lining the streets around the plaza.

Tubac's historical remains are displayed at the **Tubac Presidio State Historic Park**, which encompasses the foundations of the original presidio in an underground display, as well as several historic buildings, including the delightful Old Tubac Schoolhouse built in 1885. The Presidio Museum, which is also situated here, contains artifacts from the various periods of settlement in Tubac's history, including American Indian and Spanish. Exhibits include beautifully painted altarpieces and colonial furniture.

Colorful pottery display outside a shop in the small town of Tubac

Mission church at Tumacacori National Historical Park near Tubac

Environs

Just 3 miles (5 km) south of town lies **Tumacacori National Historical Park**, with its beautiful ruined mission. The present church was built in around 1800 on the ruins of the original 1691 mission established by Jesuit priest Father Eusebio Kino *(see p45)*. Abandoned in 1848, today the mission, with its weatherbeaten ocher façade, brick columns, arched entry, and carved wooden door, is an evocative reminder of former times. The cavernous interior is wonderfully atmospheric, with patches of exposed adobe brick and faded murals on the sanctuary walls. A small museum provides an excellent background on the mission builders and Pima Indians. Weekend craft demonstrations, including tortilla-making, basketry, and Mexican pottery, are occasionally held September through June. During the first weekend in December, La Fiesta de Tumacacori *(see p39)*, which celebrates the cultural heritage of the upper Santa Cruz Valley, is held on the mission grounds.

🏛 **Tubac Presidio State Historic Park**
Burruel St & Presidio Dr. **Tel** (520) 398-2252. **Open** 9am–5pm daily. **Closed** Dec 25. 🏛 ♿ 📷
W **azstateparks.com/parks/tupr**

🏛 **Tumacacori National Historical Park**
Tel (520) 377-5060. **Open** 9am–5pm daily. **Closed** Thanksgiving, Dec 25.
🏛 ♿ 📷 W **nps.gov/tuma**

⑩ Nogales

Road map C5. 🗺 22,000. 🚌
🛈 Nogales Chamber of Commerce, 123 W Kino Park, (520) 287-3685.
W **thenogaleschamber.org**

Nogales is really two towns straddling the US border with Mexico. This is a busy port of entry, handling huge amounts of freight, including much of the winter fruit and vegetables sold in North America. It attracts many visitors in search of bargains on both sides of the border. Decorative blankets, crafts, and furniture are good value.

Mexican pottery found in Nogales

There is a profound contrast between the US side and the ramshackle houses across the border, and visitors should be aware that the Mexican Nogales can be crowded with continuous hustle from street vendors eager for business. Still, it is a popular day-trip, and

there are several good restaurants here. Visitors are advised to leave their cars on the US side, where attendants mind the parking lots, and to walk across the border. Those who drive across the border should check that their car insurance is valid in Mexico. Visas are required only for those traveling farther south than the town and for stays of more than 72 hours. US and Canadian citizens should carry a passport for identification. US dollars are accepted everywhere.

⑪ Bisbee

Road map C5. 🗺 5,300. 🚌
🛈 Visitor Center, 478 Dart Rd, (520) 432-3554. W **discover bisbee.com**

This is one of the most atmospheric mining towns in the Southwest. The discovery of copper here in the 1880s sparked a mining rush, and by the turn of the century Bisbee was the largest city between St. Louis and San Francisco. Victorian buildings such as the landmark Copper Queen Hotel still dominate the historic town center, while attractive clusters of houses cling to the sides of the surrounding mountains.

Today, visitors can tour the mines that once flourished here, such as the deep underground Queen Mine or, a short drive south of town, the Lavender Open Pit Mine. Exhibits at the Bisbee Mining and Historical Museum illustrate the realities of mining and frontier life here.

The Victorian mining town of Bisbee

⑫ Tombstone

Road map C5. ⚑ 1,300.
ℹ Chamber of Commerce, 109 S
4th St, (888) 457-3929. Visitor Center:
395 E Allen St, (520) 457-3929.
W tombstonechamber.com

The town of Tombstone is a
living legend, forever known as
the site of the 1881 gunfight at
the OK Corral between the Earp
brothers and the Clanton gang
(see p33). The town's historic
streets and buildings form one
of the most popular attractions
in the Southwest.

Tombstone was founded
by Ed Schieffelin, who went
prospecting on Apache land
in 1877 despite a warning that
"all you'll find out there is
your tombstone." He found a
mountain of silver instead, and
his sardonically named shanty
town boomed with the ensuing
silver rush. One of the wildest
towns in the Wild West,
Tombstone was soon full
of prospectors, gamblers,
cowboys, and lawmen. In its
heyday, the town was larger
than San Francisco. More than
$37 million worth of silver was
extracted from the mines
between 1880 and 1887, when
miners struck an aquifer and
flooded the mine shafts.

In 1962 "the town too tough
to die" became a National
Historic Landmark, and, with
much of its historic downtown
immaculately preserved, it
attracts many visitors, all

Re-enactment of the gunfight at the OK Corral, Tombstone

eager to sample the unique
atmosphere. Allen Street,
with its wooden boardwalks,
shops, and restaurants, is the
town's main thoroughfare.
The **OK Corral** is preserved as
a museum, and re-enactments
of the infamous gunfight
between the Earp
brothers, Doc Holliday
and the Clanton
gang are staged
daily at noon, 2pm,
and 3:30pm.

**Tombstone
Courthouse** on
Toughnut Street
was the seat of
justice for the
county from 1882 to 1929, and
is now a State Historic Site. This
imposing building contains a
museum featuring the restored
courtroom, and many historical
exhibits and artifacts, including
photographs of some of the
town's famous characters.

Tombstone Courthouse in the town
center, now a museum

Toughnut Street used to be
known as "Rotten Row" as it
was once lined with miners'
tents, bordellos, and more
than 100 bars.

Among other buildings worth
looking for in the downtown
area is the **Rose Tree
Museum**, home of
what is reputedly
the world's largest
rosebush. There is
also the **Bird Cage
Theater**, once a
bawdy dance
hall and
bordello, and
so-named for
the covered
"crib" compart-ments, or cages,
hanging from the ceiling, from
which ladies of the night plied
their trade. Nearby is the once
rowdy Crystal Palace Saloon,
which is still a bar.

Just north of town, the
well-known **Boothill Cemetery**
is full of the graves of those
who perished in Tombstone,
peacefully or otherwise. This
evocative place is not without
the occasional spot of humor.
Look for the marker lamenting
the death of George Johnson,
hanged by mistake in 1882,
which reads: "He was right,
we was wrong, but we strung
him up, and now he's gone."

🏛 **OK Corral**
Allen St. **Tel** (520) 457-3456. **Open**
9am–5pm daily. **Closed** Thanksgiving,
Dec 25. ♿ 👓 **W** ok-corral.com

🏛 **Tombstone Courthouse**
223 E Toughnut St. **Tel** (520) 457-
3311. **Open** 9am–5pm daily.
Closed Dec 25. ♿ 👓 **W** azstate
parks.com/parks/toco

Boardwalk in Tombstone

⓫ Kartchner Caverns State Park

Road map C5. **Tel** (520) 586-4100 (info), (520) 586-2283 (reservations). **Open** 8am–5pm daily (cave tours: hours vary by season, reservation required). **Closed** Dec 25. 🎥 ♿ 📷 obligatory. 🅰 **w** azstateparks. com/parks/kaca

The Kartchner Caverns are one of Arizona's great natural wonders. Located in the Whetstone Mountains, the caves were discovered in 1974 when two cavers crawled through a sinkhole in a hillside that led them into 7 acres (3 ha) of caverns filled with colorful formations. Out of concern to protect the caves, they kept their discovery a secret for 14 years as they explored this wonderland of speleotherms, or cave form-ations, made of layers of calcite deposited by dripping or flowing water over millions of years. In 1988 the land was purchased by the state, but it took 11 years to complete the development that would allow public access while conserving the special conditions that enable these caves to continue growing.

Before entering the caves, visitors are introduced to the geology of the formations at the Discovery Center. Once inside, visitors must not touch the features, as skin oils stop their growth. Along with huge stalactites and stalagmites, there is an abundance of other types of formation such as the aptly named 21-ft- (132-m-) high soda straw, and the turnip shields.

Orange and white column formations at Kartchner Caverns

⓮ Amerind Foundation

Tel (520) 586-3666. **Open** 10am–4pm Tue–Sun. **Closed** public hols. 📷 **w** amerind.org

The Amerind Foundation is one of the most important private archaeological and ethnological museums in the country. The name Amerind is a contraction of "American Indian," and this collection contains tens of thousands of artifacts from different Native American cultures. All aspects of Native American life are shown here, with displays covering Inuit masks, Cree tools, and sculpted effigy figures from Mexico's Casas Grandes.

The adjacent Amerind Art Gallery has a fine collection of Western art by such prominent artists as William Leigh (1866–1955) and Frederic Remington

(1861–1909). The delightful pink buildings, designed in the Spanish Colonial Revival style *(see p28)*, are also of interest.

⓯ Chiricahua National Monument

Road map D5. **Tel** (520) 824-3560. **Open** 8:30am–4:30pm daily. **Closed** Dec 25. 📷 ♿ 📷 🅰 **w** nps.gov/chir

The Chiricahua Mountains were once the homeland of a band of Apache people, and an impenetrable base from which they launched attacks on settlers in the late 1800s. This 19-sq-mile (23-sq-km) area now preserves amazing rock formations, which were created by a series of volcanic eruptions around 27 million years ago. Massive rocks balanced on small pedestals, soaring rock spires, and enormous stone columns make up the bizarre landscape, viewed from the monument's scenic drive and hiking trails.

The nearby town of Willcox houses the intriguing **Rex Allen Arizona Cowboy Museum**, which is devoted to a native son who became a famous movie cowboy, starring in 19 films in the 1950s.

🏛 **Rex Allen Arizona Cowboy Museum** 150 N Railroad Ave. **Tel** (520) 384-4583. **Open** 10am–1pm Mon, 11am–3pm Tue–Sun. **Closed** public hols. 📷 ♿ **w** rexallenmuseum.org

Massive rock spires formed by million-year-old volcanic eruptions at Chiricahua National Monument

THE FOUR CORNERS

Dominated by the Navajo reservation, which is the size of Connecticut, and presenting sweeping panoramas of mesas, canyons, and vast expanses of high desert, the Four Corners is perfect for those wanting to experience Native culture and the real West.

Although it receives less than 10 in (25 cm) of rainfall per year, this arid land has supported life since the first Paleo-Indians arrived about 12,000 years ago. The people now known as the Ancestral Puebloans lived here from about AD 500 until the 13th century. They are responsible for the many evocative ruins found here, including those at Mesa Verde, Chaco Canyon, and Hovenweep National Monument. Their descendants include the Hopi, whose pueblos are said to be the oldest continuously occupied towns in North America. The Navajo arrived here in the 15th century and their spiritual center is Canyon de Chelly with its 1,000-ft- (330-m-) high red rock walls.

Monument Valley's impressive landscape has been used as a backdrop for countless movies and TV shows. The region is also popular for hiking, fishing, and whitewater rafting.

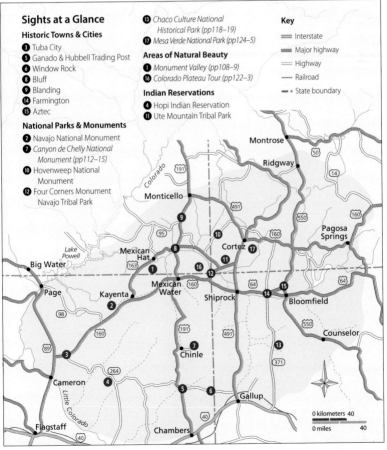

Sights at a Glance

Historic Towns & Cities
- ❸ Tuba City
- ❺ Ganado & Hubbell Trading Post
- ❻ Window Rock
- ❽ Bluff
- ❾ Blanding
- ⓮ Farmington
- ⓯ Aztec

National Parks & Monuments
- ❷ Navajo National Monument
- ❼ Canyon de Chelly National Monument (pp112–15)
- ❿ Hovenweep National Monument
- ⓬ Four Corners Monument Navajo Tribal Park
- ⓭ Chaco Culture National Historical Park (pp118–19)
- ⓱ Mesa Verde National Park (pp124–5)

Areas of Natural Beauty
- ❶ Monument Valley (pp108–9)
- ⓰ Colorado Plateau Tour (pp122–3)

Indian Reservations
- ❹ Hopi Indian Reservation
- ⓫ Ute Mountain Tribal Park

Key
- ▬▬ Interstate
- ▬▬ Major highway
- ▭▭ Highway
- ──── Railroad
- ▬▪ State boundary

Montrose

Ridgway

Colorado {191}

Monticello

Lake Powell

Big Water

Page

Kayenta

Mexican Hat {163}

Mexican Water {160}

Shiprock

Cortez

Pagosa Springs

Pagosa Springs

Bloomfield

Counselor

Cameron

Little Colorado

Chinle

Gallup

Flagstaff

Chambers

0 kilometers 40

0 miles 40

◀ Breathtaking scenery at Canyon de Chelly National Monument in Arizona

For keys to symbols *see back flap*

❶ Monument Valley

From scenic Highway 163, which crosses the border of Utah and Arizona, it is possible to see the famous towering sandstone buttes and mesas of Monument Valley. These ancient rocks, soaring upward from a seemingly boundless desert, have come to symbolize the American West, largely because Hollywood has used these breathtaking vistas as a backdrop for hundreds of movies, TV shows, and commercials since the 1930s.

The area's visitor center sits within the boundary of Monument Valley Navajo Tribal Park, but many of the valley's spectacular rock formations and other sites are found just outside the park boundary.

Visitor Center
At the visitor center you can pay to go on one of the Navajo-guided 4WD tours of the valley. These tours offer an excellent way to see places in the park that are otherwise inaccessible. The visitor center also has a restaurant that is open during the summer months and serves Navajo and American cuisine.

Three Sisters
The Three Sisters are one of several distinctive pinnacle rock formations at Monument Valley. Others include the Totem Pole and the "fingers" of the Mittens. The closest view of the sisters can be seen from John Ford's Point, and is one of the most photographed sights here.

Left Mitten

Art & Ruins
Petroglyphs such as this bighorn sheep can be seen on Navajo-guided tours of rock art sites, which are dotted around the valley's ancient ruins.

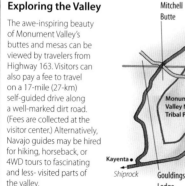

Exploring the Valley

The awe-inspiring beauty of Monument Valley's buttes and mesas can be viewed by travelers from Highway 163. Visitors can also pay a fee to travel on a 17-mile (27-km) self-guided drive along a well-marked dirt road. (Fees are collected at the visitor center.) Alternatively, Navajo guides may be hired for hiking, horseback, or 4WD tours to fascinating and less-visited parts of the valley.

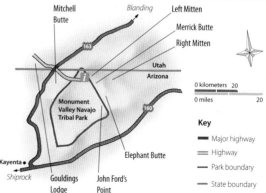

Mitchell Butte

Blanding

Left Mitten

Merrick Butte

Right Mitten

163

Utah
Arizona

160

Monument Valley Navajo Tribal Park

Elephant Butte

Kayenta

Shiprock

Gouldings Lodge

John Ford's Point

0 kilometers 20
0 miles 20

Key

━━ Major highway
═══ Highway
— Park boundary
— State boundary

John Ford's Point

The most popular stop along the valley drive is John Ford's Point, which is said to be the film director's favorite view of the valley. Various stands offer a range of Navajo handicrafts. A nearby *hogan (see p113)* serves as a gift shop where Navajo weavers demonstrate their craft.

VISITORS' CHECKLIST

Practical Information
Road map C2.
PO Box 360289, Monument Valley, (435) 727-5870. **Open** sunrise–sunset daily. Scenic drive: 8am–5pm daily (May–Sep: 6am–8pm). **Closed** Jan 1, Thanksgiving, Dec 25. visitor center only.
W navajonationparks.org

Right Mitten

Merrick Butte

Navajo Weaver

Navajo women are usually considered to be the finest weavers in the Southwest. One rug can take months to complete and sells for thousands of dollars. Using the natural colors of the land, the weavers often add a "spirit line" to their work to prevent their spirit being "trapped" within the rug.

Monument Valley

Monument Valley is not really a valley. The tops of the mesas mark what was once a flat plain. Millions of years ago, this plain was cracked by upheavals within the earth. The cracks widened and eroded, until all that is left today are the formations rising from the desert floor.

Gouldings Lodge

The lodge offers accommodations, a restaurant, and guided bus tours of the valley. The original trading post is now a museum of the valley's cinematic history.

Ancestral Puebloan ruins of Keet Seel at Navajo National Monument

❷ Navajo National Monument

Road map C2. **Tel** (928) 672-2700.
Open end May–mid-Sep: 8am–
5:30pm daily; mid-Sep–end May:
9am–5pm daily. **Closed** Jan 1,
Thanksgiving, Dec 25. 🐾 🏕
W nps.gov/nava

Named for its location on
the Navajo Reservation, this
monument is actually known
for its Ancestral Puebloan ruins.
The most accessible ruin here
is the beautifully preserved,
135-room pueblo of Betatakin,
which fills a vast, curved niche
in the cliffs of Tsegi Canyon.
An easy 1-mile (2-km) trail from
the visitor center leads to an
overlook where Betatakin is
visible on the far side, near the
canyon floor. This is a lovely
hike through piñon pines and
juniper trees. From late May to
early September (and some
winter weekends) there are
3- to 5-hour hiking tours to
Betatakin, which allow a close
look at the ruins of these
ancient houses.

A much more demanding
17-mile (27-km) hike leads to
Keet Seel, a more impressive
ruin. Only 20 permits to visit the

ruin are issued each day. This
hike has optional overnight
camping in summer at a site
with only the most basic
facilities. Keet Seel was a
larger and more successful
community than Betatakin.
Construction began on Keet
Seel in about 1250, but the
site is thought to have been
abandoned by 1300.

These two sites are
considered to mark the pinnacle
of development of the area's
Ancestral Puebloan people.

❸ Tuba City

Road map C2. 🚍 8,800. **i** Tuba City
Trading Post, (928) 283-5441.

Named for Tuuvi, a Hopi Indian
who converted to the Mormon
faith, Tuba City is best known
for the 65-million-year-old
dinosaur tracks found just off
the main highway, 5 miles
(8 km) southwest of the
town. Beyond that, this is the
largest community in the
western section of the Navajo
Reservation and is a good spot
from which to explore both the
Navajo National Monument and
the Hopi Reservation.

❹ Hopi Indian Reservation

Road map C3. 🚍 10,000. **i** Hopi
Cultural Center, Hwy 264, Second
Mesa, (928) 734-2401. **Open** May–
Sep: 6am–9pm daily; Oct–Apr: 7am–
8pm daily. **Closed** Jan 1, Thanksgiving,
Dec 25. **W** hopiculturalcenter.com

Arizona's only Pueblo Indians,
the Hopi *(see pp30–31)* are direct
descendants of the Ancestral
Puebloan people, whom they
call the Hisatsinom. The Hopi
Reservation is surrounded by the
lands of the Navajo. The landscape is harsh and barren, yet the
Hopi have cultivated the land
here for 1,000 years. They worship,
through the *kachina*, the living
spirits of plants and
animals, believed
to arrive each
year to stay with
the tribe during
the growing
season. Most of the
Hopi villages are
located on or near
one of three mesas,
or flat-topped
elevations
named First,
Second, and Third
Mesa. The artisans
on each of the
mesas specialize in
particular crafts: on First
Mesa these are carved dolls
representing the *kachina* spirits
and painted pottery; on Second
Mesa, silver jewelry and coiled
baskets are made; and on Third
Mesa, craftspeople fashion
wicker baskets and woven rugs.

Kachina doll

Walpi, the ancient pueblo on
First Mesa, was first inhabited
in the 12th century. To reach
Walpi, visitors drive up to
the Mesa from the Pollaca
settlement to the village of
Sichomovi. Nearby, the Ponsi

Historic pueblo town of Walpi on First Mesa at Hopi Indian Reservation

A range of merchandise in the general store at Hubbell Trading Post

Visitor Center is the departure point for the 1-hour Walpi tours. Walpi was built to be easily defended, and straddles a dramatic knife edge of rock, extending from the tip of First Mesa. In places Walpi is less than 100 ft (33 m) wide with a drop of several hundred feet on both sides. The Walpi tour includes several stops where visitors can purchase *kachina* dolls and distinctive hand-crafted pottery, or sample the Hopi *piki* bread.

Those wishing to shop further can continue on to Second Mesa, which has an array of Hopi arts and crafts. The Hopi Cultural Center is home to a restaurant *(see p143)* and the only hotel *(see p133)* for miles around, as well as a museum that has an excellent collection of photographs depicting scenes of Hopi life.

On Third Mesa, Old Oraibi pueblo, thought to have been founded in the 12th century, is of note only because of claims that it is the oldest continually occupied human settlement in North America.

Walpi
[i] (928) 737-2670. Walking tours available 9am–3pm daily except during ceremonies or inclement weather.

❺ Ganado & Hubbell Trading Post

Road map D2. 👤 1,200. [i] Hubbell Trading Post, Hwy 264, (928) 755-3254. [w] nps.gov/hutr

A small, bustling town in the heart of the Navajo Reservation, Ganado's major attraction is the

Hubbell Trading Post National Historic Site. Established in the 1870s by John Lorenzo Hubbell, this is the oldest continually operating trading post in the Navajo Nation. Trading posts like this one were once the economic and social centers of the reservations. The Navajo traded sheep, wool, blankets, turquoise, and other items in exchange for tools, household goods, and food. The trading posts were also a resource during times of need. When a smallpox epidemic struck in 1886, John Lorenzo helped care for the sick, using his house as a hospital.

Today, the trading post still hums with traditional trading activities. One room is a working general store, the rafters hung with frying pans and hardware, and shelves stacked with cloth, medicines, and food. Another room is filled with beautiful hand-woven rugs, Hopi *kachina* dolls, and

Navajo bracelet at Hubbell Trading Post

Navajo baskets. Another department has a long row of glass cases displaying an impressive array of silver and turquoise jewelry.

Visitors can tour Hubbell's restored home and view a significant collection of Southwestern art. At the visitor center Navajo women demonstrate rug weaving.

Hubbell Trading Post National Historic Site
A2264, near Ganado. [i] (928) 755-3475. **Open** 8am-5pm daily (summer: to 6pm). **Closed** Jan 1, Thanksgiving, Dec 25. [w] nps.gov/hutr

❻ Window Rock

Road map D2. 👤 2,700. [i] Navajo Nation Visitor Services, Hwy 264, (928) 871-6436.

The capital of the Navajo Nation is named for the natural arch found in the sandstone cliffs about a mile north of the main strip on Highway 12. The **Navajo Nation Museum** located here is one of the largest Native American museums in the US. Opened in 1997, the huge *hogan*-shaped building houses displays that cover the history of the Ancestral Puebloans and the Navajo.

Navajo Nation Museum
Hwy 264 & Post Office Loop Rd. **Tel** (928) 871-7941. **Open** 8am–5pm Mon & Sat; 8am–8pm Tue–Fri. [w] navajonationmuseum.org

Eroded sandstone opening of Window Rock, near Highway 12

❼ Canyon de Chelly National Monument

Few places in North America can boast a longer or more eventful history of human habitation than Canyon de Chelly. Archeologists have found evidence of four periods of Native culture, starting with the Basketmaker people around AD 300, followed by the Great Pueblo Builders, who created the cliff dwellings in the 12th century. They were succeeded by the Hopi, who lived here seasonally for around 300 years, taking advantage of the canyon's fertile soil. In the 1700s, the Hopi left the area and moved to the mesas, returning to the canyon to farm during the summer months. Today, the canyon is the cultural and geographic heart of the Navajo Nation. Pronounced "d'Shay," de Chelly is a Spanish corruption of the Navajo word *Tsegi*, meaning Rock Canyon.

Yucca House Ruin
Perched just below the mesa top, this ruin of an Ancestral Puebloan house sits in a rock hollow, precariously overhanging a sheer drop to the valley floor.

Mummy Cave Ruin
The two pueblos in Mummy Cave, separated by a central tower, were built in the 1280s by Ancestral Puebloans, who had inhabited the caves for more than 1,000 years. An overlook provides a good view of this impressive ruin.

Stone and adobe cliff dwellings were home to the Ancestral Puebloans from the 12th to the 14th centuries and were built to face south toward the sun, with cooler areas within.

Navajo Fortress
This imposing rock tower was the site of a three-month siege in late 1863 to early 1864, when a group of Navajos reached the summit via pole ladders to escape Kit Carson and the US army. The persistence of Carson and starvation led them to surrender and they were marched to a camp in New Mexico (*see p115*).

Canyon Landscape

The sandstone cliffs of Canyon de Chelly reach as high as 1,000 ft (300 m), towering above the neighboring meadows and desert landscape in the distance. The canyon floor around the cliffs is fringed with cottonwood bushes, watered by the Chinle Wash.

The pale walls of the White House cliff drop 550 ft (160 m) to the canyon floor.

Hogan Interior

The *hogan* is the center of Navajo family life. Made of horizontal logs, it has a smoke hole in the center to provide contact with the sky, while the dirt floor gives contact with the earth. A door faces east to greet the rising sun.

White House Ruins

This group of rooms, tucked into a tiny hollow in the cliff, seems barely touched by time. The dwellings were originally situated above a larger pueblo, much of which has now disappeared. The only site within the canyon that can be visited without a Navajo guide, it is reached via a steep 2.5-mile (5-km) round-trip trail that winds to the canyon floor and offers magnificent views.

Massacre Cave

The canyon's darkest hour was in 1805, when a Spanish force under Lieutenant Antonio Narbona entered the area. The Spanish wanted to subdue the Navajo, claiming they were raiding their settlements. While some Navajo fled by climbing to the canyon rim, others took refuge in a cave high in the cliffs. The Spanish fired into the cave, and Narbona boasted that he had killed 115 Navajo including 90 warriors. Navajo accounts are different, claiming that most of the warriors were absent (probably hunting) and those killed were mostly women, children, and the elderly. The only Spanish fatality came when a Spaniard attempting to climb into the cave was attacked by a Navajo woman and both plunged over the cliff, gaining the Navajo name "Two Fell Over." The Anglo name is "Massacre Cave."

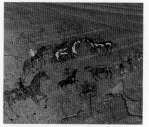

Pictograph on a canyon wall showing invading Spanish soldiers

Exploring Canyon de Chelly

Canyon de Chelly is startlingly different from the sparse desert landscape that spreads from its rim. Weathered red rock walls, just 30-ft- (9-m-) high at the canyon mouth, rise to more than 1,000-ft- (300-m-) high within the canyon, creating a sheltered world. Navajo *hogans (see p113)* dot the canyon floor; Navajo women tend herds of sheep and weave rugs at outdoor looms, and everywhere Ancestral Puebloan ruins add to the canyon's appeal. Navajo-led 4WD tours along the scenic North and South Rims are a popular way to view the site.

Antelope House Ruin
Named for a pictograph of an antelope painted by Navajo artists in the 1830s, Antelope House has ruins dating from AD 700. They can be seen from the Antelope House Overlook.

Canyon Vegetation
Within the canyon, cottonwood and oak trees line the river washes; the land itself is a fertile oasis of meadows, alfalfa and corn fields, and fruit orchards.

Chinle •

Ledge Ruin Overlook

Antelope House Overlook

Chinle Wash

White House Overlook

Canyon de Chelly

South Rim Drive

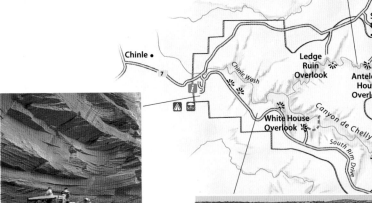

Canyon Tour
Half- and full-day tours from Sacred Canyon Lodge carry passengers in open flatbed or large 6WD army trucks. Of varying length and difficulty, the tours are the best way to see the ruins up close.

Tsegi Overlook
This high curve along the South Rim offers good general views of the farm-studded canyon floor and surrounding landscape.

For hotels and restaurants see pp132–3 and pp141–3

Hiking in the Canyon
Canyon de Chelly is a popular destination for hikers, but only the White House Ruins Trail may be walked without a guide. The visitor center *(see p113)* offers Navajo-guided hikes on trails of varying lengths.

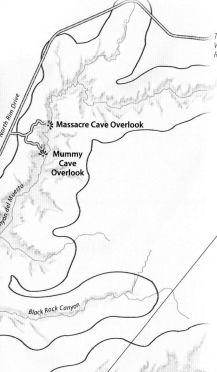

Key

═══	Highway
▪ ▪	Hiking route
───	Park boundary

To Tsaile
Window
Rock

North Rim Drive

☀ **Massacre Cave Overlook**

☀ **Mummy Cave Overlook**

Canyon del Muerto

Black Rock Canyon

Spider Rock Overlook ☀

Kilometers 3

miles 3

Spider Rock
Rising more than 800 ft (245 m), this is where, according to Navajo legends, Spider Woman lived and gave them the skill of weaving.

Kit Carson and the "Long Walk"

In 1863, the US government sent Kit Carson under the command of General James A. Carlton to settle the problem of Navajo raids. To avoid outright slaughter Carson led his soldiers through the region, destroying villages and livestock as the Navajo fled ahead of them. In January 1864, Carson entered Canyon de Chelly, capturing the Navajo hiding there *(see pp112–13)*. They were among 9,000 Navajo who were driven on the "The Long Walk," a forced march of 370 miles (595 km) from Fort Defiance to Bosque Redondo in New Mexico. There, in a pitiful reservation, more than 3,000 Navajo died before the US government accepted the resettlement as a failure and allowed them to return to the Four Corners.

Fur trapper and soldier Kit Carson (1809–68)

Dramatic mesas and buttes in the Valley of the Gods near Bluff

❽ Bluff

Road map D1. 🏔 300. ℹ️ Bluff Fort, 550 Black Locust Ave, (435) 672-9995. 🏕 W bluffutah.org

The charming town of Bluff was settled in 1880 by Mormons who dynamited their way through Glen Canyon's rock walls along what is now called the Hole-in-the-Rock Road. Float trips along the San Juan River include stops at Ancestral Pueblo ruins that can be reached only by boat.

Environs
About 12 miles (20 km) north is a 17 mile (27 km) dirt road through the **Valley of the Gods**. Like Monument Valley (see pp108–9), it features high rock spires, buttes, and mesas, but none of the crowds. On a quiet day, visitors may have the place all to themselves and imagine what it looked like to the first settlers.

❾ Blanding

Road map D1. 🏔 3,800. ℹ️ 12N Hwy 191, (435) 678-3662. W blandingutah.org

A tidy Mormon town at the base of the Abajo Mountains, Blanding is home to the **Edge of the Cedars State Park** (see pp122–23). The park contains modest Ancestral Puebloan ruins, including a small *kiva*, or religious chamber. The park museum has well-thought-out displays on the history of these ancient people and other cultures that have inhabited the region.

🏛 **Edge of the Cedars State Park**
ℹ️ Park Museum, 660 W 400 N, (435) 678-2238. **Open** Mar: 9am–5pm Mon–Sat; Apr–Oct: 9am–5pm Mon–Sat, noon–4pm Sun; Nov–Feb: noon–5pm Mon–Sat. **Closed** Thanksgiving, Dec 25. 🅿️ 🏔 W stateparks.utah.gov/parks/edge-of-the-cedars

❿ Hovenweep National Monument

Road map D1. East of Hwy 191. **Tel** (970) 562-4282. **Open** Visitors' Center: 9am–5pm daily (mid-Oct–mid-Apr: Thu–Mon). **Closed** Jan 1, Thanksgiving, Dec 25. 🅿️ 🚻 🏔 W nps.gov/hove

One of the most mysterious Ancestral Puebloan sites in the Southwest, the Hovenweep ruins lie along the rims of several shallow canyons. These well-preserved ruins, which include unique round, square, and D-shaped towers, look much as they did when W. D. Huntington, leader of a Mormon expedition, first came upon the site in 1854. The site was named in 1874, after an Ute word meaning "Deserted Valley." Little is known

of the people who inhabited these ruins, and researchers have speculated that the towers at Hovenweep might have been defensive fortifications, astronomical observatories, storage silos, or the community religious structures.

The six separate sets of ruins at Hovenweep can be visited by walking along either of the two self-guiding trails that link them.

⓫ Ute Mountain Tribal Park

Road map D2. ℹ️ Junction of Hwys 160 & 666, (970) 565-9653. **Open** Daily tours at 9am, by reservation only. 🅿️ 🚻 obligatory. W utemountaintribalpark.info

The ruins of Ute Mountain Tribal Park are one of the better-kept secrets of the Southwest. The Ancestral Puebloan people first arrived here in about AD 400. They closely followed the Mesa Verde (see pp124–5) pattern of development, creating numerous magnificent cliff dwellings, including the 80-room Lion House. These

Ancient brick tower at Hovenweep National Monument

ruins have few visitors because of their inaccessibility. Visitors can use their own vehicles and join the tours led by local Ute guides, or pay an extra charge to be driven.

⑫ Four Corners Monument Navajo Tribal Park

Road map D2. Junction of Hwys 160 & 41. **Tel** (928) 871-6647. **Open** from 8am daily; closing times vary, see website for details. **Closed** Jan 1, Thanksgiving, Dec 25. 🚻 ⚡
W navajonationparks.org

There is something oddly compelling about being able to put one foot and hand in each of four states. It is the whole premise of the Four Corners Monument – the only place in the US where four states meet at one point.

⑬ Chaco Culture National Historical Park

See pp118–19.

⑭ Farmington

Road map D2. 🚹 45,000. ✈ 🚌
ℹ 3041 E Main St, (505) 326-7602.
W farmingtonnm.org

A dusty, hard-working ranch town, Farmington is a good base for exploring the surrounding monuments. It is home to one of the most unusual museums in the Southwest. The **Bolack Museum of Fish & Wildlife** covers over 30,000 sq ft (2,800 sq m) and houses one of the largest accumulations of mounted game animals in the world. It is divided into nine themed game rooms, including African, Asian, European, and Russian. The museum's newest addition is a 10,000 sq ft (929 sq m) display of electromechanical equipment that traces America's golden age of development in electrical power generation and TV and radio broadcasting. The **Farmington Museum** focuses on the history and geology of

the area. A permanent exhibit, "From Dinosaurs to Drillbits," features a simulated ride down inside of an oil well. The museum also offers popular interactive displays for adults and children.

Environs
About 25 miles (40 km) west of Farmington is **Shiprock**, named for the spectacular 1,500-ft (457-m) rock peak that thrusts up from the valley floor about 5 miles (8 km) west of town. To the Navajo, this rock is sacred, and to early Anglo-American settlers it was a landmark that reminded them of a ship's prow. Now it is possible for sightseers to observe the peak only from the roadsides of Highways 64 or 33.
   The **Salmon Ruins**, which once housed a Chaco settlement, are situated 8 miles (12 km) to the south. These ruins were protected from grave diggers by the Salmon family, who homesteaded here in the 1870s. As a result, a century later archaeologists recovered more than a million artifacts, many of which are on display in the museum at the site.

🏛 Bolack Museum of Fish & Wildlife
3901 Bloomfield Hwy. **Tel** (505) 325-4275. **Open** 9am–3pm Mon–Sat, appointment only. **Closed** public holidays. 🚻 ⚡ 🚗 obligatory.
W bolackmuseums.com

🏛 Farmington Museum
3041 E Main St. **Tel** (505) 599- 1174.
Open 8am–5pm Mon–Sat. 🚻 ⚡ 🚗
W farmingtonmuseum.org

🏛 Salmon Ruins
6131 Hwy 64. **Tel** (505) 632-2013.
Open May–Oct: 8am–5pm daily (from 9am Sat–Sun); Nov–Apr: 8am–5pm daily (from 9am Sat, from noon Sun).
Closed Jan 1, Easter, Thanksgiving, Dec 25. 🚻 ⚡ 🚗 **W** salmonruins.com

Interior of the Great Kiva at Aztec Ruins National Monument, Aztec

⑮ Aztec

Road map D2. 🚹 6,000. **ℹ** 110 North Ash St, (505) 334-9551.
Open 9am–4pm Tue–Sat.

This small town was named for its ruins, which are Ancestral Puebloan and not Aztec as originally believed. Preserved as a National Monument, the site's 500-room pueblo was a flourishing settlement in the late 1200s. Visitors can look inside a rebuilt *kiva (see p42).*

🏛 Aztec Ruins National Monument
N of Hwy 516 on Ruins Rd. **Tel** (505) 334-6174. **Open** 8am–5pm daily (to 6pm Labor Day–Memorial Day).
Closed Jan 1, Thanksgiving, Dec 25.
🚻 ⚡ 🚗 **W** nps.gov/azru

The spectacular red peak of Shiprock near Farmington

⓭ Chaco Culture National Historical Park

Chaco Canyon is one of the most impressive cultural sites in the Southwest, reflecting the sophistication of the Ancestral Puebloan civilization *(see pp42–3)* that existed here. With its six "great houses" and many lesser sites, the canyon was once the political, religious, and cultural center for settlements that covered much of the Four Corners. At its peak during the 11th century, Chaco was one of the most impressive pre-Columbian cities in North America. Despite its size, it is thought that Chaco's population was small because the land could not have supported a larger community. Archaeologists believe that the city was mainly used as a ceremonial gathering place, with a year-round population of less than 3,000. Probably the social elite, the inhabitants supported themselves largely by trading.

Architectural Detail
Chaco's skilled builders had only stone tools to work with to create this finely wrought stonework.

KEY

① **The many kivas** here were probably used by visitors arriving for religious ceremonies.

② **This great house** was four stories high.

③ **Hundreds of rooms** within Pueblo Bonito show little sign of use and are thought to have been kept for storage or for guests arriving to take part in ceremonial events.

Chetro Ketl
A short trail from Pueblo Bonito leads to another great house, Chetro Ketl. Almost as large as Pueblo Bonito, at 3 acres (2 ha), Chetro Ketl has more than 500 rooms. The masonry used to build the later portions of this structure is among the most sophisticated found in any Ancestral Puebloan site.

Casa Rinconada
Also known as a great *kiva*, Casa Rinconada is the largest religious chamber at Chaco, measuring 62 ft (19 m) in diameter. It was used for spiritual gatherings.

Pueblo Alto
Pueblo Alto was built atop the mesa at the junction of several ancient Chacoan roads. Reaching the site requires a 2-hour hike, but the views over the canyon are well worth it.

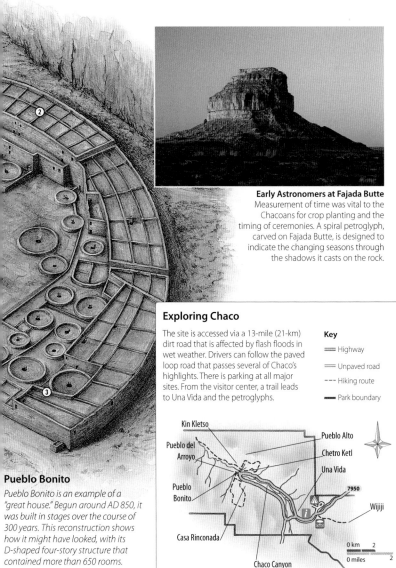

Early Astronomers at Fajada Butte
Measurement of time was vital to the Chacoans for crop planting and the timing of ceremonies. A spiral petroglyph, carved on Fajada Butte, is designed to indicate the changing seasons through the shadows it casts on the rock.

Exploring Chaco
The site is accessed via a 13-mile (21-km) dirt road that is affected by flash floods in wet weather. Drivers can follow the paved loop road that passes several of Chaco's highlights. There is parking at all major sites. From the visitor center, a trail leads to Una Vida and the petroglyphs.

Key
▬▬ Highway
══ Unpaved road
--- Hiking route
▬▬ Park boundary

Kin Kletso
Pueblo del Arroyo
Pueblo Alto
Chetro Ketl
Una Vida
Pueblo Bonito
7950
Wijiji
Casa Rinconada
Chaco Canyon

0 km   2
0 miles   2

Pueblo Bonito
Pueblo Bonito is an example of a "great house." Begun around AD 850, it was built in stages over the course of 300 years. This reconstruction shows how it might have looked, with its D-shaped four-story structure that contained more than 650 rooms.

For keys to symbols *see back flap*

Visitors riding horses near Spider Rock at Canyon de Chelly, Arizona ▶

⑯ Colorado Plateau Tour

The haunting beauty of the high plateau country, with its deep canyons and ancient, mysterious ruins, is the star of this tour, which follows some of the loneliest but loveliest roads in America. This area is very popular with hiking, mountain biking, river paddling, and 4WD enthusiasts. The plateau rises from around 2,000 ft (610 m) in elevation near Monument Valley to over 7,000 ft (2,135 m) at Monticello, Utah. The area is dotted with the ruins of the Ancient Puebloan civilization. Some, such as Hovenweep and Mesa Verde, were large complex towns, while others, for instance the ruins at Edge of Cedars State Park on a vast plain below the snowcapped Abajo Mountains, were small outposts.

③ Bluff
This small town, known for its Navajo Twin Rocks, was founded by Mormon pioneers in 1880. Today, it makes a great base for exploring the region, and is the starting point for rafting tours of the San Juan River *(see p153)*.

④ Valley of the Gods
A 17-mile- (27-km-) long dirt road winds through this valley of eroded red rock spires. Recommended for high-clearance vehicles, this road presents the remote beauty of the Southwest that existed before modern roads were built.

⑤ Goosenecks State Park
A set of incredibly tight switchbacks on the San Juan River give this overlook its name. The viewpoint is 1,500 ft (460 m) above the sinuous curves of the river, which travels 6 miles (10 km) to move 1.5 miles (2.5 km) forward.

Mexican Hat

A R I Z O N A

Flagstaff

⑥ Monument Valley
Made famous through Western movies, the valley's buttes and bluffs were once ground level, before wind and water sculpted the landscape *(see pp108–9)*.

⑦ Hovenweep National Monument
These evocative ruins are different from other Ancient Pueblo sites. Archeologists are still arguing about the purpose of the round and square towers built along this canyon *(see p116)*.

② **Edge of Cedars State Park** These small, well-preserved ruins are dwarfed by the surrounding high plateau. The park museum has a superb collection of Ancient Pueblo pottery and artifacts *(see p116)*.

Tips for Drivers

Tour length: 290 miles (467 km).
When to go: Spring and fall. Snow in winter is a possibility.
Stopping-off points: The best bets for restaurants and accommodations are Bluff and Cortez.
Note: This route can be driven in either direction. There are long distances, up to 50 miles (80 km), without services, so fill up the gas tank, and review desert driving safety *(see pp166–7)*.

① **Mesa Verde National Park**
The vast complex of ruins that lies scattered around the cliffs and canyons of this 1,000-ft- (300-m-) high mesa is among the best preserved in the Southwest *(see pp124–5)*.

Key
■ Tour route
═ Other road

⓱ Mesa Verde National Park

This high, forested mesa overlooking the Montezuma Valley was home to the Ancestral Puebloan people *(see pp42–3)* for more than 700 years. Within canyons that cut through the mesa are some of the best preserved and most elaborate cliff dwellings built by these people. Mesa Verde, meaning "Green Table," was a name given to the area by the Spanish in the 1700s, but the ruins were not widely known until the late 19th century. This site provides a fascinating record of these people from the Basketmaker period, beginning around AD 550, to the complex society that built the many-roomed cliff dwellings between AD 1000 and 1250. Displays at the Visitor and Research Center and the Chapin Mesa Museum provide a good introduction.

Spruce Tree House
These three-story structures were probably home to as many as 100 people. They are currently closed, but overlooks offer superb views of the dwellings.

Guided Tours
Ranger-led tours give visitors a chance to actually enter the ruins and get a feel of the daily lives of these ancient people.

Cliff Palace

With 150 rooms, this is the largest Ancestral Puebloan cliff dwelling found anywhere, and is the site that most visitors focus on. The location and symmetry suggest that architecture was important to the builders. Begun around 1200, it was vacated around 1275.

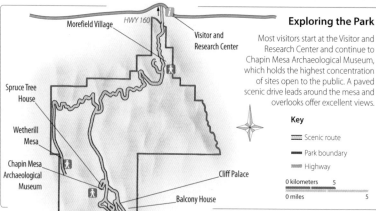

Morefield Village
HWY 160
Visitor and Research Center
Spruce Tree House
Wetherill Mesa
Chapin Mesa Archaeological Museum
Cliff Palace
Balcony House

Exploring the Park

Most visitors start at the Visitor and Research Center and continue to Chapin Mesa Archaeological Museum, which holds the highest concentration of sites open to the public. A paved scenic drive leads around the mesa and overlooks offer excellent views.

Key

▦ Scenic route
▬ Park boundary
▨ Highway

0 kilometers   5
0 miles   5

Balcony House
Possibly built for defense, Balcony House could not be seen from above, and access was (and still is) difficult. Visitors on tours must climb three ladders high above the canyon floor, then crawl through a tunnel to exit the site.

Towers were probably used for signaling or as lookouts for defense.

Square Tower House
Early cowboys named this ruin for the prominent, tower-like central structure, which was actually a vertical stack of rooms that was once surrounded by other rooms. It may have been used as a dwelling or for ceremonial purposes.

The 23 *kivas* at this site may have served a variety of ceremonial, social, and utilitarian purposes, and may indicate that many different clans lived here at various times.

Wetherill Mesa Long House
A scenic 12-mile (17-km) drive on a winding mountain road leads to Wetherill Mesa, named for the local rancher Richard Wetherill, who found Cliff Palace in the 1880s. Two cliff dwellings here, Step and Long houses, are open to visitors.

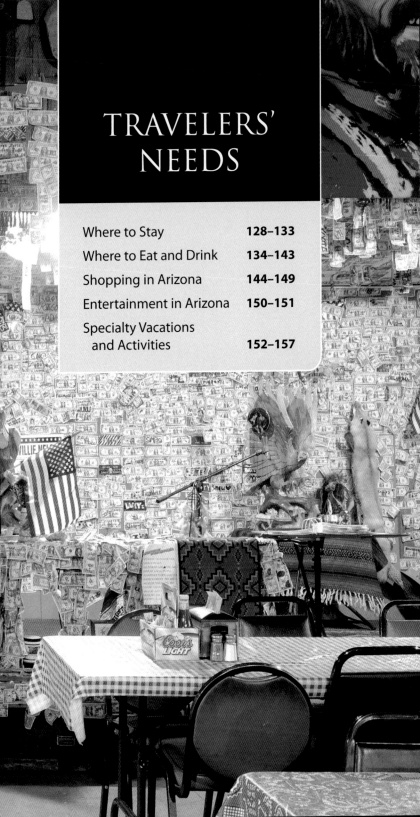

TRAVELERS' NEEDS

WHERE TO STAY

Arizona has a long history of hospitality that is reflected in the wide variety of places to stay. From lavish five-star resorts to simple rustic lodges, there is a wealth of options for visitors. You can choose historic or "boutique" hotels, cozy bed-and-breakfasts, inns, convenient motels, or fully equipped apartments. For those seeking Western-style adventure, there are dude ranches, many of which provide luxurious lodgings with horseback riding and outdoor activities. Accommodations in all

price categories usually offer private bathrooms in addition to clean, comfortable rooms. Historic hotels provide a glimpse into Arizona's early, pioneering years, and the lobby areas of these impressive hotels are worth a visit even when staying elsewhere.

Hotel prices in the region tend to vary according to season. The listings provided on pages 130–33 recommend places in all price ranges, each representing the best of their kind for that area.

Teepees at the Wigwam Motel on Route 66 in Holbrook, Arizona *(see p130)*

Hotel Classifications

The tourist industry throughout Arizona is recognized for quality lodgings. A guideline for travelers is the diamond rating system of the American and Canadian Automobile Associations (AAA and CAA). Visit www.aaa.com and www.caa.ca for more information. Every establishment, from the one-diamond motel to the five-diamond resort hotel, is rated for service, cleanliness, and the facilities offered. AAA members also benefit from discounts when they book in advance.

Taxes

Accommodation tax varies across the region as it is charged by both state and city or county governments. Expect to pay between 10 and 14 per cent of the room price in tax. Prices given for hotels in this book include taxes.

Luxury Hotels

In Arizona, hotels come in every shape and size, including historic showplaces, such as the Grand

Canyon's El Tovar *(see p130)*, which was originally built to impress East Coast investors and prove that the Southwest was an exciting tourist destination. Today, some of the most lavish hotels in Arizona are large resort hotels located in the Scottsdale and Phoenix area. A prime example is the Fairmont Scottsdale Princess *(see p131)*, with its two championship 18-hole golf courses, and spa facilities. The areas around Sedona, Phoenix, and Tucson are famous for both luxury health spas and golf resorts. Small, independently owned "boutique" hotels offer opulent facilities with an intimate atmosphere and attentive service.

There are also many hotels aimed at business travelers, offering weekly rates, computer and internet services in rooms; although these services are now available in a range of hotels.

Chain Hotels and Motels

For the most part, you can count on efficient service, moderate prices, and comfortable (if bland) surroundings at a chain hotel. The most popular chains include **Best Western** and **Holiday Inn**. Chain hotels also offer central reservation systems that can help you find a room at peak times. Motels provide rooms that are usually accessible from the parking area. They are often the only option in remote areas, and can vary from nostalgic Route 66 places *(see pp34–5)* to such bargain lodgings as Motel 6.

Historic Inns and Bed-and-Breakfasts

There are hundreds of excellent inns and bed-and-breakfasts located throughout Arizona. Generally, inns are larger, with more spacious public areas and a dining room. Bed-and-

A hotel in the Best Western chain

breakfast establishments tend to be smaller and more homey. These may be found in restored or reconstructed historic buildings, and many are located in charming Victorian houses in historic towns. These lodgings pride themselves on providing a warm welcome and friendly service. For bookings, contact **Arizona Association of Bed & Breakfast Inns**, **Arizona Trails Travel Services**, and **Mi Casa Su Casa**.

◀ The bar and restaurant at Oatman Hotel – an establishment on Route 66 *(see p137)*

Exterior view of The Peaks Resort and Golden Door Spa, Telluride *(see p133)*

Western Hotels and Dude Ranches

If you have ever wanted to indulge your "Wild West" fantasies, there are plenty of historic hotels in which to do so. Between 1880 and 1920, Western towns gained a reputation for the quality and grandeur of their hotels, and many had extravagantly ornate decor. Today, several of them have been restored to their original splendor and offer great settings for a vacation. Prescott's Hotel St. Michael *(see p131),* for example, with its grand lobby and attractive rooms, is both a historic hotel and an oasis for a relaxing, pampered stay. Dude ranches offer visitors the chance to experience Western life. They first appeared in the 1920s – the name "dude" is a colloquialism meaning "a city-dweller unfamiliar with life on the range." Choices range from relaxing vacations that include leisurely horseback rides to working ranches where you participate in such activities as cattle roundups. Meals, accommodations, and horseback riding are usually included in the price. Arizona has a **Dude Ranch Association** to help you find the perfect Western vacation.

Campgrounds and RV Parks

Campgrounds for both tents and RVs (recreational vehicles) are found all over Arizona, and are especially popular in the national parks. The **National Forest Service** provides information on forest campgrounds, which range from extremely basic to those with running water and limited RV hookups.

Lodge on the Desert, a pretty hacienda-style luxury hotel in Tucson *(see p132)*

Recommended Hotels

The hotels on pages 130–33 of this guide are a selection of the best luxury, bed and breakfast and value-for-money hotels in Arizona. They are first listed alphabetically by area, and then ordered by price range. Most of the hotels are spread across the main tourist areas, although a number that are farther afield are included if they offer particularly good value for money, facilities, service or charm. There are also lodges, resorts and apartments. What they all have in common is that, regardless of category and price, they have something special to offer.

Where a hotel has an exceptional feature, such as great-value rates, or spectacular views it has been highlighted as a DK Choice.

Where to Stay

Grand Canyon & Northern Arizona

CAMP VERDE: Fort Verde Suites $
Value for money   Map B3
628 S Main St, AZ 86322
Tel (928) 567-0275
W fvsuites.com
Conveniently located, this family-run motel has tastefully appointed rooms. Complimentary breakfast.

COTTONWOOD: Best Western Cottonwood Inn $
Value for money   Map B3
993 S Main St, AZ 86326
Tel (928) 634-5575
W bestwesterncottonwoodinn.com
Located close to many attractions, this hotel has stylishly simple rooms and a relaxing, seasonal pool. Continental breakfast served.

FLAGSTAFF: Arizona Mountain Inn & Cabins $
Value for money   Map C3
4200 Lake Mary Rd, AZ 86001
Tel (928) 774-8959
W arizonamountaininn.com
Tudor-style inn with 17 cottages scattered in a pine forest, fully stocked for romantic getaways or family gatherings.

FLAGSTAFF: Hilton Garden Inn $
Resort   Map C3
350 W Forest Meadows St, AZ 86001
Tel (928) 226-8888
W hiltongardeninn.com
Bask in modern luxury with well-equipped rooms, indoor pool, sauna, and whirlpool spa.

FLAGSTAFF: Hotel Weatherford $
Historic   Map C3
23 N Leroux St, AZ 86001
Tel (928) 779-1919
W weatherfordhotel.com
Charming hotel with quaint rooms and an electric ambience. Live musicians perform regularly.

DK Choice

FLAGSTAFF: Little America Hotel
Luxury $$
          Map C3
2515 E Butler Ave, AZ 86004
Tel (928) 779-2741
W littleamerica.com/flagstaff
Nestled in a large ponderosa pine forest, this hotel is infused with a distinctive charm and has spacious rooms, free Wi-Fi, seasonal heated outdoor pool, airport shuttle, and impeccable hospitality. Hiking trails link with the Flagstaff urban trail system.

GRAND CANYON: Phantom Ranch Lodge $
          Map B2
Grand Canyon, AZ 86023
Tel (303) 297-2757
W grandcanyonlodges.com
Sleep in bunk beds in dormitory-style rooms at this lodge, which is reached by rafting the Colorado River, by hiking or by mule.

GRAND CANYON: (NORTH RIM) Grand Canyon Lodge $
Lodge   Map B2
Grand Canyon, AZ 86052
Tel (877) 386-4383
W grandcanyonforever.com/lodging
Choose from rustic or luxurious log cabins at this mountain lodge on the edge of the canyon. Open seasonally; reserve ahead.

GRAND CANYON: (SOUTH RIM) Bright Angel Lodge $
Historic   Map B2
Grand Canyon Village, AZ 86023
Tel (303) 297-2757
W grandcanyonlodges.com
Listed in the National Register of Historic Places, this iconic log-and-stone lodge offers rooms and cabins.

DK Choice

GRAND CANYON: (SOUTH RIM) El Tovar Hotel $$
Historic   Map B2
Grand Canyon Village, AZ 86023
Tel (303) 297-2757
W grandcanyonlodges.com
This celebrated, historic landmark pine and limestone lodge is the premier place to stay on the South Rim. The 12 suites have a unique appeal and are very popular. The hotel has hosted luminaries such as Albert Einstein and Bill Clinton. Book at least a year in advance.

A view inside the gift shop at El Tovar Hotel, a historical hotel in Grand Canyon

GRAND CANYON: (SOUTH RIM) Thunderbird and Kachina Lodges $$$
Lodge   Map B2
Grand Canyon Village, AZ 86023
Tel (303) 297-2757
W grandcanyonlodges.com
The comfortable, contemporary, well-stocked family rooms offered here have partial canyon views.

HOLBROOK: Wigwam Motel $
Value for money   Map C3
811 West Hopi Dr, AZ 86025
Tel (928) 524-3048
W sleepinawigwam.com
On Route 66, this 1950s-style motel offers individual rooms in concrete Native American-style wigwams. The retro rooms have full bath and cable TV.

JEROME: Ghost City Inn Bed & Breakfast $$
Historic   Map B3
541 Main St, AZ 86331
Tel (928) 634-4678
W ghostcityinn.com
An 1890s miner's boarding house is now a tastefully decorated inn with cozy, eclectic rooms.

KINGMAN: Best Western A Wayfarer's Inn & Suites $
Value for money   Map A3
2815 E Andy Devine Ave/Route 66, AZ 86401
Tel (928) 753-6271
W bestwesternarizona.com
Close to the Powerhouse Museum, this chain hotel has comfortable rooms, a seasonal outdoor pool, and a spa.

LAKE HAVASU CITY: Hampton Inn $$
Resort   Map A3
245 London Bridge Rd, AZ 86403
Tel (928) 855-4071
W hamptoninn3.hilton.com
Adjacent to the lake, this hotel has plush rooms with lovely lake views. Breakfast bags (Mon–Fri only) are available for those in a hurry.

LAKE HAVASU CITY: Heat Hotel $$
Resort   Map A3
1420 McCulloch Blvd, AZ 86403
Tel (928) 645-2466
W heathotel.com
This waterfront hotel with contemporary design offers lavish rooms with views of the bridge and Bridgewater Channel.

The opulent exteriors of the Arizona Biltmore, a luxury hotel in Phoenix

PAGE: Best Western View of Lake Powell Hotel
Resort $$
                          Map C2
208 N Lake Powell Blvd, AZ 86040
Tel *(928) 645-5988*
W bestwesternarizona.com
Enjoy views over Glen Canyon Dam or Lake Powell at this spot, a peaceful base amid adventure.

PAGE: Courtyard Page at Lake Powell
Luxury $$$
                          Map C2
600 Clubhouse Dr, AZ 86040
Tel *(928) 645-5000*
W courtyard.com
Rest in this hotel's opulent rooms, lounge by the pool, book a golf package, or visit Lake Powell.

PRESCOTT: Hotel St. Michael $
Historic   Map B3
205 W Gurley St, AZ 86301
Tel *(928) 776-1999*
W stmichaelhotel.com
Built in 1901 and reputedly haunted, this hotel has Western-style rooms and a historic saloon.

SEDONA: Star Motel $
Value for money   Map B3
295 Jordan Rd, AZ 86336
Tel *(928) 282-3641*
W starmotelsedona.com
This small, family-run motel is a real gem. Attractive, homely rooms.

SEDONA: Amara Resort & Spa $$$
Luxury   Map B3
100 Amara Lane, AZ 86336
Tel *(928) 282-4828*
W amararesort.com
The Amara has fine luxury, unmatched comfort, modern-Native decor, and an infinity pool.

SEDONA: Enchantment Resort $$$
Luxury   Map B3
525 Boynton Canyon Rd, AZ 86336
Tel *(928) 282-2900*
W enchantmentresort.com
Stay in adobe casitas amid the red rocks of Boynton Canyon. The majestic resort offers many leisure activities.

WAHWEAP: Lake Powell Resort $$$
Luxury   Map C2
100 Lakeshore Dr, AZ 86040
Tel *(928) 645-2433*
W lakepowell.com
Overlooking Wahweap Marina, this ritzy resort offers fancy rooms; boat rentals and cruises.

WILLIAMS: Grand Canyon Railway Hotel $$
Historic   Map B3
235 N Grand Canyon Blvd, AZ 86046
Tel *(928) 635-4010*
W thetrain.com
While the lobby is reminiscent of yesteryear's railroad hotels, the rooms here are stylishly modern.

WINSLOW: La Posada $
Historic   Map C3
303 E 2nd St (Route 66), AZ 86047
Tel *(928) 289-4366*
W laposada.org
La Posada is considered architect Mary Colter's masterpiece and the last great railroad hotel. Classy rooms on landscaped grounds.

Phoenix & Southern Arizona

APACHE JUNCTION: Best Western Apache Junction Inn $
Value for money   Map F5
1101 W Apache Trail, AZ 85220
Tel *(480) 982-9200*
W bestwestern.com
Enjoy striking views of Superstition Mountain from the rooms at this hotel. The outdoor pool has a whirlpool.

BISBEE: Bisbee Grand Hotel $$
Historic   Map C5
61 Main St, AZ 85603
Tel *(520) 432-5900*
W bisbeegrandhotel.com
Uniquely themed rooms with handsome period antiques exude an old world charm at this Victorian hotel.

BISBEE: Copper Queen Hotel $$
Historic   Map C5
11 Howell Ave, AZ 85603
Tel *(520) 432-2216*
W copperqueen.com
Early 1900s Old West Victorian era hotel with comfortable rooms and antique furnishings.

PHOENIX: Wyndham Garden Phoenix Midtown $$
Resort   Map B4
3600 N 2nd Ave, AZ 85031
Tel *(602) 604-4900*
W wyndham.com
Upscale family hotel with an enchanting garden, heated outdoor pool, and tennis courts.

PHOENIX: Arizona Biltmore $$$
Historic   Map B4
2400 E Missouri Ave, AZ 85016
Tel *(602) 955-6600*
W arizonabiltmore.com
This hotel has classic elegance and modern convenience in a garden setting. Guests can enjoy afternoon tea, play lawn chess, or swim in one of eight pools.

DK Choice

PHOENIX: Arizona Grand Resort & Spa $$$
Luxury   Map B4
8000 S Pointe Parkway, AZ 85044
Tel *(602) 438-9000*
W arizonagrandresort.com
Family-friendly resort offering golf, tennis, horseback riding, and a spa. Its *pièce de résistance*, exclusive to guests, is The Oasis, a seasonal waterpark with a slide, wave pool, and the Zuni River. Each balcony suite has a living room and a wet bar. Miles of hiking trails in the adjacent South Mountain Preserve.

PHOENIX: The Wigwam Resort $$$
Luxury   Map B4
300 E Wigwam Blvd, Litchfield Pk, AZ 85340
Tel *(623) 935-3811*
W wigwamarizona.com
The charms of a bygone era and contemporary comfort blend at this stately resort with elegant casita-style rooms, three golf courses, and water slides.

SCOTTSDALE: Fairmont Scottsdale Princess $$$
Luxury   Map F4
7575 E Princess Dr, AZ 85255
Tel *(480) 585-4848*
W fairmont.com/scottsdale
This fine retreat has glamorous Spanish-style architecture, alluring landscapes, two golf courses, and world-class amenities.

For more information on types of hotels *see pages 128–9*

Chic furnishings in a guest room at Hotel Valley Ho in Scottsdale

SCOTTSDALE: Hotel Valley Ho $$$
Luxury   Map F4
6850 E Main St, AZ 85251
Tel (480) 248-2000
W HotelValleyHo.com
Glossy urban-resort, close to major attractions, with retro-chic rooms opening onto private balconies.

SCOTTSDALE: The Phoenician $$$
Luxury   Map F4
6000 E Camelback Rd, AZ 85251
Tel (480) 941-8200
W thephoenician.com
Lavish opulence – in the art collection, cactus garden, the spa's Meditation Atrium – mixes with nature's beauty at this resort.

TOMBSTONE: Landmark Lookout Lodge $
Value for money   Map C5
781 N Hwy 80, AZ 85638
Tel (520) 457-2223
W lookoutlodgeaz.com
Near Downtown Tombstone, this lodge has pleasant rooms with views of the Dragoon Mountains.

TOMBSTONE: The Tombstone Grand Hotel $
B&B   Map C5
580 W Randolph Way Tombstone, AZ 85638
Tel (520) 457-9057
W tombstonegrand.com
Families enjoy fun game nights at this hotel with immaculate service and intimate rooms.

TUCSON: El Presidio Inn $
B&B   Map C5
297 N Main Ave, AZ 85701
Tel (520) 623-6151
W elpresidiobbinn.com
Close to the Tucson Museum of Art, this 1886 Victorian inn has a lush courtyard garden and offers sumptuous gourmet breakfasts.

TUCSON: Arizona Inn $$
Luxury   Map C5
2200 E Elm St, AZ 85719
Tel (520) 325-1541
W arizonainn.com
Historic pink-stucco hotel with casita-style rooms spread throughout the lush lawns. Poolside ice creams in summer.

TUCSON: Royal Elizabeth Bed & Breakfast Inn $$
B&B   Map C5
204 S Scott Ave, AZ 85701
Tel (520) 670-9022
W royalelizabeth.com
This 1878 Victorian mansion, with original antiques and beautiful woodwork, has pastel rooms, a pretty garden, and a heated pool.

TUCSON: Lodge on the Desert $$$
Luxury   Map C5
306 N Alvernon Way, AZ 85711
Tel (520) 320-2000
W lodgeonthedesert.com
An urban oasis with views of the Santa Catalina Mountains. Lodging in hacienda-style rooms, with high, wood-beamed ceilings, fireplaces, and tiled patios.

DK Choice

TUCSON: White Stallion Ranch $$$
Luxury   Map C5
9251 W Twin Peaks Rd, AZ 85743
Tel (520) 297-0252
W wsranch.com
In the Sonoran Desert, this working cattle ranch offers riding opportunities for every level. Guests can ride Western-style among the saguaro cacti, and take hayrides to cookouts. The outdoor games, petting zoo, and pool make it a great stay for families.

YUMA: La Fuente Inn & Suites $
Value for money   Map A4
1513 E 16th St, AZ 85365
Tel (928) 329-1814
W www.lafuenteinn.com
Guests here enjoy airy rooms, a pool shaded by palm trees, and complimentary breakfast.

The Four Corners

AZTEC: Microtel Inn & Suites $
Value for money   Map D2
623 Phoenix CT, NM 87410
Tel (505) 334-4014
W microtelinn.com
Near the canyons and lakes, this comfy spot has good facilities. Spa at the pool and free breakfast.

BLANDING: Stone Lizard Lodging $
Value for money   Map D1
88 W Center St, UT 84511
Tel (435) 678-3323
W stonelizardlodging.com
Located between Moab and Monument Valley, this restored motel has cozy rooms.

BLUFF: Recapture Lodge $
Lodge   Map D1
220 Main St, UT, 84512
Tel (435) 672-2281
W recapturelodge.com
A homely, clean retreat amid red sandstone cliffs along San Juan River. Shuttles to the river for kayaks and rafts can be arranged.

BLUFF: Desert Rose Inn & Cabins $$$
Luxury   Map D1
701 Main St, UT, 84512
Tel (435) 672-2303
W desertroseinn.com
The nouveau-rustic rooms at this hotel have tasteful Southwestern art and quilted wood-framed beds. Stunning views from the pool area.

CAMERON: Cameron Trading Post $
Value for money   Map C2
466 Hwy 89, AZ 86020
Tel (928) 679-2231
W camerontradingpost.com
Balconied rooms at this hotel overlook a serene desert garden or the Little Colorado River Gorge. A Native arts gallery completes the Southwestern experience.

CHINLE: Best Western Canyon de Chelly Inn $
Value for money   Map D2
100 Main St, AZ 86503
Tel (928) 674-5874
W bestwesternarizona.com
Sleek, modest rooms in this chain hotel with a nice restaurant, steam room, and picnic area.

CHINLE: Thunderbird Lodge $
Lodge   Map D2
Canyon de Chelly Rural Route 7, AZ 86503
Tel (928) 674-5842
W thunderbirdlodge.com
Nestled amid cottonwoods, this Native American lodge offers tours with experienced Navajo guides, on horseback or in jeeps.

CORTEZ: Kelly Place Bed & Breakfast/Retreat Center $
B&B   Map D1
14537 Rd G, CO, AZ 81321
Tel (970) 565-3125
W kellyplace.com
Near the Canyons of the Ancients, with their many Puebloan sites, this B&B offers rustic quarters.

**CORTEZ: Retro Inn at
Mesa Verde** $
Value for money **Map** D1
2040 E Main St, Cortez, CO 81321
Tel (970) 565-3738
W retroinnmesaverde.com
Swanky rooms in a retro building,
and hearty breakfasts are offered
here. Friendly staff.

**CORTEZ: Holiday Inn Express
Mesa Verde** $$
Resort **Map** D1
2121 E Main St, CO, 81321
Tel (970) 565-6000
W coloradoholiday.com
Reliable chain hotel with desert-
inspired decor, a well-appointed
gym, and generous breakfasts.

DURANGO: Rochester Hotel $$
Historic **Map** D1
726 E Second Ave, CO, 81301
Tel (970) 385-1920
W rochesterhotel.com
This well-restored 1892 hotel
has attractive Old West and
cowboy decor. Airy rooms
with 19th-century furnishings.

DK Choice

DURANGO: Strater Hotel $$
Historic **Map** D1
699 Main Ave, CO, 81301
Tel (970) 247-4431
W strater.com
Built in 1887, this iconic,
gorgeous red-and-white Old
West Victorian building is a
prominent landmark in
downtown Durango. The
elegant rooms are decorated
with period antiques and
wallpaper. Located in the heart
of the San Juan Mountains, this
is an ideal base for a variety of
outdoor activities.

**MESA VERDE NATIONAL PARK:
Far View Lodge** $
Lodge **Map** D2
Mile Marker 15, Mancos, CO, 81328
Tel (970) 564-4300
W visitmesaverde.com
Tranquil and modern, this
adobe-style lodge boasts idyllic
views over the Montezuma
Valley. All of the spacious rooms
feature handcrafted furniture and
a private balcony.

**MEXICAN HAT: Valley of the
Gods Bed & Breakfast** $$
B&B **Map** C2
Valley of the Gods Rd, UT, 84531
Tel (970) 749-1164
W valleyofthegodsbandb.com
Soak up the stunning views
and relax on the long porch of
this solar- and wind-powered
remote and rustic home.

MOAB: Inca Inn $
Value for money **Map** D1
570 N Main St., UT 84532
Tel (435) 259-7261
W incainn.com
Close to Arches National Park,
this small motel has pleasant
rooms and offers free breakfast.

**MOAB: Sorrel River Ranch
Resort & Spa** $$$
Luxury **Map** D1
HC 64, Mile 17 Hwy 128, UT 84532
Tel (435) 259-4642
W sorrelriver.com
Nestled in red rock wilderness,
this arty log cabin resort blends
Old West decor with modern
comfort. Enjoy guided horseback
trail rides.

**MONUMENT VALLEY:
Goulding's Lodge** $$
Lodge **Map** C2
off Hwy 163, UT, 84536
Tel (435) 727-3231
W gouldings.com
Tucked into a mesa opposite
Monument Valley, this lodge
has brilliant views of the park
buttes. Cozy rooms and a
bustling restaurant.

**MONUMENT VALLEY:
The View Hotel** $$
Resort **Map** C2
Hwy 163, Monument Valley Tribal
Park, UT 84536
Tel (435) 727-5555
W monumentvalleyview.com
This contemporary hotel provides
secluded cabins and appealing
rooms all with spectacular views
of the monuments.

**SECOND MESA, HOPI
RESERVATION: Hopi Cultural
Center Inn** $
Value for money **Map** C2
Route 264, AZ 86043
Tel (928) 734-2401
W hopiculturalcenter.com
This Pueblo-style inn with
simple rooms serves as an
excellent base for touring all
three mesas.

**SILVERTON: Inn of the Rockies
at the Historic Alma House** $$
B&B **Map** E1
220 E 10th St, CO 81433
Tel (970) 387-5336
W innoftherockies.com
A Victorian house with eccentric
decor, homey rooms, excellent
breakfast, and warm service.

TELLURIDE: The Victorian Inn $$
B&B **Map** D1
401 W Pacific Ave, CO, 81435
Tel (970) 728-6601
W TheVictorianInn.org
Sublime mountain views, leisure
activities, such as skiing, and a
touch of the American West
make this B&B a great option.

DK Choice

**TELLURIDE: New Sheridan
Hotel** $$$
Historic **Map** D1
231 W Colorado Ave, CO, 81435
Tel (970) 728-4351
W newsheridan.com
This restored and renovated
1895 hotel, offers luxury service
and modern accommodations
with period furnishings. Rooftop
terrace with mountain views
and hot tubs.

**TELLURIDE: The Peaks Resort
& Spa** $$$
Luxury **Map** D1
136 Country Club Dr, CO, 81435
Tel (970) 728-6800
W thepeaksresort.com
Offering modern luxury and views
of the Rocky Mountains, this resort
is the perfect spot for ski access in
winter and kayaking in summer.

**WINDOW ROCK: Quality Inn
Navajo Nation Capital** $
Value for money **Map** D2
48 W Hwy 264, AZ 86515
Tel (928) 871-4108
W qualityinnwindowrock.com
Guests here enjoy impeccable
service, clean rooms, an inviting
restaurant, and free breakfast.

The grand outdoor seating area with panoramic vistas at The Phoenician in Scottsdale

For more information on types of hotels see pages 128–9

WHERE TO EAT AND DRINK

In addition to excellent regional cuisine, Arizona offers many exciting eating experiences, especially in its larger cities. Phoenix, Scottsdale, Tucson, and Sedona rival any city in the United States for the quality of ingredients and variety of cuisines available, with ambiences ranging from rustic to romantic. In keeping with the international status it has acquired over the years, Southwestern cuisine is served in a growing number of casual but stylish cafés. Steakhouses, too, abound in this region. Local restaurants usually serve the best Mexican food, and there are also eateries with a cowboy or Mexican theme, where you can get an inexpensive meal and great entertainment. In small towns, the best dishes are served in hotel restaurants. The establishments on pages 136–43 have been chosen for their quality, location, and good value. Some typical Mexican dishes available in Arizona are described in the box at the bottom of this section.

Prices and Tipping

Eating out in Arizona is very reasonable, and even expensive restaurants offer good value. Light meals in cafés and diners usually cost under $10, while chain restaurants serve complete dinners for under $15. Mexican restaurants offer combination plates, which generally include rice, beans, tacos, and some variety of meat for $8 to $12. At finer restaurants, dinner entrées range from $15 to $30, and diners can still buy a three-course meal, excluding wine, for under $50.

The standard tip is 15 per cent of the cost of the meal. However, leave up to 20 per cent if the service is good. Sales tax is not shown on the menu and will add around 5 to 7 per cent to the cost of a meal.

Mr. D'z Route 66 Diner, a famous fast-food restaurant in Kingman *(see p137)*

Types of Food and Restaurants

Dining establishments in Arizona range from small and friendly diners and cafés, offering hearty burgers and snacks, to gourmet restaurants that serve the latest Southwestern and fusion cuisine, to lavish dining rooms in upscale resorts found in and around Phoenix, Scottsdale, and Tucson.

Fast food is a way of life throughout the state, and a string of outlets such as McDonald's, Burger King, Wendy's, and Arby's are found along the main strips of most towns in the state. They all serve the usual, inexpensive variations of burgers, fries, and soft drinks. Chains such as Applebee's and Denny's offer more variety, with soups, salads, sandwiches, meals, and desserts. These are generally good value, but the quality varies from one establishment to the next. Pizza chains are also ubiquitous in the region.

A wide range of eating places can be found in shopping malls, including various ethnic cuisines such as Italian, Greek, Chinese, Japanese, and Indian.

Native American food is widely available, and is generally moderately priced.

Regional Dishes and Specialties

Southwestern food reflects the region's strong Hispanic and Native cultures. Mexican food and the more refined Southwestern cuisine, enjoy a following around the globe. One of the pleasures of a visit to Arizona is discovering the great variety of restaurants that serve dishes made with the freshest ingredients, and cooked with great expertise. The chile pepper is a staple of Southwestern cuisine, and some pack a powerful bite, but there are other milder varieties that add flavor without heat. Most menus in restaurants frequented by tourists provide an explanation of the dishes, and friendly staff offer advice. The region's other favorite is beef, and there is no shortage of good steaks and burgers in most areas.

Avocados

Enchiladas are rolled tortillas filled with cheese, chicken, or beef, topped with a red chile sauce and melted cheese.

Fry bread forms the base of many meals, and is often topped with meat, beans, cheese, lettuce, and tomatoes.

Steakhouses serving steaks, mesquite barbecue, and ribs are found across Arizona in a wide variety of price ranges. Some of these restaurants also serve fresh mountain-trout and seafood, and provide live Western-style entertainment.

Mexican restaurants are popular and are located all over the state. They vary from roadside stands and snack bars to plush restaurants. New Mexican cuisine, inspired by the cooking methods of the Pueblo culture, is widespread. The distinctive taste of the dishes comes from the use of piñon pine nuts, *nopales* (the fruit of the prickly pear cactus), and the *chayote*, which is similar to zucchini.

Southwestern cuisine is a fusion of Native American, Hispanic, and international influences, and is increasingly showcased in Arizona's finest restaurants. The most important ingredients are chiles, corn, beans, cilantro, tomatillos, and pine nuts. Restaurants visited by locals tend to serve hotter chiles than those catering to tourists.

Vegetarian

Southwestern cuisine is largely meat based. Vegetarians may not be able to find much variety outside the larger cities and resorts. However, salad bars are

A colorful restaurant housed in a massive teepee along Route 66

available everywhere, from fine restaurants to fast food chains. Salads can be a complete meal, as they often come with meat and seafood, but vegetarian orders are usually accommodated. A number of fast food chains serve soups and baked potatoes as well.

The more expensive restaurants, and those affiliated with hotels, are usually willing to provide vegetarian meals on request. It is a good idea to call ahead.

Disabled Facilities

Restaurants are required to provide wheelchair access and a ground-level restroom by law, but check with older establishments in advance.

Alcohol

Beer, particularly the many kinds of *cervezas* imported from Mexico, is the most popular drink in the region. Typical

brands include San Miguel and Corona. Arizona has a growing brew-pub and micro-brewery industry as well. Wine and other alcoholic drinks are also available, except on Native reservations. The finer restaurants usually serve a variety of beverages. Visitors must be 21 to buy alcohol. Make sure you carry ID as you may be requested to show it.

Recommended Restaurants

The restaurants listed on pages 136–43 of this guide cover a comprehensive range of cuisines and have been selected for their value, good food, location and atmosphere.

Entries marked as DK Choice, have been highlighted in recognition of a special feature – a historic venue, use of unusual ingredients, outstanding dishes, excellent value, spectacular views, or a combination of these.

Huevos rancheros, fried eggs on a soft tortilla with chile, cheese, and refried beans, are eaten at breakfast.

Tacos are crisp-fried tortillas filled with ground beef, beans, cheese, and salad, and served with guacamole.

Chile relleno is a whole green chile stuffed with cheese, meat, or rice, dipped in light batter and then deep-fried.

Where to Eat and Drink

Grand Canyon & Northern Arizona

BOULDER CITY: Coffee Cup $
Diner   Map A2
512 Nevada Way, NV 89005
Tel *(702) 294-0517*
Food is cooked to order at this family-friendly eatery, featured on Television Food Network. Breakfast and lunch menus offer American classics and Southwestern fare such as pork chili verde omelet.

CAMP VERDE: Moscato Ristorante Italiano $$
Italian   Map B3
396 S Main St, AZ 86322
Tel *(928) 567-7417*   **Closed** *Sun*
This restaurant's rustic exterior belies an elegant ambience inside. The menu features Italian classics such as fettuccine with salmon and shrimp scampi linguini.

FLAGSTAFF: Charly's Pub & Grill $
Southwestern   Map C3
23 N Leroux St, AZ 86001
Tel *(928) 779-1919*
Feast on Navajo tacos, posole, steaks and delectable pies while enjoying wines and cocktails from the bar. Housed in the historic Hotel Weatherford (*see p130*).

FLAGSTAFF: Downtown Diner $
American   Map C3
7 E Aspen Ave, AZ 86001
Tel *(928) 774-3492*
Located close to Route 66, this 1950s-style diner offers hearty breakfasts. Burgers, homemade soups, and fresh trout from Oak Creek are served round the clock.

FLAGSTAFF: Black Bart's Steakhouse, Saloon & Musical Revue $$
Steakhouse   Map C3
2760 E Butler Ave, AZ 86004
Tel *(928) 779-3142*
Named after a 1870s stagecoach robber, Black Bart's menu features flavorful seafood, ribs and oat-grilled steaks. A nightly musical review involves Broadway and jazz performances and songs from the 1960s and 70s.

FLAGSTAFF: Josephine's $$
American   Map C3
503 N Humphreys St, AZ 86001
Tel *(928) 779-3400*
Experience fine dining in a historic Craftsman Bungalow with fireplaces and a pretty patio. The produce is seasonal and the wine list is impressive.

FLAGSTAFF: Pasto Cucina Italiana $$
Italian   Map C3
19 E Aspen Ave, AZ 86001
Tel *(928) 779-1937* **Closed** *Sun & Mon*
Known for its innovative Italian dishes, this delightful downtown restaurant has a courtyard patio and a wine lodge. Try the chicken parmesan, lasagna verde, and strawberry vanilla panna cotta.

DK Choice

FLAGSTAFF: Cottage Place Restaurant $$$
American   Map C3
126 W Cottage Ave, AZ 86001
Tel *(928) 774-8431*   **Closed** *Mon & Tue*
A romantic bungalow restaurant with award-winning creative gourmet cuisine and a monthly changing tasting menu by the chef. Try the Chateaubriand for Two or choose from a range of entrées such as gorgonzola encrusted filet, grilled white shrimp in chimichurri, and forest mushroom ravioli.

GRAND CANYON: Phantom Ranch Canteen $
American   Map B2
Grand Canyon, AZ 86023
Tel *303-297-2757*
This place caters to the adventurous going down to the canyon bottom, which means early breakfast and dinner, and a sack lunch option. There are set meal timings. Book ahead.

Diners enjoying the panoramic views from the North Rim at the Grand Canyon Lodge

Price Guide

Price categories include a three-course meal for one, a glass of house wine, and all extra charges, including tax.

$	under $50
$$	$50–70
$$$	over $70

GRAND CANYON: Canyon Star Steakhouse $$
Southwestern   Map B2
Grand Hotel at the Grand Canyon, 149 State Hwy 64, AZ 86023
Tel *(888) 634-7263 (in US), (303) 265-7000 (international)*
A feast of steaks, barbecue, and American entrées are offered at the Canyon Star. The timbered dining room and the adjacent bar have western saddles for seats.

GRAND CANYON: Coronado Room $$
American   Map B2
Best Western Grand Canyon Squire Inn, SR64, AZ 86023
Tel *(928) 638-2681*
Enjoy a menu of European and Southwestern-inspired dishes: escargot, spinach enchiladas, and sizzling fajitas, along with prime-rib steaks and seafood.

GRAND CANYON: (NORTH RIM) Grand Canyon Lodge $
American   Map B2
Grand Canyon, AZ 86052
Tel *(928) 638-2611 (summer), (928) 645-6865 (winter)*
Beef, chicken, and American buffalo are on the menu at this beautiful, remote restaurant. Astounding views of the Kaibab Plateau. Reserve ahead in summer.

GRAND CANYON: (SOUTH RIM) Bright Angel Restaurant $
Southwestern   Map B2
Grand Canyon Village, AZ 86023
Tel *(928) 638-2631*
Try a Harvey House Steak or the Colter Quesadilla at this family-friendly eatery. Seating is on a first-come, first-served basis.

DK Choice

GRAND CANYON: (SOUTH RIM) El Tovar $$
American   Map B2
Grand Canyon Village, AZ 86023
Tel *(928) 638-2631*
A wide range of wines with a menu of Southwestern and classic dishes are offered at the historic El Tovar. Savor the views of the Grand Canyon from the veranda or the dining room. Reservations advised.

JEROME: The Asylum Restaurant $
American   **Map** B3
Jerome Grand Hotel, 200 Hill St, AZ 86331
Tel *(928) 639-3197*
Snug eatery serving New American dishes such as Pacific king salmon with prickly pear barbecue sauce and grilled pork tenderloin with chipotle apricot sauce. Beautiful views of the Verde Valley and a selection of the choicest wines.

JEROME: The Flatiron $
Southwestern   **Map** B3
416 Main St, AZ 86331
Tel *(928) 634-2733* **Closed** *Tue & Wed*
Cozy café that uses locally sourced produce to create breakfasts (served until noon) and lunches, including vegan and gluten-free fare.

DK Choice

KINGMAN: Mr D'z Route 66 $
Diner   **Map** A3
105 E Andy Devine Ave, AZ 86401
Tel *(928) 718-0066*
With its kitschy interiors, memorabilia from the 1950s and picnic tables outside, this diner is the perfect spot to sip homemade root beer and devour sweet potato fries. Oprah Winfrey is among those who have stopped by for a burger and onion rings.

LAKE HAVASU CITY: Juicy's River Cafe $
American   **Map** A3
42 S Smoketree Ave, AZ 86403
Tel *(928) 855-8429*
Extensive breakfast, lunch, and dinner menus including burgers, ribs, fish, and pasta. Try the daily specials. Pleasant ambience and top-notch service.

LAKE HAVASU CITY: Shugrue's $
American   **Map** A3
1425 McCulloch Blvd, AZ 86403
Tel *(928) 453-1400*
A fine dining restaurant that offers steak and seafood entrées with wine, beer, and cocktails. The Dijon garlic-crusted halibut with sea scollops is a favorite. Fine views of London Bridge.

OATMAN: Oatman Hotel $
American   **Map** A3
181 Main St, AZ 86433
Tel *(928) 768-4408*
The walls at this quirky place (formerly a hotel, *see p79*) are covered with hundreds of dollar bills. Feast on tasty pulled-pork sandwiches and buffalo burgers. There is a small museum upstairs.

The well-stocked kitchen area at The Flatiron in Jerome

PAGE: Bonkers $
American   **Map** C2
810 N Navajo Drive, AZ 86040
Tel *(928) 645-2706*
Natural meats and seasonal produce are used at Bonkers to create delicious dishes. It has Italian favorites and Turf and Surf as entrée categories, plus a low-calorie menu. Friendly staff.

PAGE: Dam Bar and Grille $
American   **Map** C2
644 N Navajo Dr, AZ 86040
Tel *(928) 645-2161*
This fine dining restaurant, with a contemporary vibe, is known for its excellent steak, seafood, and pasta. Soak in the sunset while dining on the patio or relax at the sports bar.

PAGE: El Tapatio Mexican Restaurant $
Mexican   **Map** C2
25 Lake Powell Blvd, AZ 86040
Tel *(928) 645-4055*
A traditional Mexican restaurant with a festive atmosphere and an outdoor patio, El Tapatio is popular for its flaming fajitas, huge margaritas, and imported *cerveza* (beer). Good vegetarian options. Generous servings.

PRESCOTT: El Gato Azul $
Southwestern   **Map** B3
316 W Goodwin St, AZ 86303
Tel *(928) 445-1070*
Relish homemade chorizo, roasted chiles, sherry chicken crêpes, and Dagwood sandwiches at this eclectic Southwestern restaurant. Check out the tapas menu.

PRESCOTT: Murphy's $$
American   **Map** B3
201 N Cortez St, AZ 86301
Tel *(928) 445-4044*
Premium eatery serving fresh seafood, including yellowfin tuna and mesquite-grilled shrimp brochette. Slow-roasted prime rib is among the specialties. Excellent list of wines and micro-brewed beers.

SEDONA: Black Cow Café $
Café   **Map** B3
229 N Hwy 89A, AZ 86336
Tel *(928) 203-9868*
Photographs of Sedona from the 1950s and 60s adorn the walls of this café, built as a yesteryear ice cream parlor. Scrumptious homemade pies, pastries, and smoothies have made this eatery popular as a dessert café.

SEDONA: El Rincon Restaurante Mexicano $
Mexican   **Map** B3
Tlaquepaque Village, 336 S Hwy 179, Suite A112, AZ 86336
Tel *(928) 282-4648*
Dine al fresco on the patio or within the stylish Spanish interiors at this restaurant. The Arizona-style Mexican dishes, with hints of native Navajo, can be rounded off with the fruit-filled chimichanga à la mode.

SEDONA: Takashi Japanese Restaurant $
Japanese   **Map** B3
465 Jordan Rd, AZ 86336
Tel *(928) 282-2334* **Closed** *Mon*
The elaborate menu here includes a selection of sushi, soft-shell crabs, teriyaki, sukiyaki, tempura, and teppanyaki dishes. Try the combination plates, which bring together different cooking styles.

SEDONA: Dahl & Diluca Ristorante Italiano $$
Italian   **Map** B3
2321 W Hwy 89A, AZ 86336
Tel *(928) 282-5219*
Delicious veal picatta and eggplant (aubergine) parmigiana are among the dishes on this farm-to-table menu. The Tuscan villa atmosphere evokes the romance of old Italy.

For more information on types of restaurants *see page 134–5*

Outdoor tables under the trees at Etch Kitchen & Bar, Sedona

SEDONA: The Heartline Café $$
American **Map** B3
1610 W Hwy 89A, AZ 86336
Tel (928) 282-3365 (daytime), (928) 282-0750 (after 4pm)
An assortment of Mediterranean, Southwestern, and Asian dishes served in a relaxed, contemporary ambience. Signature dishes include pecan-crusted local trout with Dijon sauce, Asian barbecued tuna, and bacon-wrapped filet mignon.

SEDONA: Javelina Cantina $$
Mexican **Map** B3
Hillside Courtyard, 671 Hwy 179, AZ 86336
Tel (928) 282-1313
Overlooking Shugrue's famous red rocks, this restaurant serves sizzling fajita platters, *carne asada* (sliced beef) plates, fish tacos, and a wide range of tequilas and margaritas, plus domestic and Mexican beers. Sit in the airy dining room or the large terrace.

SEDONA: Etch Kitchen & Bar $$$
American **Map** B3
L'Auberge de Sedona, 301 Little Lane, AZ 86336
Tel (928) 204-4350
The menu changes seasonally here and makes use of local produce, imported truffles, and artisan cheeses. Extensive wine list. Splendid views of the creek and forest.

SHOW LOW: Cattlemen's Steakhouse $
Steakhouse **Map** C3
1231 E Deuce of Clubs, AZ 85901
Tel (928) 537-9797
Specialties at this steakhouse and lounge include lip-smacking hand-cut prime rib and steaks,

chicken, pork, and lobster. There are separate kids' and twilight menus. Try the salad bar.

WILLIAMS: Pine Country Restaurant $
American **Map** B3
107 N Grand Canyon Blvd, AZ 86046
Tel (928) 635-9718
Pine Country serves large breakfast portions, sumptuous sandwiches and melts for lunch, and salads, pasta, chops, and Shepherd's Pie for dinner. The delicious home-style cooking is delivered to the tables by the amiable staff.

WILLIAMS: Red Raven Restaurant $
American **Map** B3
135 W Route 66, AZ 86046
Tel (928) 635-4980
This casual and creative spot has an eclectic menu featuring salads, Southwest-inspired steaks, seafood, and pasta dishes. The kitchen also whips up delectable desserts. The list of wines and beers is extensive.

WILLIAMS: Rod's Steak House $
Steakhouse **Map** B3
301 E Route 66, AZ 86046
Tel (928) 635-2671 **Closed** Sun
Rocky Mountain trout, barbecue ribs, and fried chicken are on the menu here, with slow-cooked prime rib and steaks being favorites. Look out for the red neon sign of Rod's mascot, Domino the Steer, a landmark on Route 66.

WILLIAMS: Twisters 50's Soda Fountain & The Route 66 Place $
American **Map** B3
417 E Route 66, AZ 86046
Tel (928) 635-0266 **Closed** Sun
This 1950s diner is popular for its banana splits, sundaes, and floats. Groove to retro music while having a dinner of burgers, sandwiches, chile dogs, and steaks. Route 66, Elvis, and Coca-Cola collectibles are for sale.

Phoenix & Southern Arizona

APACHE JUNCTION: Mining Camp Restaurant & Trading Post $
American **Map** F5
6100 E Mining Camp St, AZ 85217
Tel (480) 982-3181 **Closed** May–Oct; Mon–Thu
A favorite for many years, this place has long wooden tables and generous platters of food, which are ideal for groups to share. Team up roast chicken,

oven-baked ham, and barbecue ribs with bowls of coleslaw and baked beans.

BENSON: Mi Casa Restaurant $
Mexican **Map** C5
723 W 4th St, AZ 85602
Tel (520)-245-0343
A family-run eatery in a small house that blends authentic Mexican flavors with those of New Mexico. The enchiladas banderas, shrimp tacos, and flan are highly recommended.

BISBEE: Café Roka $$
American **Map** C5
35 Main St, AZ 85603
Tel (520) 432-5153 **Closed** Days vary seasonally
Italian, Californian, and Mediterranean influences can be seen in chef Kass's cooking at this eatery. Local organic produce, grass-fed meats, and sustainable seafood are used to create unique flavors. Special dietary requests are accommodated.

CASA GRANDE: BeDillon's Cactus Garden & Restaurant $$
Southwestern **Map** B4
800 N Park Ave, AZ 85122
Tel (520) 836-2045
This beautiful adobe home is surrounded by a cacti garden. Hand-cut charboiled steaks, prime rib, and chicken are on the varied menu. House favorites include seafood raul with scallops, shrimp and crab in a Monterey sauce.

GILA BEND: Little Italy Pizza & Italian $
Italian **Map** B4
502 E Pima St, AZ 85337
Tel (928) 683-2221
A family-run restaurant specializing in hand-tossed pizzas. A lengthy menu of Italian entrées includes penne al pesto, eggplant (aubergine) parmigiana, and chicken marsala.

GLOBE: Chalo's Casa Reynoso $
Mexican **Map** C4
902 E Ash St, AZ 85501
Tel (928) 425-0515
Home-style enchiladas, burritos, tacos, and chili are served in this cozy, family restaurant. One of the signature dishes is the spicy or mild Mexican sopaipillas filled with beef and pork.

GLOBE: Copper Bistro $
American **Map** C4
2118 E Hwy 60, AZ 85501
Tel (928) 473-4442
An elaborate lunch and dinner menu is offered at this friendly café. Try the salads, burgers,

barbecue, sandwiches, or pasta. Specials include prime rib, mango shrimp, and Cornish pasties. The desserts are a must-have.

NOGALES: Cocina La Ley $
Mexican   Map C5
226 W 3rd St, AZ 85621
Tel (520) 287-4555   **Closed** Tue
A pleasant little eatery with flavorful, traditional fare. Pescado con camaron (fish soup), tacos de cabeza (beef cheek), and horchata (rice and cinnamon beverage) are some of the popular dishes.

NOGALES: La Roca Restaurant $
Mexican   Map C5
Calle Elias 91, Nogales, Mexico
Tel (520) 313-6313
For authentic flavors, dine at this romantic Spanish colonial hacienda (landed estate) across the border. Entrées include shrimp ceviche, grilled beef tenderloin, and chicken with sweet pepper sauce.

PHOENIX: Aunt Chilada's Squaw Peak $
Mexican   Map B4
7330 N Dreamy Draw Dr, AZ 85020
Tel (602) 944-1286
A rustic space with an abundance of flowers, the garden patio at Aunt Chilada's offers the option of dining al fresco. Sip a margarita while feasting on the chicken-breast mole with sesame seeds.

PHOENIX: Courtyard Café at Heard Museum $
Southwestern   Map B4
Heard Museum, 2301 N Central Ave, AZ 85004
Tel (602) 251-0204
Salads, gourmet sandwiches, and entrées are put together using local ingredients. The meatloaf with ground bison, ground beef, and smoked bacon is a house specialty. Save room for the fry bread sundae.

PHOENIX: Matt's Big Breakfast $
American   Map B4
825 N 1st St, AZ 85004
Tel (602) 254-1074
Office workers flock here for sandwiches and salads during the week and at weekends people drop in for a salami scramble and waffle. Matt's uses only grain-fed meats, organic produce when possible, and cage-free eggs.

PHOENIX: Pizzeria Bianco $
Pizzeria   Map B4
623 E Adams St, AZ 85004
Tel (602) 258-8300   **Closed** Sun
A small eatery with a simple menu. The wood-fired Neapolitan pizzas here are legendary.

Toppings include fennel sausage, wood-roasted onion, and fresh house-smoked mozzarella. Located in a brick building with large picture windows.

PHOENIX: Crudo $$
Italian   Map B4
Gaslight Square, 3603 E Indian School Rd, AZ 85018
Tel (602) 358-8666   **Closed** Mon
Modern, spacious restaurant specializing in raw fish prepared the Italian way, using basil and olives. It also serves salmon in fata, grilled short ribs, and cheese dishes such as ricotta with walnut sauce and honey. Good cocktail and wine list.

PHOENIX: The Stockyards Restaurant $$
Steakhouse   Map B4
5009 E Washington St #115, AZ 85034
Tel (602) 273-7378
Open since 1947, this historic steakhouse puts up the finest stockyard steaks and prime rib of beef. Seafood, such as salmon and rainbow trout, is also on the menu. Excellent desserts and wines.

PHOENIX: Tarbells $$
American   Map B4
3213 E Camelback Rd, AZ 85018
Tel (602) 955-8100
Chef and owner Mark Tarbell pairs contemporary cuisine with fine wines at this upscale restaurant. Try Scotch Beef with mashed potatoes or salmon with home-made ribbon pasta. For dessert, don't miss the cheesecake with rosemary carmel sauce. Perfect for a romantic evening.

PHOENIX: Compass Arizona Grill $$$
American
Hyatt Regency, 122 N 2nd St, AZ 85004
Tel (602) 440-3166
The city's only revolving rooftop restaurant offers views of the

Valley of the Sun. The menu of American regional dishes such as filet mignon with blue cheese potato mash, is complemented by an international wine list.

PHOENIX: Litchfield's $$$
American
Wigwam Resort, 300 E Wigwam Blvd, Litchfield Pk, AZ 85340
Tel (623) 935-3811 **Closed** Sun & Mon
The cuisine here is crafted from farm-to-table ingredients and can be enjoyed in the casual indoor dining room or on the garden veranda. The wide-ranging menu includes entrées such as Arizona buffalo strip steak. Vegetarian and gluten-free options are available.

DK Choice

PHOENIX: Vincent's on Camelback $$$
Southwestern
3930 E Camelback Rd, AZ 85018
Tel (602) 224-0225   **Closed** Sun & Mon
Juxtaposing Southwestern and Provençal flavors, chef and owner Vincent Guerithault's innovative menu sets the standard for fine dining. Try the corn ravioli with white truffle oil, followed by wild boar loin with parsnip purée and habenero sauce. Attentive service and extensive wine list.

PINETOP-LAKESIDE: Charlie Clark's Steakhouse $
Steakhouse
1701 E White Mountain Blvd, AZ 85935
Tel (928) 367-4900
A western-style restaurant, Charlie Clark's is renowned for producing one of the area's finest mesquite-grilled aged steaks and slow-roasted or black-ened prime rib of beef.

Bright decor with art on the walls at La Roca Restaurant, Nogales

For more information on types of restaurants see page 134–5

SCOTTSDALE: Frank & Lupe's $
Mexican   Map F4
4121 N Marshall Way, AZ 85251
Tel *(480) 990-9844*
This small, old town restaurant packs flavor into popular New Mexican dishes such as poblano cream enchiladas, chalupas, chimichangas, and tamales. Beer and mixed drinks are available.

SCOTTSDALE: Roaring Fork $
Steakhouse   Map F4
4800 N Scottsdale Rd, Ste. 1700, AZ 85251
Tel *(480) 947-0795*
Lamb, pork, and fresh fish are on the menu, along with Southwestern wood-fired entrées such as fish tacos, burgers, buttermilk-fried chicken, and filet mignon with green-chile macaroni.

SCOTTSDALE: Cowboy Ciao $$$
American   Map F4
7133 E Stetson Dr, AZ 85251
Tel *(480) 946-3111*
Creative dishes, such as smoked brisket with a whiskey and cider sauce, and exotic mushroom pan fry, can be accompanied by global wines at this restaurant. There is a horseshoe bar and an open kitchen, as well as Multiple spaces for private dining.

SCOTTSDALE: J&G Steakhouse $$$
Steakhouse   Map F4
The Phoenician Resort, 6000 E Camelback Rd, AZ 85251
Tel *(480) 214-8000*
At J&G take in the view of the valley and watch the sun go down while dining on premium meats, a selection of fish from around the world, and oysters from both coasts. There is a tasting menu available and an excellent wine list.

SCOTTSDALE: Sassi $$$
Italian   Map B4
10455 E Pinnacle Peak Pkwy, AZ 85255
Tel *(480) 502-9095*   **Closed** *Mon*
Bold and rustic Italian flavors are accompanied by Italian wines at Sassi; the menu features pasta, seafood, and poultry. Spectacular views, outdoor patios, and the southern Italian villa design enhance the overall experience.

SUPERIOR: Los Hermanos Restaurant & Lounge $
Mexican   Map C4
835 W US Hwy 60, AZ 85273
Tel *(520) 689-5465*
Enjoy hearty breakfasts and American fare with favorites including chicken tenders, fries,

Neatly arranged tables at J&G Steakhouse, a fine dining restaurant in Scottsdale

and pies, with homemade tortillas, enchiladas, tacos, and chile rellenos. Margaritas and imported Mexican beer are available.

TOMBSTONE: Big Nose Kate's Saloon $
American   Map C5
417 E Allen St, AZ 85638
Tel *(520) 457-3107*
This cowboy bar, named after gunfighter and gambler Doc Holliday's girlfriend, is a former hotel that is full of collectibles from the west. Goldie's over-stuffed Reuben sandwich with corned beef, sauerkraut and Swiss cheese is the most popular item. Live country music is played here daily.

TOMBSTONE: The Crystal Palace Saloon $
American   Map C5
436 E Allen St, AZ 85638
Tel *(520) 457-3611*
Housed in a historic 1879 brewery building, this saloon serves Angus steaks, seafood, chicken wings, sandwiches, and pizza. Barbecue ribs with blackened cajun is a favorite. There's karaoke every Wednesday.

TUBAC: Elvira's $
Mexican   Map C5
2221 Interstate 19 E Frontage Road A-101, AZ 85646
Tel *(520) 398-9421*   **Closed** *Mon*
Inventive cuisine from the south of the border that blends the traditional with the modern is served at this vibrant place. Signature dishes include the moles, flank steak molcajete in salsa verde, and grilled flounder mango Caribe style. Good tequila and cocktails.

DK Choice

TUCSON: Café Poca Cosa $
Mexican   Map C5
110 E Pennington St, AZ 85701
Tel *(520) 622-6400*   **Closed** *Sun & Mon*
Café Poca Cosa serves authentic Neuvo Mexican cuisine prepared with regional ingredients. The menu, in English and Spanish, is changed twice daily. Try the *plato de poca cosa* – a chicken, beef, and vegetarian sample of the day's entrées. Chic but casual.

TUCSON: La Cocina $
Mexican   Map C5
Old Town Artisans, 201 N Court Ave, AZ 85701
Tel *(520) 622-0351*
Sculptures by old town artisans decorate the interiors of La Cocina. Globally inspired dishes such as chile relleno plate, lemon caper penne, and lemongrass coconut curry are on the menu. Meals can also be enjoyed in the lovely shaded courtyard.

TUCSON: El Charro Café $
Mexican   Map C5
311 N Court Ave, AZ 85701
Tel *(520) 622-1922*
Located in the historic El Presidio district, El Charro serves traditional Sonoran-style and innovative Tucson-style dishes. The secret ingredients in the *carne seca* (shredded sun-dried beef) create mouth-watering flavors.

TUCSON: El Corral $
Steakhouse   Map C5
2201 E River Rd, AZ 85718
Tel *(520) 299-6092*
Stop by for the special slow-roasted prime rib or mesquite-grilled prime steaks, baby-back ribs, and chicken. Inviting decor with fireplaces, flagstone floors, and wood-beamed ceilings.

TUCSON: Feast $
American   Map C5
3719 E Speedway Blvd, AZ 85712
Tel *(520) 326-9363*   **Closed** *Mon*
Entrées at this sophisticated eatery may include sea bass with *huitlacoche* sauce and butternut steak. The monthly changing menu offers interesting pairings with wines and cocktails. Try the ricotta-almond fritters with aniseed glaze for dessert.

TUCSON: La Parrilla Suiza $
Mexican   Map C5
5602 E Speedway Blvd, AZ 85712
Tel *(520) 747-4838*
Tacos, meat, and cheese dishes are grilled or cooked over

charcoal and served with sauces made of indigenous ingredients at this Mexican. Don't miss the Bistek tacos – flour tortillas stuffed with beef, covered in piquillo sauce, and a side of guacamole, refried beans, lettuce, and rice.

TUCSON: Li'l Abner's Steakhouse $$
Steakhouse **Map** C5
8501 N Silverbell Rd, AZ 85743
Tel *(520) 744-2800*
This no-frills Old Western-style Steakhouse has a mesquite grill out back to cook delicious steaks, chicken, and ribs. Patio seating and bar service.

TUCSON: The Grill at Hacienda Del Sol $$$
American **Map** C5
Hacienda del Sol, 5501 N Hacienda del Sol Rd, AZ, 5718
Tel *(520) 529-3500*
A plush restaurant with outdoor seating and gorgeous views. The crispy Thai snapper puttanesca and New York steak with pasilla mole should not be missed. Lavish brunch buffet on Sundays and award-winning wine list.

TUCSON: Maynards Market & Kitchen $$$
American **Map** C5
400 N Toole Ave, AZ 85701
Tel *(520) 545-0577*
Maynards' seasonal cuisine is inspired by the French bistro tradition. Entrées include dry-aged steaks, wild salmon, lamb shank and bouillabaisse. Book in advance for the Chef's Table.

TUMACACORI: Wisdom's Café $
Mexican **Map** C5
1931 Frontage Rd, AZ 85640
Tel *(520) 398-2397* **Closed** *late May–mid-Jul; Sun*
This family-run café is known for the unique Fruit Burro dessert – hot, crispy burrito filled with fruit,

rolled in cinnamon, and served with vanilla ice cream. There is a separate vegetarian and vegan menu. Beer and wine on tap.

YUMA: The Garden Café $
American **Map** A4
250 Madison Ave, AZ 85364
Tel *(928) 783-1491* **Closed** *Jun–Sep; Mon*
Sit back on this café's multi-tiered patio and enjoy breakfast or lunch of Southwestern-inspired chicken taco salad, tortilla soup, quiche, and well-seasoned steaks. Save room for the tempting desserts.

The Four Corners

AZTEC: Rubio's $
Mexican **Map** D2
116 S Main Ave, NM 87410
Tel *(505) 334-0599* **Closed** *Sun*
Come here for classic New Mexican cuisine. Try the eggs, burritos and *huevos rancheros* (Mexican-style fried eggs) for breakfast. Lunch and dinner are also served and patio seating is available. Open only for breakfast on Saturdays.

BLANDING: Patio Drive In $
Diner **Map** D1
95 North Grayson Parkway, UT 84511
Tel *(435) 678-2177*
Breakfast, lunch, and dinner are cooked to order at this diner serving burgers, sandwiches, and wraps. Try one of the thick shakes alongside Mexican specials such as mahi mahi fish tacos.

BLUFF: Cottonwood Steakhouse $
Steakhouse **Map** D1
409 W Main St, Hwy 191, UT, 84512
Tel *(435) 672-2282* **Closed** *winter*
This restaurant serves sizeable portions of chicken, steak, shrimp, or catfish with a generous helping of green salad, all to be washed

down with beer or malt coolers. Guests can choose to eat under the cottonwood tree outside.

BLUFF: Twin Rocks Café $
Café **Map** D1
913 E Navajo Twins Dr, UT, 84512
Tel *(435) 672-2341*
This café's all-day menu features reasonably priced sandwiches, salads, and the unique Navajo pizza (fry bread or ash bread with toppings). Take time to also visit the trading post.

CAMERON: Cameron Trading Post $
Southwestern **Map** C2
Route 89, AZ 86020
Tel *(928) 679-2231*
American, Mexican, and Native American fare is served here throughout the day, along with the house special Navajo taco. The dining room has a pressed tin ceiling with Native American artworks adorning the walls.

CHINLE: Garcia's Restaurant $
Southwestern **Map** D2
Garcia Trading Post at Canyon de Chelly, Navajo Route 7, AZ 86503
Tel *(928) 674-5000* **Closed** *Limited hours in winter*
Located in the Holiday Inn, Garcia's serves mouth-watering Native American and Mexican dishes such as mutton stew, fajitas, and marinated sirloin steak.

CHINLE: Junction Restaurant $
Southwestern **Map** D2
100 E Main St, AZ 86503
Tel *(928) 674-8443*
Housed in Chinle's Best Western Hotel, Junction's is a good place for classic Native American-inspired dishes including savory beef stew and Navajo fry bread, as well as generous portions of comfort food, pizzas, and ice cream sundaes.

CHINLE: Thunderbird Lodge $
Southwestern **Map** D2
Canyon de Chelly, Navajo Route 7, AZ 86503
Tel *(928) 674-5841*
American and continental dishes are served at this pleasant cafeteria located in the Navajo reservation in Canyon de Chelly. Navajo rugs and artwork decorate the walls.

CORTEZ: La Casita De Cortez $
Mexican **Map** D1
332 E Main St, CO 81321
Tel *(970) 565-0023*
This friendly eatery offers authentic flavorful dishes such as enchiladas, moles, and chili relleno. Sit at the bar or the outside tables and enjoy a margarita during summer.

Navajo rugs decorate the dining room at the restaurant Cameron Trading Post, Cameron

For more information on types of restaurants *see page 134–5*

CORTEZ: The Farm Bistro $
American   Map D1
34 W Main St, CO 81321
Tel *(970) 565-3834*   **Closed** *Sun*
Comfort foods based on local
produce and meats are the focus
at The Farm. The menu has
options such as chicken pot pie,
Moroccan lamb meatballs, as
well as vegetarian dishes. The
lounge serves Colorado-made
wine, beer, and spirits.

CORTEZ: Shiloh Steakhouse $
Steakhouse   Map D1
5 S Veach St, CO 81321
Tel *(970) 565-6560*
Enjoy soups, salads, burgers, and
sandwiches for lunch or char-
grilled steaks, seafood, and
chicken for dinner. Gluten-free
options are also available. Guests
can choose between dining inside
or outside on the garden patio.

**DURANGO: Carver
Brewing Co.** $
Southwestern   Map D1
1022 Main Ave, CO 81301
Tel *(970) 259-2545*
Carver has been brewing light
lagers to hardy oatmeal stouts
since the 1980s. There is a
covered beer garden in the
back. Stop by for the famed
breakfast or a meal of steaks,
seafood, and pasta.

DURANGO: Ken & Sue's $$
American   Map D1
636 Main Ave, CO 81301
Tel *(970) 385-1810*
The diverse menu here is
complemented by the pleasant
environment and great service.
The signature dishes are inspired
by Asian cuisine. Try the excellent
molten chocolate cake for dessert.
Gluten-free options also available.

Sweeping views of the Mesa Verde National
Park at Metate Room, Colorado

**DURANGO: The Red
Snapper** $$
Seafood   Map D1
144 E 9th St, CO, 81301
Tel *(970) 259-3417*
Housed in a historic downtown
building, The Red Snapper is
a haven for seafood lovers, as
well as a good place to enjoy
steaks and pasta. It also has a
salad bar.

DURANGO: Ore House $$$
Steakhouse   Map D1
147 E College Drive, CO, 81301
Tel *(970) 247-5707*
Ore House offers a comfortable
setting and Old Western charm.
The kitchen serves the choicest
steaks, organic poultry, and wild-
caught seafood. Locally grown
seasonal produce is used to
prepare salads and sides.

FARMINGTON: Clancy's Pub $
Southwestern   Map D2
2703 E 20th St, NM, 87402
Tel *(505) 325-8176*
This Irish *cantina* (tavern) in
an adobe-style building has an
eclectic menu featuring burgers,
steaks, and sushi, along with daily
lunch and dinner specials.

**FARMINGTON: St. Clair Winery
& Bistro** $
American   Map D2
5150 E Main St, NM 87402
Tel *(505) 325-0711*
New Mexican wines are paired
well with the varied dishes on
the menu at St. Clair. Gluten-
free and vegetarian options are
also available. The dining room
is spacious and there's also
seating outdoors.

GALLUP: Badlands Grill $
Steakhouse   Map D3
*2201 West Highway 66, Gallup,
NM 87301*
Tel *(505) 722-5157*   **Closed** *Nov–
Feb Sun*
Describing itself as a steak and
seafood supper club, Badlands
is known for succulent double-
cut pork chops and hand-cut
beef wet-aged for 21 days. Salads,
burgers, sandwiches, pasta,
ribs, and seafood also feature
on the menu.

GALLUP: Jerry's Cafe $
Mexican   Map D3
406 W Coal Ave, NM 87301
Tel *(505) 722-6775*   **Closed** *Sun*
Local artwork adorns the walls
of this popular diner that serves
large portions of Mexican
comfort food. Loyal customers
keep coming for the honey
sopaipillas (quick bread). Friendly
and efficient service.

KAYENTA: Amigo Café $
Mexican   Map C2
Hwy 163, AZ 86033
Tel *(928) 697-8448*   **Closed** *Sun*
This small town establishment is
frequented by both locals and
tourists. The combo plate is a
great way to sample the Mexican
fare. Navajo tacos and fry bread
are also on the menu.

**MESA VERDE NATIONAL PARK:
Spruce Tree Terrace Café** $
American   Map D2
Mile Marker 15, Mancos, CO, 81328
Tel *(970) 529-4444*   **Closed** *major
holidays*
Order takeout or sit on the
patio to enjoy the scenic view
of the park while feasting on
the popular Navajo tacos and
Southwestern dishes at this
cafeteria. Located opposite
the Chapin Mesa Museum.

DK Choice

**MESA VERDE NATIONAL
PARK: Metate Room** $$
Southwestern   Map D2
Mile Marker 15, Mancos, CO, 81328
Tel *(970) 529-4422*   **Closed** *late-
Oct–mid-Apr*
Metate Room is recognized for
its sustainable cuisine inspired
by the traditional Puebloan
culture. The menu springs a
surprise each time with dishes
such as crispy prickly pear pork
belly, rattlesnake and pheasant
sausage, seared sockeye salmon,
and elk Wellington with red
wine reduction. Enjoy these
with a bottle of local wine.

MOAB: Eklecticafe $
Café   Map D1
352 N Main, UT 84532
Tel *(435) 259-6896*
An amiable café serving an all-
day breakfast of cinnamon rolls,
omelets, *huevos rancheros*, and
pancakes. Lunch options include
an array of sandwiches, wraps,
gyros, salads, and soups.

DK Choice

MOAB: Desert Bistro $$
Southwestern   Map D1
36 South 100 West, UT 84532
Tel *(435) 259-0756*   **Closed** *Dec–
Feb; Mon*
Gourmet cuisine at Desert
Bistro bends traditional
cooking rules to create complex
flavors with beef, pork, lamb,
free-range chicken, fresh
seafood, and vegetarian fare.
Located downtown just off
the main street.

Exquisitely lit interiors and views of the mountains from Alfred's Restaurant in Telluride

MOAB: Jeffrey's Steakhouse $$
Steakhouse   Map D1
218 N 100 W, UT 84532
Tel *(435) 259-3588*
Jeffrey's serves seafood, lamb, chicken, and pork entrées in an upscale and casual dining room with Southwestern decor. Only the finest hormone-free Wagyu beef is used for the flavorful steaks.

MONUMENT VALLEY: Stagecoach Dining Room $
Native American   Map C2
Goulding's Lodge, UT, 84536
Tel *(435) 727-3231*
Southwestern entrées with the preferred Navajo taco and beef stew with Navajo fry bread are on the menu here. Perched on top of a hill with picturesque views.

MONUMENT VALLEY: The View Hotel Restaurant $
Native American   Map C2
Hwy 163 Monument Valley Tribal Park, UT 84536
Tel *(435) 727-5555*
Come to The View to indulge in Navajo specialties such as green chili stew and Navajo taco, along with classic American steaks, chops, and vegetarian dishes. There are breathtaking views of the Monument Valley.

OURAY: Bon Ton Restaurant $$
Italian   Map E1
St. Elmo Hotel, 426 Main St, CO, 81427
Tel *(970) 325-4951*   **Closed** *Wed in winter*
Intimate Bon Ton serves high-quality Angus beef and fresh seafood. There is a martini bar and an award-winning wine list.

OURAY: The Outlaw $$
American   Map E1
610 Main St, CO, 81427
Tel *(970) 325-4366*   **Closed** *Mon in winter*
Savor a variety of steaks, seafood, and pasta at the oldest operating restaurant in Ouray. House specialties include tender lamb chops in a brown cognac sauce, pepper steak, and baby back pork ribs. There's also a separate kids' menu.

SECOND MESA, HOPI RESERVATION: Hopi Cultural Center Restaurant $
Native American   Map C3
Route 264, AZ 86043
Tel *(928) 734-2402*
This well-loved eatery with a salad bar serves the traditional Hopi specialty of steaming mutton stew with hominy and roasted chiles – a real crowd-pleaser.

SILVERTON: Handlebars Restaurant & Saloon $
American   Map E1
117 W 13th St, CO 81433
Tel *(970) 387-5395*   **Closed** *Nov–Apr*
The history of the mining town of Silverton comes to life with the Old West decor at Handlebars. Feast on good steaks, chicken, and burgers. Friendly service.

SILVERTON: Mattie and Maud's $
American   Map E1
1124 Greene St, CO 81433
Tel *(970) 387-9918*   **Closed** *Sun*
Pop into this delightful family-run café for a hearty breakfast of cinnamon rolls, omelets, and Frito Pie, or a tasty lunch of Navajo tacos and chicken quesadilla.

TELLURIDE: Brown Dog Pizza $
Pizzeria   Map D1
110 E Colorado Ave, CO 81435
Tel *(970) 728-8046*
This place serves award-winning Detroit Square, American Classic, Thin Crust, and Sicilian-Style pizzas. Wings, burgers, subs, pasta, and gluten-free options are also available. Choose to sit in the sports bar or at one of the quieter tables. There's a separate menu for kids.

TELLURIDE: 221 South Oak St $$$
American   Map D1
221 S Oak, CO, 81435
Tel *(970) 728-9507*
Set in a historic home, just steps away from the gondola, guests at this intimate restaurant can dine on the garden patio in summer or by the fireplace in winter. The wine list is crafted to enhance the flavors of the eclectic menu. Mussels and Martini Night on Wednesdays.

DK Choice

TELLURIDE: Alfred's Restaurant $$$
Steakhouse   Map D1
Take the free gondola to Station St. Sophia at the top of the mountain, CO 81435
Tel *(970) 728-7474*
The adventurous menu here features lamb, steak, sustainable-sourced elk, and seafood, with sides of fresh local vegetables and salads. Enjoy panoramic views of Telluride and the mountain range from the open, airy dining room. Slippers are provided for skiers!

TELLURIDE: Cosmopolitan $$$
American   Map D1
Hotel Columbia, 301 W San Juan Ave, CO 81435
Tel *(970) 728-1292*
At Cosmopolitan savor contemporary fare or seasonal fusion cuisine featuring quality Wagyu beef and seafood, as well as pork, chicken, and lamb. Classic dining room with an enclosed patio.

TELLURIDE: New Sheridan Chop House $$$
Steakhouse   Map D1
New Sheridan Hotel, 233 W Colorado Ave, CO 81435
Tel *(970) 728-9100*
Specialties at this modern fine-dining restaurant include dry-aged prime steaks. Local ingredients, organic poultry, and non-threatened fish varieties are used in the entrées and Fresh seafood is flown in daily.

TUBA CITY: Hogan Restaurant $
Native American   Map C2
Main St and Moenave Rd, AZ 86045
Tel *(928) 283-5260*
In the heart of the Navajo tribal lands, Hogan is a perfect stop for traditional mutton stew and Navajo tacos. Take in the beautiful view of desert landscapes while enjoying Mexican and American dishes.

For more information on types of restaurants *see page 134–5*

SHOPPING IN ARIZONA

With such an exciting range of Native American, Hispanic, and Anglo-American products, shopping in Arizona is a cultural adventure. Native crafts, including rugs, jewelry, and pottery, top the list of things that people buy. The Southwest is also known as a center for the fine arts, with Scottsdale and Sedona famous for their many galleries, selling everything from Arizona-inspired landscapes and the latest contemporary work, to kitsch bronze sculptures of cowboys and Indians. Across the state, specialty grocery stores and supermarkets stock a range of Southwestern products from hot chile sauces to blue corn tortilla chips. Western clothing, including boots, hats, and belts can be found in shops across the state. In the major cities, there is a choice of chic fashion districts, usually situated in air-conditioned, landscaped malls. Phoenix and Scottsdale rank shopping among their top attractions, and themed malls and boutique shopping areas attract hundreds of thousands of visitors each year.

Western Clothing

Among the most popular souvenirs bought in Arizona are hand-tooled cowboy boots, cowboy hats, and decorative leather belts. Western clothing is made to high standards throughout the Southwest. Phoenix is well-known as a center for cowboy clothes. **Az-Tex Hats** of Scottsdale has the largest selection of cowboy hats in the Southwest, while **Saba's Western Store** has been outfitting customers in Western fashions since 1927. The **Boot Barn** has locations throughout Arizona and offers an extensive selection of boots, hats, accessories, and Western wear.

Regional Food

Arizonans are proud of their Southwestern cuisine, and in most shopping areas you will

Chile peppers hanging from a wooden cart

find grocery stores and specialty shops selling an extensive array of Arizona-made sauces, salsas, dips, and gourmet food items. Many of these foods are chile based, ranging from the mild jalapeño to the super-hot habañero peppers. The mesquite-smoked jalapeño pepper, known as *chipotle*, is medium hot and has a smoky flavor. Salsa is a popular condiment made from tomatoes, chile, garlic, and cilantro.

Farmers' markets are another good source of local produce, and usually stock a range of dried chile strings, known as *ristras*. Several companies have websites where you can order such regional gourmet foods as handmade corn tortillas, chile-stuffed olives, hot-spiced microwave popcorn, mesquite bean candy, chile peanut butter, and prickly pear jam.

Colorfully adorned cowboy boots on sale in a store in Arizona

A large number of bookstores and shops offer a variety of cookbooks with recipes on Arizonan and Southwestern cuisine, from easy-to-prepare dishes to traditional and fusion recipes using all the favorite ingredients.

Gems and Minerals

With Arizona's fascinating geology and long mining history, it is not surprising to find glittering gems and minerals on display in shops across the state. Rock shops and museum shops everywhere provide reasonably priced and beautiful minerals such as turquoise, azurite, and malachite; quartz crystals of varied shapes and sizes; and gold and silver. The

Rocks and minerals on display during the Tucson Gem & Mineral Show

A typical Route 66 souvenir shop, in the small town of Seligman

knowledgeable staff in these shops enjoy talking about Arizona's minerals and geology. While visitors to Petrified Forest National Park are of course forbidden to pick up specimens, several local shops, including **Jim Gray's Petrified Wood** in Holbrook, sell beautifully polished petrified wood acquired from legitimate sources. **Tucson Mineral & Gem World** carries a large selection of both Arizonan and other minerals and crystals for novices and collectors alike. **Mystical Bazaar** in Sedona specializes in making custom jewelry using Arizona gemstones.

Besides shopping, Arizona hosts two of the world's largest gems and minerals shows during January and February each year in Quartzsite and Tucson *(see p39)*. Rockhounds, gem and mineral dealers and enthusiasts from around the world are known to gather in Arizona for these shows.

Route 66 Memorabilia and Tourist Kitsch

Memories, memorabilia, kitsch, and souvenirs from the golden age of the automobile can be found in shops all along Arizona's Route 66. The **Historic Route 66 Association of Arizona** in Kingman is a non-profit corporation that is dedicated to the preservation, promotion, and protection of Route 66 and its memories. The association's gift shop offers books, videos, and souvenirs all about the road. The **Route 66 Gift Shop** in Seligman is a museum, visitor center, and gift shop with shirts, hats, license plates, signs, and much more. In Williams, **Twisters 50s Soda Fountain and The Route 66 Place** provides Route 66 information and mementos, including T-shirts, jackets, vests, and signs and shields, as well as Coca-Cola, John Deere, Betty Boop, and 1950s memorabilia.

Antiques

Antiques, and especially those that evoke memories of the Wild West, are very popular in Arizona. Western, Native, and cowboy antiques include saddles, hats, spurs, badges, Navajo rugs, silver, and turquoise jewelry. In addition you can also buy lanterns and wagon wheels.

In the Phoenix area, the **Old Towne Shopping District** in downtown Glendale is the main antiques district, with more than 70 antiques shops and specialty stores. One of Arizona's largest collector's shows, the **Arizona Antique Market**, is held on several weekends throughout the year in Chandler.

Prescott is also known for its antiques shops, many of which are located in the central town square area of downtown Prescott. In Tucson, the Fourth Avenue shopping district has several antiques stores between 4th and 7th Streets.

Vintage car outside an antiques store in Old Town Cottonwood

Outside view of Scottsdale's El Pedregal Festival Marketplace

Flea Markets

Across the state, flea markets offer everything Arizonan and much more. Flea markets are usually open on weekends, and sometimes on Fridays or other weekdays. Advertised as the largest open-air flea market in the Southwest, **Phoenix Park 'n Swap** offers a broad range of products, from clothing, tools, and jewelry, to furniture, luggage, and athletic footwear. **Mesa Market Place Swap Meet** features 1,600 booths filled with new and used items, antiques, home furnishings, clothing, jewelry, toys, and food products. In Tucson, 800 vendors at the **Tanque Verde Swap Meet** flea market sell antiques and collectibles, fresh produce, Southwestern crafts, and coins and stamps. **Peddler's Pass** of Prescott Valley has a range of antiques and collectibles, plus clothing, crafts, and fresh produce. Quartzsite has more than a dozen festive flea markets from November to March, including the **Rock & Gem Show** in January, which sells gems and minerals.

Malls

Southern Arizona has some of the most stunning malls in the US, featuring air conditioning, plant-filled atriums, and fine restaurants. The largest of these is Phoenix's **Metrocenter**, with more than 125 stores. Large department stores

such as Neiman Marcus can be found at the **Scottsdale Fashion Square**. Phoenix's **Biltmore Fashion Park** offers Chico's, Brooks Brothers, and Saks Fifth Avenue, and has some of the best dining options in town.

Themed malls are abundant in the region. The **Arizona Center** in Phoenix has restaurants and shops set among gardens, fountains, and a waterfall. The **El Pedregal Festival Marketplace** in Scottsdale has a festive Moroccan atmosphere with a handful of boutique shops.

Tucson has several large shopping malls, including one of the largest in the state, **Tucson Mall** with over 200 stores. **El Con Center** has a great selection of department and specialty stores.

Art Galleries

Arizona can boast a vibrant artistic tradition with skilled artists and numerous galleries across the state displaying works of art that reflect the unique colors, light, and landscapes of the Southwest. Scottsdale is Arizona's premier fine art center. The city has over 100 galleries that stock the works of internationally recognized artists in many disciplines. The popular **Scottsdale ArtWalk**, which takes place on Thursday evenings, features special exhibits and artist receptions in the galleries.

The downtown area of Tucson is home to over 40 art galleries, including the **DeGrazia Gallery in the Sun**. The co-operative **Desert Artisans Gallery**, near the Catalina Foothills in northeastern Tucson, displays works by a diverse assortment of local artists.

Sedona has an active art scene, and Western art can be found in 40 galleries in the city. **Tlaquepaque** is a small art village in Spanish Colonial style with courtyards and gardens, offering primarily Southwestern and Native art. Bisbee, Jerome, and Tubac all have galleries and craft shops, many of which display the work of emerging artists.

One-of-a-kind Shops

Arizona-style independence and creativity have created unique products that go beyond the expected. Part of the delight of shopping in Arizona is finding shops such as **Poisoned Pen**, one of the country's largest bookstores, specializing in mystery titles. Mystery book buffs can browse through 15,000 titles, and appreciate the special events and talks given by authors.

Architect Paolo Soleri built Arcosanti, the experimental town in the high desert of Arizona *(see p87)*, to the north of Phoenix. **Cosanti Originals**, located in Paradise Valley, offers unique, one-of-a-kind Soleri sculptures in the form of windbells, and their sales help fund research into alternative living.

Paintings and drawings on adobe walls at DeGrazia Gallery in the Sun in Tucson

DIRECTORY

Western Clothing

Az-Tex Hats
3903 N Scottsdale Rd,
Scottsdale, AZ 85251.
Tel (800) 972-2116,
(480) 481-9900.
w aztexhats.com

The Boot Barn
3776 S 16th Ave,
Tucson, AZ 85713.
Tel (520) 622-4500.

Saba's Western Store
3965 N Brown Ave,
Scottsdale, AZ 85251.
Tel (877) 342-1835,
(480) 947-7664.
w sabas.com

Gems and Minerals

Jim Gray's Petrified Wood
147 Hwy 180, Holbrook,
AZ 86025.
Tel (928) 524-1842.
w shop.jimgrays
petrifiedwoodco.com

Mystical Bazaar
1449 State Rd 89A,
Sedona, AZ 86336.
Tel (928) 204-5615.
w mysticalbazaar.com

Tucson Mineral & Gem World
2801 S Kinney Rd,
Tucson, AZ 85735.
Tel (520) 883-0682.
w tucsonmineral.com

Route 66 Memorabilia and Tourist Kitsch

Historic Route 66 Association of Arizona
120 W Andy Devine Ave,
Kingman, AZ 86401.
Tel (928) 753-5001.
w azrt66.com

Route 66 Gift Shop
217 E Route 66,
Seligman, AZ 86337.
Tel (928) 422-3352.
w route66giftshop.com

Twisters 50s Soda Fountain and The Route 66 Place
417 E Route 66, Williams,
AZ 86046.
Tel (928) 635-0266.
w route66place.com

Antiques

Arizona Antique Market
860 N 54th St
Chandler, AZ 85226.
Tel (602) 717-7337.
w azantiqueshow.com

Old Towne Shopping District
East of 59th Avenue,
Glendale, AZ 85308.
Tel (877) 800-2601.

Flea Markets

Mesa Market Place Swap Meet
10550 E Baseline,
Mesa, AZ 85209.
Tel (480) 380-5572.
w mesamarket.com

Peddler's Pass
6201 E Hwy 69, Prescott
Valley, AZ 86314.
Tel (928) 775-4117.
w peddlerspass.com

Phoenix Park 'n Swap
3801 E Washington St,
Phoenix, AZ 85034.
Tel (800) 772-0852.
w americanpark
nswap.com

Quartzsite Rock & Gem Show
Tyson Wells Show
Grounds, Quartzsite,
AZ 85346.
Tel (928) 927-6364.
w tysonwells.com

Tanque Verde Swap Meet
4100 S Palo Verde Rd,
Tucson, AZ 85714.
Tel (520) 294-4252.
w tucsonswap.com

Malls

Arizona Center
400 E Van Buren St,
Phoenix, AZ 85004-2240.
Tel (602) 271-4000.
w arizonacenter.com

Biltmore Fashion Park
2502 E Camelback Rd,
Phoenix, AZ 85016.
Tel (602) 955-8400.
w shopbiltmore.com

El Con Center
3601 E Broadway Blvd,
Tucson, AZ 85701.
Tel (520) 795-9958.
w elconcenter.com

El Pedregal Festival Marketplace
34505 N Scottsdale Rd,
Scottsdale, AZ 85251.
Tel (480) 488-1072.
w elpedregal.com

Metrocenter
9617 Metro Parkway,
Phoenix, AZ 85051.
Tel (602) 997-8991.

Scottsdale Fashion Square
7014 E Camelback Rd,
Scottsdale, AZ 85251.
Tel (480) 941-2140.
w fashionsquare.com

Tucson Mall
4500 N Oracle Rd,
Tucson, AZ 85705.
Tel (520) 293-7330.
w tucsonmall.com

Art Galleries

DeGrazia Gallery in the Sun
6300 N Swan, Tucson,
AZ 85718.
Tel (520) 299-9191,
(800) 545-2185.
w degrazia.org

Desert Artisans Gallery
6536 E Tanque Verde RD,
Tucson, AZ 85715.
Tel (520) 722-4412.
w desertartisans
gallery.com

Scottsdale Arts District & ArtWalk
Scottsdale, AZ 85251.
Tel (480) 421-1004.
w scottsdalegalleries.
com

Tlaquepaque
336 Hwy 179, Sedona,
AZ 86351.
Tel (928) 282-4838.
w tlaq.com

One-of-a-kind Shops

Cosanti Originals
6433 E Doubletree Ranch
Rd, Paradise Valley,
AZ 85253.
Tel (800) 752-3187.
w cosanti.com

Poisoned Pen
4014 N Goldwater Blvd,
Suite 101, Scottsdale,
AZ 85251.
Tel (888) 560-9919.
w poisonedpen.com

Native Arts and Crafts

See pp148–9.

Cameron Trading Post
Highway 89, Cameron,
AZ 86020.
Tel (928) 679-2231.
w camerontrading
post.com

Heard Museum Shop
2301 N Central Ave,
Phoenix, AZ 85004-1323.
Tel (800) 252-8344,
(602) 252-8844.
w heardmuseumshop.
com

Hopi House
Main St, Grand Canyon,
AZ 86023.
Tel (928) 638-2631.

Hubbell Trading Post
Highway 264, Ganado,
AZ 86505.
Tel (928) 755-3254.
w nps.gov/hutr

Sewell's Indian Arts
7087 E 5th Ave,
Scottsdale, AZ 85251.
Tel (480) 945-0962.
w buyindianarts.com

Shopping for Native Arts and Crafts

One of the most rewarding parts of a trip to Arizona is shopping for Native arts and crafts *(see pp26–7)*. Now valued as collectors' items, many modern crafts, such as pottery and basket making, can trace their history to centuries-old tribal life. There is intense competition between Native artisans, and the quality of traditional arts continues to be high. At the same time, a new wave of Native artists are successfully blending traditional art with modern media and styles from around the world.

Whether shopping in trading posts, art galleries, or museum shops *(see p147)*, a skillful eye can result in bargains. Purchasing work direct from Native artists offers the opportunity to meet the artisans.

Rug-making is practiced by the Navajo. A large rug created by a master weaver can fetch thousands of dollars.

Trading Posts

*The **Cameron Trading Post** and the **Hubbell Trading Post** originated in the mid-1800s, and are thriving Native arts and crafts centers today. Trading posts are classic middlemen. They benefit the tribes by nurturing Native artists and offering a ready market for their work. For visitors, they provide advice and a generous variety of crafts for comparison shopping.*

Basket making is one of the oldest Native American crafts, dating back hundreds of years. Virtually all tribes in Arizona practice basket making, but the baskets of the Apache and the Hopi are particularly refined.

Pottery is practiced by many tribes, but Hopi pottery is considered to be the best. Made from local clays, it features both contemporary and traditional designs, many taken from nature, with names such as "birdwing," "dragonfly," "hummingbird," or "rain."

Silverwork, often with turquoise arrays, has been produced by Navajo, Zuni, and Hopi peoples for centuries. Since the mid-19th century, Navajo jewelers have incorporated Spanish styles. Hopi and Zuni silver is different, with an intricate overlay process that has raised silver patterns against a dark background.

Galleries and Museums

Some of the very best traditional and contemporary Native art can be found in fine art galleries and museum shops, such as **Hopi House** at the Grand Canyon or the **Heard Museum Shop**. Prices in these shops tend to be higher, but careful shopping can still result in bargains. These galleries and museum shops often have long-established relationships with some of the very best Native artisans, and can provide shoppers with information on art trends, investment considerations, and provenance (documented information on the artist, and the background and history of the artwork).

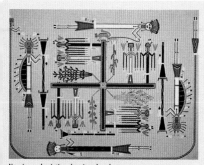
Navajo sand painting showing abundant crops

Buying Directly from Natives

One of the most gratifying shopping experiences is purchasing crafts directly from Native artisans, who are found at the major tourist destinations. These craftsmen are either beginners or mid-level artisans, and the prices are usually very reasonable.

- Exercise normal caution. Look for flaws such as uneven edges or curling in rugs, and lopsidedness in pottery.
- Do not purchase expensive articles if you do not know how to determine quality. Avoid making large purchases from unknown vendors.
- Don't be too aggressive while bargaining. A good price is usually 70 to 80 per cent of the originally offered price.
- Remember Native etiquette. Speak softly and clearly. Don't point, and if you shake hands, do so gently.
- If you want a photograph of the artist, they may ask for money ($5–$10 is normal).

Navajo weaver working outdoors

Carvings are primarily represented by *kachina* or *katsina* dolls – beautifully painted, ornate representations of the *kachina* spirits of the Hopi and the Pueblo peoples. Although popular with tourists, they have deep significance for the Hopis, and should be handled and treated with respect. Other tribes occasionally make *kachina*-like dolls for the tourist trade.

ENTERTAINMENT IN ARIZONA

Arizona's lively blend of cultures and increasing population have made it a thriving center for arts and entertainment. The large cities of Phoenix and Tucson have vibrant artistic communities, and offer opera, ballet, classical music, and major theatrical productions. Sedona is famous for its resident painters and sculptors, and regularly hosts prestigious touring productions, as well as

regional theater, dance, and musical events. Also, almost every city and major town has a lively nightlife that includes popular music such as country, jazz, and rock, and dinner theater and standup comedy.

Sport is a popular pastime in Arizona, and fans can find major league and college football, baseball, and basketball teams playing across the state.

Bull riding, a popular rodeo event in Arizona

Old Tucson Studios (see pp96–7), offer tours of their working movie sets. Similar entertainment can be found at **Rawhide**, north of Scottsdale, which has a museum, an old-fashioned ice cream parlor, and a famous music venue. Goldfield, near Apache Junction, which was once the richest gold mining town in America, offers a train tour of the original gold mine site, a working saloon, a zipline, and a bordello museum.

Information

The best information source on entertainment and events are local newspapers.

Phoenix's *The Arizona Republic* and Tucson's *Daily Star* are useful, and they also have websites with up-to-date information. Several magazines also review events and nightlife. Most hotels offer magazines, such as *Where* and *Key*, that feature dining, attractions, and entertainment. **Jazz in Arizona**'s website details upcoming events. You can book tickets for most events through **Ticketmaster** outlets, or via their online booking service.

Rodeos, Wild West Shows, and Historical Tours

Since Buffalo Bill's first Wild West show in the 1880s, Arizona has been a mecca for Western-style entertainment. Traditional cowboy skills, such as roping steers and breaking wild mustangs, are now part of rodeo contests that offer substantial money prizes. Rodeo is the

Spanish word for round-up, harking back to the 19th century when herds of cattle crossed the Southwest on their way to California. Today's rodeo circuit is very competitive and dangerous, attracting full-time professionals whose high pay reflects this risky career. Some of the most popular rodeos in Arizona are Tucson's Fiesta de los Vaqueros Rodeo, The Payson Rodeo, The Summer Rodeo Series in Williams, and Frontier Days Rodeo in Prescott.

Arizona offers plenty of opportunities to sample the Wild West atmosphere, either in the many ghost towns or in historic frontier towns such as **Tombstone** (see p104), which stages mock-gunfights at the OK Corral. Western towns that were built as film studios, such as

Sports

The three most popular spectator sports in Arizona, as in the rest of the United States, are football, baseball, and basketball. The state's largest concentration of major teams is in the Phoenix area. The **Arizona Cardinals**, who play their home games at the University of Phoenix Stadium, are the state's only major league football team, and the oldest continually operating NFL team in the country. The Arizona Diamondbacks baseball team joined the major league in 1998 and is based at the $275-million **Chase Field** in Phoenix. Professional basketball is represented by the Phoenix Suns, who share the

Troy Brohawn of the Arizona Diamondbacks

Talking Stick Resort Arena with the American Football team, the Arizona Rattlers.

While tickets may be hard to obtain for league games, it is relatively easy to gain entrance to the many college games in any sport throughout the region. Phoenix's warm climate also attracts the Cactus League, a series of training games for seven major league baseball teams in February and March.

Classical Music, Ballet, and Opera

Phoenix has an excellent reputation for music. Both the Phoenix Symphony and Arizona Opera perform at the **Phoenix Symphony Hall** building. The city's $14-million refurbishment of the Spanish Baroque-style **Orpheum Theater** has created the state's top venue for big name Broadway shows, and a stunning addition to more than 20 major venues for arts, sports, and entertainment in and around Phoenix. The Arizona Theater Company occupies the **Herberger Theater Center**, offering a regular program of performances. With more than 20 theater companies in Phoenix, there is an impressive array of plays to choose from, as well as touring stage shows and big name entertainers.

In Tucson, the **Arizona Opera** stages its impressive productions at the Tucson Convention Center Music Hall, which is also home to the award-winning **Tucson Symphony Orchestra**.

Nightlife

Arizona has a vibrant nightlife which caters to most visitors.

The Museum Club on the historic Route 66, in Flagstaff

In almost every town there are restaurants, bars, and nightclubs that offer country music and dancing. Among the most famous country music venues is the Wild West theme-town of Rawhide in Scottsdale, where a large number of well-known bands play. **The Museum Club** in Flagstaff is a legendary Route 66 (see p35) roadhouse that has hosted such top country music names as Hank Williams and Willie Nelson, and still offers a lively selection of Southwestern bands.

The major cities of the state have virtually every type of evening entertainment on offer. For example, trendy dance clubs and jazz bars and cafés are gaining in popularity, and standup comedy and rock music are available in countless venues. In Tucson, **The Rialto Theatre** brings a wide variety of live entertainment – from punk rock to salsa – to the stage of this renovated 1918 playhouse. Clubs and arenas in Phoenix and Tucson are regular stops for big stars on US tours.

Phoenix Symphony Hall, home to Phoenix Symphony and Arizona Opera

SPECIALTY VACATIONS AND ACTIVITIES

With hundreds of miles of deep rock canyons, spectacular deserts, and towering, snow-capped mountains, Arizona offers a wide and tempting array of outdoor adventure activities. Much of the state's wilderness is protected by the federal government in national parks, national recreation areas, and lands administered by the National Forest Service and the Bureau of Land Management. Visitor numbers to the region are increasing, and it is now a magnet for climbers, mountain bikers, hikers, and 4WD enthusiasts. The range of organized tours includes whitewater rafting and horseback riding, as well as cultural heritage tours of the many ancient Native American sites. Wildlife enthusiasts, particularly birdwatchers, can spot rare species on the spring and fall migration routes that cross the Southwest. The region is also a center for sports activities, especially for golfers *(see pp156–7)*, who can choose from over 300 courses, some of which are the world's finest.

General Information

The main centers for outdoor activities in the region are Phoenix, Tucson, Flagstaff, and Sedona. These towns have excellent equipment shops and visitor information centers. It is advisable to spend some time planning your trip in advance.

Hikers and campers exploring national park backcountry will need permits from the National Park Service as well as detailed maps, which can be obtained from the **USDA Forest Service**, or the **US Geological Survey (USGS)**. National parks have excellent, well-marked trails, and fascinating ranger-led hikes that focus on the local flora, fauna, and geology. Advice on trails, permits, and weather conditions at most attractions can be obtained at both the state and local tourist offices. Anyone exploring desert or canyon country should be aware of the potential for flash floods, and should check weather reports daily, especially during the summer months of July and August.

Hiking

The single most popular outdoor activity in Arizona is hiking. Day hikes and longer trips attract large numbers of residents and visitors, who feel that this is one of the best ways to see the region's stunning scenery.

Hikers on the trail to Pueblo Alto at Chaco Canyon

Popular hiking areas include Mount Lemmon *(see p100)* outside Tucson, Camelback Mountain *(see p87)* and the Superstition Mountains *(see p90)* outside Phoenix, Oak Creek Canyon *(see p75)* near Sedona, and the vast desert expanses of Glen Canyon Recreation Area *(see pp68–9)*.

For easier hiking and driving tours, contact **Walk Softly Tours**, which offers single- and multi-day adventures in the Sonoran Desert and Four Corners areas. **The Grand Canyon Field Institute** arranges a year-round calendar of guided hikes and multi-day backpacking trips, on themes such as photography or natural history.

Arizona Trails is a travel agency that custom-designs hiking adventures in Arizona, matching individuals or groups to experienced guides for one- to three-day desert, canyon, or mountain hikes.

Rock Climbing

Arizona's dry, sunny climate and extensive mountains, canyons, and sheer rock faces make it one of America's most popular climbing destinations.

There are excellent, and often busy, climbing locations near each city, and nearly all the major cities have first-rate climbing shops and schools. **Arizona Climbing and Adventure School**, in Carefree, provides full- and half-day climbs across the state, for groups and individuals.

In the Phoenix and Scottsdale area, **360 Adventures** offer half- and full-day climbing adventures, as well as a full-day introduction to rock climbing targeted at beginners and intermediate-level climbers. Rates include all necessary permits and equipment.

Mountain Biking and Four-Wheel Driving

With so much wilderness crisscrossed by trails and jeep tracks, mountain biking and 4WD touring are two of the fastest growing sports in

Mountain biking on red rock in Coconino National Forest, Sedona

Arizona. Casual riders will find plenty of thrills in Phoenix's Papago Park *(see p88)*. In Tucson, there are numerous trails in the Mount Lemmon area.

Bikeapelli Adventure Tours offers single- and multi-day adventures on rough desert single-tracks and slickrock rides. Sedona is also a hotbed for 4WD adventures, and local legend **Pink Jeep Tours** offers guided 4WD tours, including one of the Grand Canyon. Monument Valley *(see pp108–9)* is a prime location for 4WD tours, which are often led by Navajo guides from **Goulding's Lodge Monument Valley Tours**. Glen Canyon National Recreation Area's miles of trails and dirt roads make it a hotspot for both mountain bikers and 4WD enthusiasts.

Whitewater Rafting and Kayaking

When people think of whitewater rafting in Arizona, they often dream of the 16-day run through the Grand Canyon. But, as incredible as this trip is, it requires time, and up to a year of advance planning. When time is short, Arizona offers plenty of other whitewater and flatwater rafting choices. If you want to see the Grand Canyon, several operators, including **Tour West**, offer three- to five-day trips through the lower Grand Canyon, beginning at Diamond Creek on Hualapai reservation and ending at Lake Mead. The Salt River is a raging torrent in the White Mountains, where **Wilderness Aware** offers one- to five-day rafting trips. On the Colorado Plateau, **Wild River Expeditions** offers a gentle one-day float through the canyons of the San Juan River that includes stops to see petroglyphs and Ancestral Puebloan ruins.

Other Watersports

Artificial lakes along the Colorado River – formed because of the damming of the river – offer a variety of watersports, including power-boating and jetskiing. Lake Powell is famous for houseboat cruises, which showcase remote beaches, canyons, and the desert beauty for which the lake is known. **Lake Powell Resorts & Marinas** rents out houseboats and powerboats.

At **Lake Mead** *(see p78)*, shops rent fishing boats and jetskis, and offer waterskiing lessons. Various types of boats, including houseboats, powerboats and ski boats, can be rented from **Callville Bay Resort & Marina**. Farther south, at Lake Havasu City, all kinds of equipment, from waterskis to tubes, can be rented from **Nautical Watersports Center**.

Fishing

Lakes Mead, Powell, and Havasu are noted as excellent fishing destinations. The lakes are well stocked with game fish during the fishing season, which runs from March to November. River anglers can also fish for salmon and trout. Fishing licenses are required almost everywhere, and catch and release is the rule in many areas. Information about licenses, tournaments, and tours can be obtained from marinas, outdoor equipment stores, local gas stations, and the **Arizona Game & Fish Department**.

Hot-Air Ballooning

Cool, still mornings, dependable sunshine, and steady breezes have made Arizona one of the top hot-air ballooning destinations in America. Around Phoenix, several operators, including **Hot Air Expeditions**, offer Champagne flights over the Sonoran Desert. You can also drift gently over the canyons of Sedona with **Northern Light Balloon Expeditions**.

Whitewater rafting trip on the Colorado River

Birdwatching

With more than 200 species of birds, including many rare breeds, birdwatching is a popular pastime in Arizona, particularly in spring, early summer, and fall. These are the peak migration seasons for many species such as warblers and flycatchers, and for shorebirds.

Cibola National Wildlife Refuge is home to a wide variety of birds, including nesting waders, ducks and a winter population of snow geese, and more than 1,000 sandhill cranes. Several habitats across the region suit desert birds such as the roadrunner and elf owl; **Saguaro National Park** (see p96), located in the Sonoran Desert, is a notable example. Southern Arizona is also home to America's greatest variety of hummingbirds. The **Southeastern Arizona Bird Observatory**, a non-profit organization, offers educational tours in the region.

Learning Vacations

Some of Arizona's most interesting learning vacations focus on Native cultures and ancient civilizations. Two organizations, **The Crow Canyon Archaeological Center** and **The Four Corners School**, offer vacation courses on geography, flora and fauna, ancient ruins, and Native arts. Archaeology courses often involve working on digs with professional archaeologists. Most programs last between four and ten days, and visitors are housed either in college campuses or in motels. Several of Arizona's top museums offer a variety of learning vacations. **Smithsonian Journeys** also offers popular programs such as the past and present arts of the Hopi and Navajo tribes.

Spa Vacations

Arizona's warm winter weather and spectacular outdoors have resulted in the blossoming of

Telemark turns on San Francisco Peaks, near Flagstaff

high-end spas in Phoenix, Tucson, and Sedona (see p74). These spas offer everything from posh pampering to serious diet and fitness programs, and a host of New Age wellness experiences.

Tucson's **Canyon Ranch**, considered one of the world's finest destination spas, offers a stunning array of programs incorporating tennis, hiking, biking, yoga, tai chi, and meditation.

Broad-billed hummingbird

Nearby, **Miraval** is famous for its blend of pampering and physical regimen, offering over 100 facial and body treatment options, including acupuncture, Shiatsu, and Trager. The spa's immaculate grounds feature waterfalls, tennis courts, stables, and a Zen garden.

Skiing and Winter Sports

Featuring 2,300 ft (700 m) of vertical drop and a network of superb trails serviced by five chairlifts, the 12,600-ft (3,840-m) **Arizona Snowbowl** (see p71), which lies just north of Flagstaff, is the undisputed champion of downhill ski resorts in Arizona.

Another major resort, **Sunrise Park**, in the White Mountains, features ten lifts and 65 runs, and is a favorite with many visitors, particularly snowboarders. Also growing in popularity is the southernmost ski resort in the country, **Mount Lemmon Ski Valley**, which is located just outside Tucson. The Grand Canyon's North Rim is particularly sought after by cross-country skiing enthusiasts.

Horseback Riding

Horseback riding is synonymous with Arizona. Even large cities have stables that offer trail rides through the desert. **OK Corral Stables**, at Apache Junction near Phoenix, offers horseback trail camping trips for one to five days. Cooler summer locations, such as Sedona and Pinetop-Lakeside, are also popular. Dude ranches offer a range of experiences, from pampered luxury with daytime trail rides, to real cattle ranches that offer visitors the chance to live and work as a cowboy. The **Arizona Dude Ranch Association** can help plan a dude ranch vacation.

Horseback riding through the desert in Arizona

DIRECTORY

Information

A wealth of information on using and enjoying public lands is available at
W **recreation.gov**

USDA Forest Service
333 Broadway SE, Albuquerque, NM 87102.
Tel (505) 842-3898.

USGS
12201 Sunrise Valley Dr, Reston, VA 20192.
Tel (888) 275-8747.
W **usgs.gov**

Hiking

Arizona Trails
16650 E Palisades Blvd, Suite 106, Fountain Hills, AZ 85268.
Tel (888) 799-4284.
W **aztrailstravel.com**

Grand Canyon Field Institute
PO Box 399, Grand Canyon, AZ 86023.
Tel (866) 471-4435.
W **grandcanyon.org**

Walk Softly Tours
PO Box 7755, Surprise, AZ 85374.
Tel (623) 444-8902.
W **walksoftlytours.com**

Rock Climbing

Arizona Climbing and Adventure School
PO Box 3094, Carefree, AZ 85377.
Tel (480) 363-2390.
W **climbingschool.com**

360 Adventures
Tel (888) 722-0360.
W **360-adventures.com**

Mountain Biking and 4WD

Bikeapelli Adventure Tours
1695 W Hwy 89a, Sedona, AZ 86336.
Tel (928) 282-1312.
W **mountain bikeheaven.com**

Goulding's Lodge Monument Valley Tours
Hwy 163, Monument Valley, UT 84536.
Tel (435) 727-3231.
W **gouldings.com**

Pink Jeep Tours
PO Box 1447, Sedona, AZ 86339.
Tel (928) 282-5000, (800) 873-3662.
W **pinkjeeptours sedona.com**

Whitewater Rafting and Kayaking

Tour West
PO Box 333, Orem, UT 84059.
Tel (800) 453-9107.
W **twriver.com**

Wild River Expeditions
2625 S Hwy 191, Bluff, UT 84512.
Tel (435) 678-2628.
W **riversandruins.com**

Wilderness Aware
PO Box 1550, Buena Vista, CO 81211.
Tel (800) 462-7238, (719) 395-2112.
W **inaraft.com**

Other Watersports

Callville Bay Resort & Marina
100 Callville Bay Rd, Overton, NV 89120.
Tel (800) 255-5561.
W **callvillebay.com**

Lake Powell Resorts & Marinas
100 Lake Shore Dr, Page, AZ 86040.
Tel (928) 645-2433, (888) 896-3829.
W **lakepowell.com**

Nautical Watersports Center
1000 McCulloch Blvd, Lake Havasu City, AZ.
Tel (928) 680-7600.
W **nauticalwatersports. com**

Fishing

Arizona Game & Fish Department
2222 Greenway Rd, Phoenix, AZ 85023.
Tel (602) 942-3000.
W **azgfd.com**

Hot-Air Ballooning

Hot Air Expeditions
702 W Deer Valley Rd, Phoenix, AZ 85027.
Tel (800) 831-7610.
W **hotairexpeditions. com**

Northern Light Balloon Expeditions
PO Box 1695, Sedona, AZ 86339.
Tel (928) 282-2274, (800) 230-6222.
W **northernlight balloon.com**

Birdwatching

Cibola National Wildlife Refuge
66600 Cibola Lake Rd, Cibola, AZ 85328.
Tel (928) 857-3253.
W **fws.gov/refuge/ cibola**

Southeastern Arizona Bird Observatory
PO Box 5521, Bisbee, AZ 85603.
Tel (520) 432-1388.
W **sabo.org**

Learning Vacations

The Crow Canyon Archaeological Center
23390 County Road K, Cortez, CO 81321.
Tel (970) 565-8975.
W **crowcanyon.org**

The Four Corners School
1117 N Main St, Monticello, UT 84535.
Tel (800) 525-4456.
W **fourcornersschool. org**

Smithsonian Journeys
PO Box 23182, Washington, DC 20077.
Tel (855) 330-1542.
W **smithsonian journeys.com**

Spa Vacations

Canyon Ranch
8600 E Rockcliff Rd, Tucson, AZ 85750.
Tel (520) 749-9000, (800) 742-9000.
W **canyonranch destinations.com**

Miraval
5000 E Via Estancia Miraval, Tucson, AZ 85739.
Tel (800) 232-3969.
W **miravalresort.com**

Skiing and Winter Sports

Arizona Snowbowl
PO Box 40, Flagstaff, AZ 86002.
Tel (928) 779-1951.
W **arizonasnowbowl. com**

Mount Lemmon Ski Valley
10300 Ski Run Rd, Mt. Lemmon, AZ 85619.
Tel (520) 576-1321.
W **skithelemmon.com**

Sunrise Park Ski Resort
PO Box 117, Greer, AZ 85927.
Tel (928) 735-7669, (855) 735-7669.
W **sunriseskipark.com**

Horseback Riding

Arizona Dude Ranch Association
PO Box 603, Cortaro, AZ 85652.
W **azdra.com**

OK Corral Stables
5470 E Apache Trail, Apache Junction, AZ 85219-8981.
Tel (480) 982-4040.
W **okcorrals.com**

Golfing in Arizona

Boasting over 300 golf courses, many of which are among the world's finest, Arizona is a golfer's paradise. With so many courses, golf enthusiasts have a dazzling array of terrains and levels of challenge to choose from. Green fees can range from nominal to expensive. Private courses are open to club members exclusively, and to those with reciprocal memberships. Semi-private courses are reserved for members, but do accept paying guests at certain times. Public courses are open to all, but golf resorts prefer guests staying with them, though they are opened to the public occasionally. The legendary Boulders Club, near Phoenix, rotates access to its two world-class courses between resort guests, private members, and the public.

A private golf course in the cooler climes of Flagstaff

Flagstaff and Northern Arizona

Golf on the Colorado Plateau, at elevations between 5,000 ft (1,520 m) and 7,000 ft (2,130 m), is played throughout the year, although some courses close in winter. In summer, the northern courses usually bustle as they are cooler by 15°F, on an average, than courses in Phoenix. Busy is relative, however, and seldom will the Northern Arizona courses be as crowded as their southern cousins.

In Sedona, the Gary Pranks-designed course at **Sedona Golf Resort** is one of Northern Arizona's must-play venues. Regularly featured in lists of the state's best courses, this par 71 course features lush greens and stunning views of the surrounding red rock canyons.

Surrounded by pine-covered mountains, Prescott is one of the busiest golf regions in Northern Arizona. One of the best deals can be found at **Antelope Hills Golf Course**. For a modest fee of about $50, players can choose from the 18-hole North Course, with its towering elm trees, classic layout, and challenging doglegs, or the links-style South Course. In nearby Prescott Valley, the par 72 **Stoneridge Golf Course**, opened in 2002, is one of Northern Arizona's rising stars with a visually stunning and physically challenging links-style course that features over 350 ft (110 m) of vertical rise and fall across its 18 holes.

Lush grass at a golf course in Scottsdale, Arizona

Phoenix and Central Arizona

The Valley of the Sun has perhaps more golf courses per capita than anywhere in the world, nearly 200 and counting, including some of the world's very best. Since this is a spot that must satisfy not only its residents, but also over a million visiting golfers every year, it's no surprise that many of the courses are public or resort courses with generous public access.

Golf is big business here, particularly in Scottsdale, a town virtually synonymous with the concept of luxurious golf resorts such as **The Boulders Club** and **Troon North Golf Club**, which offer some of the best courses in the world. In fact, the Tom Weiskopf-designed course at Troon North is a desert golfer's dream, and is listed as one of the top 100 golf courses to play by *Golf Magazine*. Like many Scottsdale courses, the amenities and services at Troon North are top-notch, but all

PGA Tour

Arizona's reliable sunshine and pleasant winter temperatures make it a favorite of the Professional Golfer's Association (PGA), which holds an important tournament here early in the year. In late January (or sometimes early February) the Waste Management Phoenix Open (see p39) attracts huge crowds to the Tournament Players Club of Scottsdale. The club's unusual layout allows for virtually unlimited viewing, and as many as 400,000 people have attended a single tournament.

Tiger Woods hits a tee shot during the Phoenix Open

Randolph North in Tucson – one of the top ten public golf courses in Arizona

this comes at a steep price, at up to $274 a round. In Phoenix, there is the **Wildfire Golf Club**, which features two first-class courses, a classic Arnold Palmer Signature course, and the desert-style Faldo Championship Course.

Those wanting to opt for a public course can head east to **Gold Canyon Resort**, which has the Sidewinder and Dinosaur Mountain courses, both top-rated public courses. Both courses are visually stunning and among the best value in this land of golf and sunshine.

Tucson and Southern Arizona

Set in the verdant Sonoran Desert, surrounded by stunning landscape and boasting over 350 days of sunshine every year, Tucson is one of America's best golf destinations. The city has fantastic offerings, including **Ventana Canyon Resort**, whose Tom Fazio-designed Mountain Course offers immaculate greens. Listed among North America's best courses, it offers enough challenge to keep even the most experienced golfers

focused. Another rewarding course is the classic **Randolph North**, with its broad water hazards and towering eucalyptus trees. A popular PGA venue in the 1980s, Randolf North now hosts LPGA events.

South of Tucson, the suburbs of Green Valley have some of the finest courses in Southern Arizona. One of these is **Torres Blancas**, a Lee Trevino-designed course with a monster 484-yard (442-m), par 4 signature 17th hole that gives players something to talk about back at the clubhouse.

DIRECTORY

General

Arizona Golf Association
7600 E Redfield Rd, St 130,
Scottsdale, AZ 85260.
Tel (602) 944-3035.
W azgolf.org

Golf Arizona
W golfarizona.com

Flagstaff and Northern Arizona

Antelope Hills Golf Course
1 Perkins Dr, Prescott,
AZ 86301.
Tel (928) 776-7888.
W antelopehillsgolf.com

Sedona Golf Resort
35 Ridge Trail Dr,
Sedona, AZ 86351.
Tel (928) 284-9355.
W sedonagolf
resort.com

Stoneridge Golf Course
1601 N Bluff Top Dr,
Prescott Valley,
AZ 86314.
Tel (928) 772-6500.
W stoneridgegolf.com

Phoenix and Central Arizona

The Boulders Club
34831 N Tom Darlington
Dr, PO Box 2090,
Carefree, AZ 85377.
Tel (480) 488-9028.
W thebouldersclub.
com

Gold Canyon Resort
6100 S Kings Ranch Rd,
Gold Canyon,
AZ 85219.
Tel (480) 982-9090.
W gcgr.com

Troon North Golf Club
10320 E Dynamite Blvd,
Scottsdale, AZ 85262.
Tel (480) 585-7700.
W troonnorthgolf.com

Wildfire Golf Club
5350 E Marriott Drive,
Phoenix, AZ 85054.
Tel (480) 473-0205,
(888) 705-7775.
W wildfiregolf.com

Tucson and Southern Arizona

Randolph North Golf Course
600 S Alvernon Way,
Pima County, Tucson,
AZ 85711.
Tel (520) 791-4161.
W tucsoncitygolf.com/
randolph-north

Torres Blancas Golf Club
3233 S Abrego Dr,
Green Valley,
AZ 85614.
Tel (520) 625-5200.
W torresblancasgolf.
com

Ventana Canyon Resort
6200 N Clubhouse Lane,
Tucson, AZ 85750.
Tel (520) 577-1400.
W ventanacanyonclub.
com

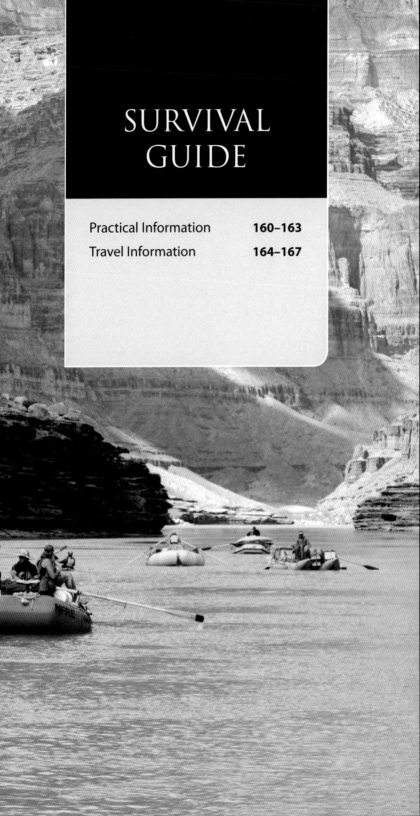

SURVIVAL
GUIDE

PRACTICAL INFORMATION

A vast region of fascinating and spectacular natural beauty, Arizona is dotted with dramatic rock formations, canyons, ancient archaeological sites, and wild desert scenery that offers visitors a choice of pleasures, including a wide variety of outdoor activities.

Arizona's cities are famous for their combination of a laid-back Southwestern culture, and sophisticated urban pursuits such as excellent museums and great dining. In addition, unique attractions located on

Native reservations provide a wonderful opportunity to observe American Indian cultures. Accommodations in the region are excellent (see pp128–33), and visitor information centers are plentiful, even in small towns.

The following pages contain useful information on planning a trip to this region. Travel Information (see pp164–7) provides information on travel by both public transportation and private car.

When to Go

Arizona is a year-round destination, and its climate is dictated by elevation. The higher elevation areas have cold, snowy winters, making them a popular destination for skiing and other winter sports activities. In contrast, lower elevations in Southern Arizona are noted for the warm and sunny winter weather, with temperatures averaging a comfortable 70°F (21°C) in Phoenix. Be aware, however, that the average temperature in the summer months of July and August touches 100°F (37°C) in Phoenix, making it one of the hottest cities outside the Middle East. Spring and fall are ideal seasons to visit Arizona – there are fewer visitors, and the milder temperatures make outdoor activities a popular option. However, some services may be closed at these times: the North Rim of the Grand Canyon (see p61) is open only between May and October. Whatever the time of year, this is a region known for having a great deal of sun, with the northern areas averaging over 200 days of sunshine each year, and the southern parts famous for having more than 300 sunny days in a year.

Tourist Information

Visitor information centers in Arizona offer everything from local maps to hotel and B&B bookings. Special tours, such

as guided history walks, ranger-led archaeological tours, and wildlife expeditions, can also be arranged through these offices. In addition, the national and state parks have their own visitor centers that provide hiking maps, safety advice, and special licenses for hiking and camping out in the wilderness.

Arizona has a department of tourism, as do all the major towns and cities in the state. Access the **Arizona Office of Tourism** website when planning your trip, and you'll find all sorts of ideas and suggestions. Websites run by local visitor centers, as well as those of individual sights, also offer information and online booking services for accommodations.

Many tourist attractions, such as Canyon de Chelly National Monument (see pp112–13), are located on Native reservations

and are managed by tribal councils. For advice on etiquette, opening times, and admission fees, contact the local **Bureau of Indian Affairs** or the **Navajo Tourism Department**.

Time Zones

The state is located in the Mountain Standard Time zone, but it does not follow Daylight Saving Time. From late spring to early fall, all of the neighboring states in the Mountain Standard Time zone (New Mexico, Colorado, and Utah) set their clocks forward by 1 hour, but not Arizona.

To confuse matters even more, it is important to be aware that the Navajo Nation (across Arizona and part of New Mexico) does use Daylight Saving Time, but the Hopi Indian Reservation (in the middle of the Navajo Reservation) does not.

Currency

American currency, based on the decimal system, has 100 cents to the dollar. Bills are all the same size and color, and they come in the following denominations: $1, $5, $10, $20, $50, and $100. American coins come in 1-, 5-, 10-, and 25-cent, as well as 50-cent and $1 dollar pieces, which are minted but rarely used. Smaller denominations are preferred in small towns, convenience stores, and gas stations. It is useful to always carry cash for tips, public transport, and taxis.

Ranger on a guided tour at Keet Seel, Navajo National Monument

◀ Rafts on the Colorado River in Grand Canyon, Arizona.

Internet

Nearly all hotels provide Wi-Fi, though many will charge a fee to use it. Eateries and coffeeshops, such as Starbucks, provide free Wi-Fi. The website openwifispots.com provides a useful directory of free Wi-Fi spots throughout the US.

Senior Travelers

Although the age when you are considered a senior is 65, a multitude of discounts are available to people over 50. Reduced rates can apply to meals, accommodations, public transportation, and entrance fees, and are often better than student discounts.

The **National Park Service** offers Golden Age Passports that reduce the cost of park tours and services. **Elderhostel** arranges educational tours, which include inexpensive accommodations, lectures, and meals. The **American Association of Retired Persons (AARP)** offers good travel discounts.

Travelers with Disabilities

Arizona has excellent facilities to cater to the physically disabled traveler. All public places and buildings are legally required to be wheelchair-accessible, and to have suitably designed restrooms. Public transportation also comes under this law, and road crossings in city centers have dropped curbs to enable easier access. Service animals, such as guide dogs for the blind, are the only animals that are allowed on public transportation.

Many national parks and archaeological sights have paved walkways for wheel-chairs. The National Park Service grants free lifetime entry to those who are disabled or blind. The **Disabled Travelers** website and the **Society for Accessible Travel & Hospitality** are two organizations that offer advice, from how to rent specially adapted cars to qualifying for parking permits.

Student Travelers

The largest provider of student travel products and services is **STA Travel**. It offers discounted accommodations, rail passes, phone cards, email options, travel packages, and cut-rate student airfares. **Student Universe** offers similar services. If you are planning to stay in youth hostels, you will need to join **Hostelling International/ American Youth Hostels (HI/AYH)**.

Water fountains in the courtyard of the Heard Museum in Phoenix

DIRECTORY

Tourist Information

Arizona Office of Tourism
1110 W Washington St, Phoenix, AZ 85007.
Tel (866) 275-5816.
🖵 visitarizona.com

Bureau of Indian Affairs
2600 N Central Ave, Phoenix, AZ 85004.
Tel (602) 379-6600.
🖵 bia.gov

Greater Phoenix Convention & Visitors Bureau
400 E Van Buren St, Suite 600, Phoenix, AZ 85004.
Tel (877) 225-5749.
🖵 visitphoenix.com

Navajo Tourism Department
PO Box 663, Window Rock, AZ 86515.
Tel (928) 871-6436.
🖵 discovernavajo.com

Senior Travelers

American Association of Retired Persons
16165 N 83rd Ave, Suite 201, Peoria AZ 85382.
Tel (866) 389-5649.
🖵 aarp.org

Elderhostel
11 Avenue de Lafayette, Boston, MA 02111.
Tel (800) 454-5768.
🖵 roadscholar.org

National Park Service
(see also under individual sights) Intermountain Area, PO Box 25287, Denver, CO 80225.
🖵 nps.gov

Travelers with Disabilities

Disabled Travelers
PO Box 492, Yucca, AZ 86438.
🖵 disabledtravelers. com

Society for Accessible Travel & Hospitality (SATH)
Tel (212) 447-7284.
🖵 sath.org

Student Travelers

Hostelling International/ American Youth Hostel (HI/AYH)
Tel (240) 650-2100.
🖵 hiusa.org

STA Travel
Tel (800) 781-4040, (800) 836-4115.
🖵 statravel.com

Student Universe
Tel (800) 272-9676.
🖵 studentuniverse. com

Personal Security and Health

Arizona is a relatively safe place as long as some general precautions are observed. Arizona's urban centers have lower crime rates in contrast to other US cities, but it is still wise to be cautious and to find out which parts are unsafe at night. When traveling across remote areas, take a reliable local map, and follow the advice of local rangers and visitor centers. These sources also offer invaluable information on survival in the wilderness and on safety procedures that should be followed during outdoor activities *(see pp64–7 & pp152–7).* It is also advisable to check the local media, such as newspapers, television, and radio, for current weather and safety conditions.

Police

The Arizona Department of Public Safety (DPS) is a law-enforcement agency that includes the Highway Patrol. The state has an additional 141 law-enforcement agencies. On federal lands, including national parks and forests, park rangers are there to protect visitors.

In an emergency call 911. To report a crime in Phoenix call the **Non-Emergency Line**.

What to be Aware of

Most tourist areas in Arizona are friendly and non-threatening, and wilderness areas are, for the most part, free of crime. However, to avoid being a victim of crime, it is wise to observe a few basic rules. Never carry large amounts of cash, wear obviously expensive jewelry, or keep your wallet in your back pocket. Wear handbags and cameras over one shoulder with the strap across your body. Keep your identification separate from your cash and traveler's checks. Most hotels have safety deposit boxes or safes in which you should store any valuables.

At night it is better to stay where there are other people and be aware of which areas could be unsafe. In general, crime is higher in the larger cities, with South Tucson having the highest crime rate. It is a good idea to carry a cell phone so that you can call 911 in an emergency.

If you are driving, be sure to lock any valuables in the trunk where they are out-of-sight, and park only in well-lit parking lots. Also, it is wise to have a roadside assistance service plan, such as AAA *(see p167),* which sends licensed service representatives in case assistance is needed. In tourist destinations, lock the car when stepping out. Parking areas in national parks, especially overlooks and trailheads, are very popular targets for thieves.

Lost and Stolen Property

If your property is lost or stolen, contact the local police at the non-emergency line to file a report. Be sure to keep a copy of the report for insurance purposes. For lost property, contact the city's visitor center or Chamber of Commerce.

For lost or stolen debit or credit cards, call your credit card or bank. It is a good idea to keep a record of your card numbers and bank phone numbers in a separate place from your purse or wallet.

For a lost passport, there are passport acceptance facilities in more populated areas such as Phoenix, Scottsdale, Tucson, Yuma, Glendale, Flagstaff, and Tempe. The greatest number of passport offices can be found in Maricopa County; or you can contact a representative on (877) 487-2778 (8am–10pm EST Mon–Fri except federal holidays).

Medical Treatment

City hospitals with emergency rooms can be found in the directory, but they are often overcrowded. Private hospitals offer more personalized treatment and are listed in the Yellow Pages. Walk-in clinics offer basic medical services, and are usually less expensive and more efficient than hospitals for non-emergencies. You may be required to provide evidence of your ability to pay before a doctor will agree to treat you, hence the importance of adequate medical insurance. Hotels will usually call a doctor or recommend a local dentist. **The Society of St. Vincent De Paul** is a national organization that helps stranded travelers.

Travel and Health Insurance

Arizona has excellent medical services, but as in the rest of the US they are very expensive. Visitors are strongly advised to make sure they have comprehensive medical and dental coverage for the duration of their stay. Visitors planning to take part in outdoor activities in

Police department sign on the Navajo Reservation

Park ranger at the Petrified Forest National Park, Arizona

remote areas or stay on Native reservations should consider including medical air evacuation insurance as well.

Outdoor Safety

The weather in the Southwest can present a number of dangerous situations, especially in Southern Arizona, where sudden summer storms may cause flash floods. Weather information can be obtained from ranger stations, through reports on radio and television, and on the Internet. If you are planning a drive or hike in remote territory, always tell someone where you are going and when you expect to return.

The dry summer heat is often underestimated, and hikers are advised to carry at least a gallon (4 liters) of drinking water per person for each day of walking. Dry conditions also pose the risk of forest fires at higher

elevations, and it is advisable to check with forest service rangers regarding fire danger before lighting any flame.

The sun is surprisingly strong at higher elevations, and an effective sunscreen and sunhat should always be worn. Temperatures can change rapidly in Arizona. It may be 80°F (26°C) during the day, and then drop to 30°F (-1°C) at night. Be prepared and dress accordingly.

Dangerous creatures are found in the wilderness *(see p25)*, but these animals generally avoid humans and it is unlikely you will be bitten if you avoid their habitats.

Do not turn over rocks or reach up to touch rock ledges. Shake out clothes and shoes that have been on the ground before putting them on. Venomous stings and bites may hurt but are rarely fatal to adults with prompt medical attention. Always carry a first aid and snakebite kit if you are going into snake country.

Traveling on the Reservations

Visitors are welcome on reservations, and will generally find Natives to be friendly and helpful. However, take the same care as when traveling in any remote rural area of the US. Services such as restaurants, motels, gas stations, and ATMs are only located in towns and at major crossroads.

Call 911 in case of an emergency. If a serious medical situation develops, you will be provided first-line treatment and then shifted to a hospital off the

reservation. Most reservations have their own highly trained police forces, which enforce the laws and assist lost tourists. It is illegal to bring alcohol onto reservations – even a bottle visible in a locked car will land you in trouble. Always ask before photographing anything, and be prepared that a fee may be requested. Do not wander off marked trails as this is forbidden. Dress respectfully – for example, the Hopi request that people do not wear shorts or halter tops.

Lone truck on rough Arizona desert road

TRAVEL INFORMATION

Phoenix, followed by Tucson, is the main gateway for visitors arriving in Arizona by air. There are other major airports in neighboring states that also serve as entry points, including the cities of Las Vegas in Nevada, Salt Lake City in Utah, and Albuquerque in New Mexico. Visitors also arrive by long-distance bus or, less frequently, by Amtrak train. However, the automobile remains the preferred mode of transport.

Arizona has an excellent, well-maintained network of highways, service stations, and comfortable, air-conditioned cars for rent.

Public transportation options are increasing in major urban centers of the state – in Phoenix, a light rail service has been implemented, and local bus systems have expanded their hours of operation. The downtown shuttle is used by visitors during weekday working hours.

An airplane flying over the Phoenix skyline at sunset

There are very few non-stop flights into Arizona from outside the US. Most international visitors have to connect via one of the country's major airports, such as Los Angeles, San Francisco, Chicago, or Dallas. Travelers from Pacific countries generally change at Honolulu, Hawaii. Foreign carriers that do have direct flights to Phoenix include **British Airways**, **Air Canada**, and AeroMexico.

Visas

Citizens of Great Britain, Ireland, and many other EU countries, as well as citizens of Japan, Singapore, Australia, and New Zealand, do not need a visa provided they have a return ticket and their stay in the US does not exceed 90 days. Regulations require visitors from these and other Visa Waiver Program countries to register with the US government's Electronic System for Travel Authorization (ESTA) before they depart for the United States. Authorization is valid for two years. It is advisable to apply well in advance.

Other citizens must apply for a nonimmigrant visa from a US consulate, while Canadians need only a passport. Before you travel, it is advisable to check the most up-to-date information, available at www.uscis.gov.

Travel Safety Advice

Visitors can get up-to-date travel safety information from the **State Department** in the US, the **Foreign and Commonwealth Office** in the UK, and the **Department of Foreign Affairs and Trade** in Australia.

Arriving by Air

Sky Harbor International in Phoenix has three terminals and receives the bulk of domestic and international arrivals. Sky Harbor and Tucson International Airport are centers for major US airlines that offer both international and domestic routes, including **American Airlines**, **Delta Airlines**, **Frontier Airlines**, **Southwest Airlines**, and **United Airlines**. American Airlines flies from Phoenix to Tucson, Flagstaff, and Yuma; **JetBlue** flies to a variety of US destinations.

Air Fares

There is an array of fare types and prices available. The cheaper tickets are usually booked early, especially between June and September, as well as around the Christmas and Thanksgiving holidays.

Direct bookings can be done through an agent, travel website or through an airline. Agents are a good source of information on bargains and ticket restrictions. Fly-drive deals, where the cost of the ticket includes car rental, may also be a lower-priced option.

Although several websites offer bargains on last-minute bookings, travel websites offer the convenience of price comparisons. Prices can change daily, so check at various times before buying tickets. However,

Airport	Information	Distance to City Center	Travel Time by Road
Phoenix	(602) 273-3300	4 miles (6 km)	15 minutes
Tucson	(520) 573-8100	8 miles (13 km)	30 minutes
Flagstaff	(928) 556-1234	7 miles (11 km)	10 minutes

A Grand Canyon Railway train on its way to Grand Canyon Village

the travel websites may not always have the best prices on tickets or packages. Your comparison shopping should include visiting the airlines websites, and calling up hotels and rental car outfits.

Traveling by Train and Bus

Train and bus travel in Arizona can be a slow but enjoyable means of exploring the region.

Amtrak offers two train routes – Southwest Chief runs daily between Chicago and Los Angeles, through the Navajo and Hopi reservations, Winslow, Gallop, and Flagstaff, while the Sunset Limited travels three times a week between Orlando and Los Angeles, passing through Tucson and Yuma. Both offer National Park Service cultural and natural heritage programs.

For rail enthusiasts, the **Grand Canyon Railway** offers both diesel and steam rail trips from Williams (see p35) to the Grand Canyon. The 2-hour trip offers packages with meals and overnight accommodations. Western entertainment – including a posse of bad guys staging an attack on the train – is included.

Long-distance **Greyhound** buses are the least expensive

Greyhound bus crossing Southwestern desert landscape

way to travel, and they also offer the widest choice of destinations. There are 27 daily routes throughout Arizona, complemented by city-run shuttle buses linking Greyhound stations to the state's main airports.

Greyhound and a number of other companies also offer package tours on luxury air-conditioned buses. Destinations include national parks, such as the Grand Canyon, and casinos, as well as urban and historical tours.

Public Transportation in Cities

With the exception of Flagstaff, which can be explored on foot, the major cities in Arizona, such as Phoenix and Tucson, are large areas and are plagued by traffic problems. Visitors could use public transportation, such as local buses, to tour these. Booking a tour can often be the best way of seeing major city sights and some remote scenery.

Phoenix and Scottsdale are covered by the **Valley Metro** bus and light rail system, as well as by **Ollie the Trolley**, a bus service that runs between Scottsdale's resorts and its shopping districts. The Phoenix–Tempe–Mesa area is served by the expanding Metro Light Rail, and there is a plan to extend service to Tucson. Tucson has the **Sun Tran** bus system.

DIRECTORY

Travel Safety Advice

Australia
Department of Foreign Affairs and Trade.
W dfat.gov.au
W smarttraveller.gov.au

UK
Foreign and Commonwealth Office.
W gov.uk/foreign-travel-advice

US
State Department
W travel.state.gov

Arriving by Air

Air Canada
Tel (888) 247-2262.
W aircanada.com

American Airlines
Tel (800) 433-7300.
W aa.com

British Airways
Tel (800) 247-9297.
W ba.com

Delta Airlines
Tel (800) 221-1212.
W delta.com

Frontier Airlines
Tel (800) 432-1359.
W flyfrontier.com

JetBlue
Tel (800) 538-2583.
W jetblue.com

Southwest Airlines
Tel (800) 435-9792.
W southwest.com

United Airlines
Tel (800) 241-6522.
W united.com

Traveling by Train and Bus

Amtrak
Tel (800) 872-7245.
W amtrak.com

Grand Canyon Railway
Tel (800) 843-8724.
W thetrain.com

Greyhound
Tel (800) 231-2222.
W greyhound.com

City Public Transit

Ollie the Trolley
Scottsdale. W dunn transportation.com

Sun Tran
Tucson. W suntran.com

Valley Metro
Phoenix.
W valleymetro.org

Traveling by Car & Four-Wheel Drive

When the movie characters Thelma and Louise, in the film of the same name, won a kind of freedom on the open roads of the Southwest, they promoted the pleasures of driving in this visually spectacular and dramatic region. However, for both residents and visitors, driving is a necessary part of life in Arizona, and a car is often the only means of reaching remote country areas. Tours of picturesque regions, such as the North Rim of the Grand Canyon *(see p61)*, Canyon de Chelly National Monument *(see pp112–13)*, or the Organ Pipe Cactus National Monument *(see p102)*, are best made by car. The entire state is served by a network of well-maintained roads, from multilane highways to winding, scenic routes that lead to even the remotest areas.

Renting a Car

Most of the major car rental businesses, such as **Alamo**, **Avis**, and **Hertz**, and some budget dealers, such as **Budget, Dollar Rent-A-Car**, and **Thrifty Auto**, have outlets at airports, and in towns and cities across Arizona. However, for those planning to fly into Phoenix, the least expensive option may be to arrange a fly-drive deal.

There is a central computerized booking system for most of the car companies – use the toll-free number and the Internet to find the best rates. Bargains can also be found by booking in advance and by traveling during the off-season.

Renting SUVs and 4WDs

Visitors planning to travel the back roads to explore places like Chaco Canyon *(see pp118–19)* or Monument Valley *(see pp108–9)* may want to rent a sports utility vehicle (SUV) or a four-wheel drive (4WD) vehicle; such vehicles provide greater road clearance. Roads that require high clearance in Arizona are usually marked as such. In wet conditions, it is safest to travel by 4WD on these roads, and it is also advisable to use 4WD vehicles on dirt roads. Most of the major car rental companies offer 4WD SUVs, but you must ask for guaranteed delivery, specify the 4WD you want, and make sure you understand the usage restrictions, if any. Also, some car rental agreements do not allow travel on unpaved roads.

For serious off-road 4WD use, **Barlow** in Sedona rents modified jeeps for 4 to 8 hours of use on designated trails.

Renting RVs

One of the most interesting and cost-effective ways of enjoying Arizona's vast and fascinating outdoors is in a recreational vehicle (RV). An RV gives you more freedom to explore on your own schedule, the ease of unpacking only once, and the convenience of cooking in your own kitchen.

Campgrounds are plentiful, and you can choose between the grounds of the National Park Service, Forest Service, Bureau of Land Management and private companies *(see pp152–55 and p161)*. The **Recreation Vehicle Rental Association (RVRA)** offers tips on selecting a rental RV, campground information, as well as rental agreement information. Make sure that the rental company provides roadside assistance if required, and that it explains the operations and usage of all the features of the RV. Also, plan to spend your first night near the dealer in case you require additional information after driving and sleeping in the RV.

Backcountry Driving

For any travel in the remote parts of Arizona, such as the

Sports utility vehicle moving through Canyon de Chelly

Recreational vehicle in Arizonan backcountry

desert regions and Native reservations, it is very important to check your route to see if a 4WD vehicle is required. Although many backcountry areas have graded dirt and gravel roads, which can be used by conventional cars, a 4WD is essential in some wild and remote areas. Monument Valley, for example, has a self-guided driving tour on dirt roads. Contact motoring organizations and tourist centers for information to assess your backcountry trip properly.

There are certain basic safety points that should be observed on any trip of this kind. Before you go, check that your car has a spare tire, and the tools required to change it, and that you know how to replace a flat tire. Carry a cell phone, blanket, and emergency food and water in case of a breakdown in a remote area. Plan your route and carry up-to-date maps. When traveling between remote destinations, inform the police or National Park Service wardens of your departure and expected arrival times. Check weather and road conditions before you start, and be aware of seasonal dangers such as flash floods. If you run out of gas or break down, call for help and stay with your vehicle since it offers protection from the elements.

Native flora and fauna must not be removed or damaged. Also, visitors should not drive off-road unless they are in a specially designated area,

and especially not on Native reservation land. If driving an RV, you must stop overnight in designated campgrounds.

Roadside Services

Although Arizona has many remote destinations, service stations are usually located in towns and at the intersections of major highways. Most have small stores that offer drinks, snacks, and basic automotive parts. Seldom are they more than 60 miles (95 km) apart. Not all stations provide mechanical assistance, so visitors may want to join a roadside assistance organization, such as the **American Automobile Association (AAA)**, that will come to their aid at a call. In the Phoenix area, Freeway Service Patrol vehicles assist stranded motorists by diagnosing minor vehicle problems, helping with repairs, and calling a tow truck.

DIRECTORY

Renting a Car

Alamo
Tel (800) 354-2322.
W alamo.com

Avis
Tel (800) 331-1212.
W avis.com

Budget
Tel (800) 527-0700.
W budget.com

Dollar Rent-A-Car
Tel (800) 800-4000.
W dollar.com

Hertz
Tel (800) 654-3131.
W hertz.com

Thrifty Auto Rental
Tel (800) 847-4389.
W thrifty.com

Renting SUVs and 4WDs

Barlow Jeep Rentals
3009 W Hwy 89A,
Sedona, AZ 86336.
Tel (928) 282-8700.
W barlows.us

Roadside Services

American Automobile Association
742 E Glendale Ave, Suite 182,
Phoenix, AZ 85027.
Tel (602) 285-6241.
W aaaaz.com

Recreation Vehicle Rental Association
3930 University Dr,
Fairfax, VA 22030.
Tel (703) 591-7130.
W rvra.org

Gas station and memorabilia store in Hackberry, on the legendary Route 66

General Index

Acknowledgments

Main Contributor
Paul Franklin is a travel writer and photographer specializing in the United States and Canada. He is the author of several guide books and magazine articles, and is based in Livingston, Texas.

Contributors
Nancy Mikula, Donna Dailey, Michelle de Larrabeiti, Philip Lee.

Factcheckers
Paul Franklin and Nancy Mikula.

Proofreader
Sonia Malik.

Indexer
Hilary Bird.

DK London Publisher
Douglas Amrine.

Publishing Managers
Fay Franklin, Jane Ewart.

Additional Picture Research
Rachel Barber, Ellen Root.

Relaunch and Revisions Team
Brigitte Arora, Hansa Babra, Claire Baranowski, Robert Barnes, Marta Bescos, Sonal Bhatt, Uma Bhattacharya, Tessa Bindloss, Subhadeep Biswas, Julie Bond, Neha Chander, Nicola Erdpresser, Mariana Evmolpidou, Anna Freiberger, Vinod Harish, Mohammad Hassan, Christine Heilman, Laura Jones, Cincy Jose, Jasneet Kaur, Juliet Kenny, Sumita Khatwani, Vincent Kurien, Tanya Mahendru, Nicola Malone, Alison McGill, Bhavika Mathur, Deepak Mittal, George Nimmo, Scarlett O'Hara, Catherine Palmi, Sands Publishing Solutions, Azeem Siddiqui, Brett Steel, Roseen Teare, Conrad Van Dyk, Ros Walford, Greg Ward, Ed Wright.

Additional Photography
Paul Franklin, Steve Gorton, Dave King, Andrew McKinney, Neil Mersh, Ian O'Leary, Tim Ridley, Rough Guides/Greg Ward, Clive Streeter.

Cartography
Uma Bhattacharya, Alok Pathak, Ben Bowles, Rob Clynes, Sam Johnston, James Macdonald (Colourmap Scanning Ltd).

Senior DTP Designer
Jason Little.

Senior Cartographic Editor
Casper Morris.

DK Picture Library
Gemma Woodward, Hayley Smith, Romaine Werblow.

Production Controller
Louise Daly.

Dorling Kindersley would like to thank the following people whose contributions and assistance have made the preparation of this book possible.

Special Assistance
Many thanks for the invaluable help of the following individuals: Juliet Martin, Heard Museum; Stacy Reading and Brett Brooks, Phoenix CVB; Barbara MacDonald and Hope Patterson, Tucson CVB; Leslie Connell and Ana Masterson, Flagstaff CVB; Michelle Mountain, Museum of Northern Arizona; Tom Pittinger, Grand Canyon National Park; Russ Bodner, Chaco Culture National Historic Park; and all the national park staff in the region.

Photography Permissions
Dorling Kindersley would like to thank all the cathedrals, churches, museums, hotels, restaurants, shops, galleries, national and state parks, and other sights for their assistance and kind permission to photograph at their establishments.

Key – a-above; b-below/bottom;c-center; f-far; l-left; r-right; t-top.

Works of art and images have been produced with the permission of the following copyright holders: Frank Lloyd Wright Foundation 29ca, 87b; University of Arizona Fine Arts Oasis Barbara Grygutis *Front Row Center* 94tl.

The publishers would like to thank the following individuals, companies, and picture libraries for their kind permission to reproduce their photographs:

4Corners: Bernhard Fichtl 2–3.

AFP: Spaceimaging.com 17t; **Alamy:** 78t, 163c; **Alamy Images:** B.A.E. Inc 139br; Bruce yuanyue Bi 31c; Stefan Binkert 68tr; Richard Cummins 151tc; Andrew Czerniak 58bc; Ian Dagnall 14tr; Susan E. Degginger 144br; Larry Geddis 95tl, 102br; Brian Green 14b; George H. H. Huey 13tr, 15br; imageBROKER 145t; Andreas Keuchel 97bl; Simon Leigh 144bl; Prisma Bildagentur AG 126–7; Whit Richardson 65tl, 108tr; Rollie Rodriguez 10tc; Kumar Sriskandan 136bc; USBR Photo 92–3; David Wall 122tr, Nik Wheeler 141bl; **Allreds:** Ben Eng Photography 143tl; **Arizona Biltmore:** 131tr; **Arizona Game & Fish Department:** Pat O'Brien 20tc; **Arizona Office of Tourism:** Chris Coe 34tr; **Arizona Science Center:** 83br; **Arizona State Library:** Archive+Public Records, Archive Division, Phoenix no.99–0281 34; **Arizona State Parks:** K. L. Day 105tl; **L'Auberge de Sedona:** 138tl; **Aura/NOAO/National Science Foundation:** 100b.

Branson Reynolds: 31b; **Bridgeman Art Library:** Christie's London Walter Ufer (1876–1936) *The Southwest* 8–9;

Frederic Remington (1861–1909) *Aiding a Comrade* c.1890 32–3, *The Conversation, or Dubious Company* 26b.

Corbis: 47t, 47clb, 47b; Art on File 29clb, 29br; Bettman *Cowboy on a Horse* Frederic Remington (1861–1909) 26cl, 32cb, 32tr, 44cb, 45bl, 49c, 115b, 164tc; Duomo/Jason Wise 156t; New Sport/Gark Newkirk 156b; James L. Amos 116t; Tom Bean 20b, 25br, 32tr, 32b, 36cra, 39b, 43cr, 55b, 66b, 74bc, 148br, 157t, 157c, 158t; Patrick Bennett 72br; Geoffrey Clements 149t; Richard A. Cooke 26b; Richard Cummins 21t, 74t, 74c, 79b; Owen Franken 167t; Marc Garanger 163b; Raymond Gehman 90cla, 91cb; Lowell Georgia 90bl, 90br; Mark E. Gibson 101b; Darrel Gulin 25tr, 25bc; Richard Hamilton 162b; Jan Butchofsky-Houser 33t, 166t; Dave G. Houser 91clb; George H. H. Huey 102c; Liz Hymans 43t; Dewitt Jones 40tr; Catherine Karnow 30ca, 74clb, 74cb, 170b; Layne Kennedy 62c, 104b; Danny Lehman 148c; James Marshall 28tr; Joe McDonald 97t; David Muench 1c, 25cr, 42–3, 57c, 79t, 91t; Marc Muench 64b; Pat O'Hara 58bl; Greg Probst 90cl; Carl & Ann Purcell 66t; Roger Ressmeyer 100c; Tony Roberts 156cl, 157t; Joel W. Rogers 67t, 164c; Bob Rowan 3c, 30tl; Pete Saloutos 153crb; Phil Schermeister 36bl; Richard Hamilton Smith 149b; Scott T. Smith 25clb; Kennan Ward 24tr; Ron Watts 54cl; Nik Wheeler 128c; **Corbis Sygma:** Stone Les 162c.

Dave G. Houser: 37b; © Mrs. Anna Marie Houser/The Allan Houser Foundation 27t; **Diana Dicker:** 42b; **Digital Clarity:** Hayden Houser 89t; **Dreamstime.com:** Bennymarty 48–9; Jon Bilous 34bl; Natalia Bratslavsky 18; Bnakano27 61br; Jerry Coli 150cb; Miroslav Liska 134c; Evgeny Moerman 52; Littleny 167br; Kathrine Martin 35cra; Paul Moore 11br; Glenn Nagel 117cra; Oksanaphoto 62–3; Phartisan 156cra; Cheryl Quigley 15c; Radekdrewek 11tl; Danny Raustadt 154br; Elzbieta Sekowska 10cl; Mark Skalny 5clb, 51br; Nickolay Stanev 106; Hilda Weges 19b; Wizreist 80.

Etch Kitchen & Bar: 138tl.

Flatiron Café: 137tr.

Getty Images: Walter Bibikow 12tc; Car Culture, Inc. 10br, 35cla; Collection Mix: Subjects/Car Culture 139tr; Richard Cummins 145br; Kerrick James 39tc; Panoramic Images 120–21; **Grand Canyon Caverns:** 34br; Grand Canyon Railway: 165tl; **Grand Canyon National Park Lodges:** 130bc; **Grand Canyon West:** 67tr; **Greyhound Lines, Inc.:** 165b; **Gouldings Lodge:** 109b.

Heard Museum: Acceptance,1997, part of the exhibit by Retha Walden Gambaro "Attitudes in Prayer" 85tl; Fred Harvey Collection/Daniel Namingha *Red-Tailed Hawk* 26–27, 84tr, 85tr; **Hopi Learning Center:** 26tr, 152cl; **Hotel Valley Ho:** 132tl; **Houserstock:** Ellen Barone 32.

Indexstock Imagery: Mark Gibson 150t; James Lemass 155b; **iStockphoto.com:** Philip Cacka 148br.

John Running: 30crb, 31t. **Kobal Collection, London:** Paramount Pictures 33b.

Leonardo Media Ltd.: 129cb.

Masterfile: G.D.Gifford 154c; **Metate Room:** 142bl; **Museum of New Mexico:** Fray Orci *Portrait of Don Juan Bautista de Anza* 1774 neg. no. 50828 45br(d); **Musical Instrument Museum:** 89bc.

NHPA: 18br; John Shaw 24clb; courtesy of the **National Park Service, Chaco Culture National Historic Park:** 44cb, 43b, 118tl; **New Mexico Tourism:** 36tc.

Paul Franklin: 21c, 56br, 61tr, 65b, 121 all, 123t, 123b, 149t; **Peter Newark Pictures:** 32cla, 33tl, 41c, 45t, 46t, 46br; **The Phoenician:** 133br, 140tc; **Photoshot:** Newscom 55cr; **Private Collection:** 7c, 45cb, 157c.

Raman Srinivasan: 103t; **Robert Harding Picture Library:** Richard Cummins 70cl; Whit Richardson 158–9.

Sharlot Hall Museum: 37t.

University of Archeology & Anthropology: 152bl; **University of Arizona:** 94tl.

Yuma Convention and Visitors Bureau: © Robert Herko 1999 101t.

Front endpaper: Dreamstime.com: Evgeny Moerman cl, Wizreist bl, Nickolay Stanev cr.

Cover
Front & Spine – **AWL Images:** Danita Delimont Stock. Back – **Dreamstime.com:** Lunamarina

All other images © Dorling Kindersley. For further information see: www.dkimages.com

Special Editions of DK Travel Guides

DK Travel Guides can be purchased in bulk quantities at discounted prices for use in promotions or as premiums. We are also able to offer special editions and personalized jackets, corporate imprints, and excerpts from all of our books, tailored specifically to meet your own needs.

To find out more, please contact:
in the United States **specialsales@dk.com**
in the UK **travelguides@uk.dk.com**
in Canada **specialmarkets@dk.com**
in Australia **penguincorporatesales@ penguinrandomhouse.com.au**

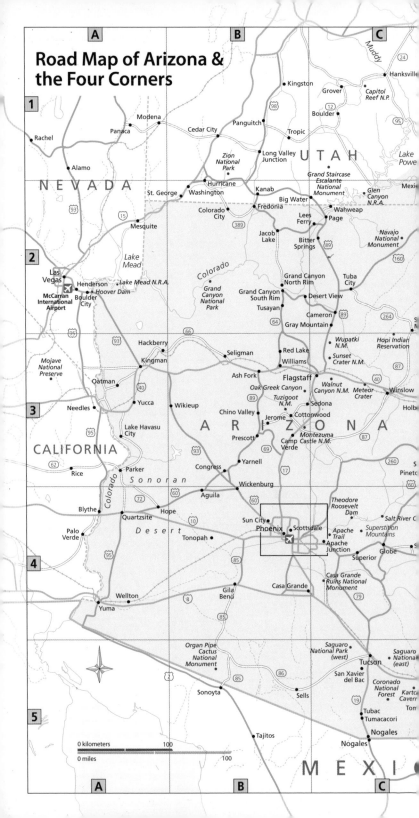

Road Map of Arizona & the Four Corners